TROUBLED WATERS

FINANCING WATER IN THE WEST

TROUBLED WATERS

FINANCING WATER IN THE WEST

Rodney T. Smith

BARBARA DYER, PROJECT DIRECTOR & EDITOR
ROGER J. VAUGHAN, GENERAL EDITOR
ROBERT POLLARD, EDITORIAL SUPPORT
NORMA P. DEFREITAS, PRODUCTION MANAGER

THE COUNCIL OF STATE PLANNING AGENCIES
HALL OF THE STATES
400 NORTH CAPITOL STREET
SUITE 291
WASHINGTON DC 20001

Cover: Map-*U.S. West*—explorations (1860); reproduced from original, Geography and Map Division of the Library of Congress.

Library of Congress Cataloging in Publication Data

Smith, Rodney T.
    Troubled waters.

    "March 1984"
    Bibliography: p.
    Includes index.
    1. Water resources development—West (U.S.)—Finance. I Title.
HD1695.A17S65 1984   338.4'333391'00978   84–21386
ISBN 0-934842-33-7

Cover Design by Donya Melanson Associates
Typography by The TypeWorks

Manufactured in the United States

The Council of State Planning Agencies is a membership organization comprised of the planning and policy staff of the nation's governors. Through its Washington office, the Council provides assistance to individual states on a wide spectrum of policy matters. The Council also performs policy and technical research on both state and national issues. The Council has been affiliated with the National Governors' Association since 1975.

Funding support for this publication was provided by the Ford Foundation. The statements, findings, conclusions, recommendations, and other data contained in this report do not necessarily represent the views of the Council of State Planning Agencies. No part of this book may be used or reproduced in any manner whatsoever without written permission except in the case of brief quotations embodied in research papers and reviews.

The Council of State Planning Agencies
Hall of States
400 North Capitol Street
Washington, D.C. 20001
(202) 624-5386

James M. Souby
Executive Director

TABLE OF CONTENTS

LIST OF FIGURES

LIST OF TABLES

FOREWORD

HISTORICALLY, WESTERN WATER INVESTMENT has been of such importance as to have shaped the political, institutional and economic fiber of the States. In spite of huge investments in the past, the need for additional capital continues to grow. States face the formidable task of balancing this demand with other vitally needed public works, during a period of high interest rates and increasing reticense by the federal government to finance projects.

States are not lacking in financial advisement. The body of literature on the infrastructure and water supply "crises" has swelled during the last few years. But to me the value of this book to Western States is outstanding in two respects. First, it recognizes that a broad range of state institutions which affect water project finance can be consciously adapted in support of many goals. States may choose among methods of reducing costs, sharing the financial burden or supporting particular projects, according to the state's priorities. At the same time, because this analysis has drawn upon the expertise of individuals responsible for water project planning, management, and finance decisions, it is responsive, pragmatic, and rooted in sound economic analysis.

Many of the options contained in this book will be controversial. But the time is at hand to rethink policies developed in a different era under assumptions which may no longer be valid. Economic and political climates have changed.

Finally, this work is applicable to states throughout the nation and for public works and infrastructure financing outside of water related facilities. It offers policymakers a fascinating glimpse into their role in the debt finance marketplace. The Council of State Planning Agencies has produced a book which I believe will assist public officials in managing and supplying the resource of primary importance to the states and their citizens.

Bruce Babbitt
Governor of Arizona

ACKNOWLEDGMENTS

AN ENDLESS PROCESSION of generous individuals have provided me assistance, criticism, advice, and encouragement in the past two years during the preparation of *Troubled Waters*.

Bruce Babbitt, Governor of Arizona, provided invaluable leadership to my research. I appreciate his role as lead governor for the Council of State Planning Agencies study team, and his Chairmanship of a day-long workshop to discuss an early draft of my book. My confidence in the future of my native western region is reaffirmed by this successful politician who has a keen interest in viewing old problems from new perspectives.

Barbara Dyer, Associate Director of CSPA and Roger Vaughan, Senior Associate for Economic Policy contributed greatly to the effort. As members of the CSPA team, we traveled extensively throughout the West and the corridors of Wall Street. At every turn, they probed my thinking, offered their own insights, and extended detailed editorial assistance. Any success which *Troubled Waters* enjoys is as much their responsibility as it is my own.

My book also benefited from many critical discussions during meetings with Principal Advisors to the CSPA team. The candor expressed and exchange of dissenting ideas was a testimony to the substantial benefits policy analysis can reap from organized forums dedicated to a rigorous exploration of policy options. I especially wish to thank George Britton, Bob Wise and Nancy Wrona with the Governor's Office in Arizona for their commitment to this effort and rigorous review of my work. Members of the editorial review panel were: Craig Bell, Western States Water Council; Kent Briggs, Executive Assistant for Policy and Planning Coordination, Governor's Office of Utah; Jo Clark, Western Governors Policy Office; Paul Cunningham, Special Assistant for Natural Resources, Governor's Office of Idaho; Bill McDonald, Director of Colorado Water Conservation Board; Don Nelson, former Administrative Aide to the Governor of Wyoming; Wes Steiner, Chief Water Engineer of Arizona; and Hank Welch, Utah Department of Natural Resources.

Representatives from the Investment Banking community generously shared their expertise and information. I extend special thanks to Donald Porter (Vice President, The First Boston Corporation, San Francisco) who not only participated in the Sun Valley workshop, but also communicated with me on numerous other occasions. Other investment bankers from whom I received assistance were: Kevin Collins (Managing Director, The First Boston Corporation), Mark Ferber (Kidder Peabody), George Friedlander (Vice President, Smith Barney, Harris, Upham & Co.), James H. Gibbs (Vice President, E. F. Hutton & Co., Inc.), and Mary Mudryk (Morgan Stanley & Co.). John J. Hallacy III (Assistant Vice President of Municipal Bond Department) and Wendy K. Stadnyk (Assistant Vice President of Municipal Finance Department) graciously introduced me to the bond rating procedures at Standard & Poor's Corporation.

Many other state officials cooperated with the CSPA study team during its travels. These individuals offered unique insights provided by their own state's experiences and shared useful criticisms of the themes advanced in *Troubled Waters*. I express my gratitude and hope that those individuals whose names I've omitted from this list forgive me for my poor record-keeping. In Arizona, I wish to thank Bill Chase, City Manager's Office of City of Phoenix, Leonard Ducker, Arizona Municipal Water Users Association, William G. Ealy, Deputy Manager of the City of Tucson, Standly L. Smith, Deputy Chief Engineer Maricopa County Flood Control District, and Grant Ward, General Manager of Roosevelt Water Conservation District. In California, thanks to Kathy Harder, State Water Resources Control Board, Melinda C. Luedtke, Executive Secretary of California Debt Advisory Commission, Ronald Robie, former Director of the California Department of Water Resources and currently Municipal Court Judge in Sacramento, David Vache, Legislative Budget Analyst and Virgil E. Whitely, California Department of Water Resources.

In Colorado, I appreciate the efforts of Bob Arnott, Director of Office of Health Protection, Department of Health, Chips Barry, Deputy Director of Department of Natural Resources, Evan Goulding, Commissioner of Department of Agriculture, Monte Pascoe, then Executive Director of Department of Natural Resources, Morgan Smith, Executive Director of Department of Local Affairs, and Lee White former Executive Director of Office of State Planning and Budgeting. In Idaho, thanks to Ken Dunn, Chief Water Engineer. In Texas, M. Reginald Arnold II, Development Fund Manager, Texas Water Development Fund, Charles Nemir, Executive Driector, Texas Department of Water Resources, Michael L. Personett, Environmental Policy Specialist, Natural Resources Policy Division, Dennis Thomas, Director of Office of Management and Budget, and Harden Wiedemann, former Director of Office of Planning and Intergovernmental Relations were all very helpful. Finally, thanks to Dee Hansen,

State Engineer and Temple A. Reynolds, Executive Director of Department of Natural Resources in Utah for their advice and support.

The book has also benefited from many discussions and reviews which I have received from academics interested in water law. My thinking has been profoundly influenced by: Terry Anderson, Montana State University; Lee Brown Jr., University of New Mexico; Charles E. Phelps, University of Rochester; and Gary Weatherford, John Muir Institute.

I must also extend thanks to the many individuals who have played important supporting roles to the research and the production of *Troubled Waters*. Robert Pollard for his editorial support, James Souby, Executive Director of CSPA, has created an excellent, supportive atmosphere for examining the contentious political issues behind water finance. Norma deFreitas of CSPA must take full credit for the excellent production of this book. I am pleased to acknowledge the skillful research assistants provided by: Robert Kaminsky, former MBA student, University of Chicago, currently at Chemical Bank; Scott Turicchi, BA student Claremont McKenna College; David Yenney, and Anthea Dunn, Stratecon, Inc.

Finally, I am also grateful for the financial support offered by the Ford Foundation. Dr. Norman Collins, Program Officer, and Susan Sechler have been patient supporters of this research.

CHAPTER 1

MAKING THE FINANCING PROBLEM MANAGEABLE

> Physically and socially, the West does not remain the same
> from decade to decade any more than other places do. [It
> exists] within the warping influence of great in-migration,
> uninterrupted boom, and unremitting technological tinker-
> ing. But these . . . are to be *understood in relation to a
> timeless condition, aridity.*
>
> Wallace Stegner

The states clustered between the Pacific Ocean and the 100th meridian are as diverse as any in our nation. Temperature ranges from
arctic to subtropical and rainfall from desert to rain forest. Cultural
heritage extends from the original inhabitants of the continent to
first-generation immigrants from Europe, Asia, and the Americas.
The West includes the nation's most populous state and some of the
least populated. Yet this group of states is bound together perhaps
more strongly than any other in the country by a regional identity.

Water has been the ultimate force drawing western states together. The perennial struggle to meet water demands shaped the
West's economic, cultural, and political systems. Western water systems are among the most developed, complex, legally encumbered,
and politically debated in our nation. Frequent items on the policy
agenda include settling disputes over water rights, allocating water
among competing uses, maintaining in-stream flows, reversing the
decline in water tables, calculating how much further development
will cost, and deciding who should pay.

Despite large investments in reclamation projects, concern per-
sists over the adequacy of water supplies. The surface supplies of the
upper Rio Grande, Gila River, and Colorado River basins are fully
claimed. The Platte River tributaries in Wyoming and Colorado are
approaching this point. Even in the Pacific Northwest, where rainfall is abundant, hydroelectric power generation creates local water
shortages. In Arizona, groundwater is being depleted at twice its
replenishment rate.

Yet, demands for increasingly valuable western water inevitably
will intensify. The U.S. Census Bureau predicts population growth

in the West to be twice that of the rest of the nation through the year 2000. Increased demands by industrial, commercial, and residential users will heighten the competition with existing demands of agriculture—far and away the dominant user of water in the West (Agriculture accounts for 93 percent in Colorado, 89 percent in Arizona, and 76 percent in Washington, according to the U.S. Census of Agriculture, 1978.) Even where rapid growth does not occur, the costs of maintaining and repairing existing water systems will rise dramatically. Communities have deferred repair work in response to tight government budgets, making the fix-up costs immense, turn-of-the-century irrigation systems need refurbishment or replacement. These costs cannot be postponed indefinitely.

The West shares with the rest of the nation a growing concern over how to preserve or restore the quality of water. Industrial waste, pesticides, and toxic chemicals have contaminated groundwater supplies, leaving many bodies of surface water neither fishable, swimmable, nor drinkable. In the San Gabriel Valley of California, 39 wells supplying water to 13 cities were closed in 1980 because of trichloroethylene pollution. As knowledge about the health effects and behavior of contaminants increases, and as the monitoring of water quality improves, the breadth and gravity of the problem may grow. The costs of safeguarding water supplies and of safely treating residential and industrial waste are likely to sky-rocket during the next decades.

Although projections of capital investments in water projects are crude, substantial investments are contemplated. The Western States Water Council (1981) surveyed western states' capital-expenditure plans, including municipal and industrial, irrigation and drainage, flood control, recreation, water quality, and other environmentally-oriented tasks. Eight states indicate that planned expenditures could exceed $100 billion over the next 25 years. These burgeoning investments will fuel the political debate surrounding water finance.

The federal government's diminishing contribution to paying for the costs of water projects compounds the problems facing western states. In 1982, all federal support was eliminated for river basin commissions, the Water Resources Council, and for direct water-resource-planning grants to states—formerly awarded under the Water Resources Planning Act of 1965. The federal government also is reassessing its traditional funding of water-development projects—no new appropriations have been awarded for proposed projects since 1976. The wastewater-treatment construction grant program—administered by the U.S. Environmental Protection Agency (EPA) to fund states' sewer construction—was cut from $3.7 billion to $2.4

billion, and the share of project costs that state and local governments must pay was raised from 25 percent to 45 percent.

This shift in federal policy signals the retreat by a major funding source for water projects. Before 1970, the federal share of cumulative government expenditures for water-resource development equaled 75.7 percent for irrigation uses, 58.9 percent for industrial uses, 74.4 percent for in-stream hydropower uses, and a minor 7.8 percent for municipal systems.[1] EPA waste-treatment grants covered 69.3 percent of local governments' capital spending in 1979.[2] Federal intergovernmental grants equaled 48 percent of total state and local spending on water quality control during 1976 to 1979.[3] Faced with shrinking federal support for water projects, western policymakers must seek low-cost ways of financing water projects and of spreading these costs equitably among users.

The difficulties of financing water projects are compounded by the changing environment in the municipal bond market. State and local governmental debt has grown steadily over the past three decades, and this trend will continue, if not accelerate, in the future. How can the bond market absorb additional state and local governmental debt? Will financing costs soar if states and municipalities expand their debt financing for water investment? Will the recent default by the Washington Public Power Supply System—the largest municipal bond issue in history—"chill" the market for new water investment?

THE PURPOSE OF THIS BOOK

Answering the questions posed above is a formidable task. The issues strike at the heart of the economics and politics of public finance. Decisionmakers are faced with choices that may prove costly, controversial, or devisive. Yet these problems need not be insurmountable. State policies can be devised to make these problems manageable.

This book explores practical options for policymakers by examining the economics of water finance. It does not attempt to evaluate specific projects nor to judge the merits of federal policy. Rather, it examines how state fiscal, statutory, and regulatory powers can be used to reduce financing costs of water development, distribution, and treatment. The book examines how costs are influenced by more efficient allocation of water among competing users and by more effective public investment in systems and facilities. The book does not presume that a state's water policies should be motivated solely by the objective of low-cost financing. However, it does recognize that the cost of water finance will influence the ease with which states can achieve other political objectives associated with water policy.

The economic issues examined in this respect include water pricing and property taxation, water law, state regulation of banking and securities, and intergovernmental fiscal and administrative relations. The analysis considers how instrumental these diverse policies are in devising financially sound answers to the following questions: 1) How, and to what extent, can state governments increase their fiscal resources to make up for the reduction in federal funds? 2) How can states assist local governments as they shoulder a greater share of the financial burden? 3) How can state/local fiscal relations be structured to reduce the cost of financing water-development projects? and 4) How can the public and private sectors better cooperate to reduce financing costs? The answers to these questions are found ultimately by examining the economic principles behind sound debt finance.

In principle, financing could proceed along two lines. A project could use debt financing when funds for current capital expenditures are secured from investors who expect repayment at a specified future date. Or it could use pay-as-you-go financing, in which funds are obtained from existing revenue sources. However, debt financing has two advantages that make it preferable to pay-as-you-go financing. First, using debt reduces the economic burden of financing because it avoids reliance on large temporary water surcharges or tax rates. Second, using debt deflects the political opposition of current residents who may protest paying for services to future residents who did not pay the temporary surcharges. How well debt financing can exploit these advantages depends on how well water-project financing can meet the standards used by the municipal bond market to assess the creditworthiness of borrowers.

BUILDING AND MARKETING COLLATERAL

A jurisdiction's economic strength in using debt to finance water facilities depends on its ability to insure a steady revenue stream to back the project. Private investors need assurance that the provisions for repayment are secure. The structure and perceived reliability of the repayment promise can be viewed as the project's or jurisdiction's *collateral*. The strength of this collateral affects the cost of financing water investments: the stronger the collateral, the lower the cost of borrowing money. State and local government policies can build collateral if they improve the financial health of a water

TABLE 1–1

State Government Policy Options

Policy	Effect of policy		
	Reduces cost to govt.	Reassigns cost among users	Exchanges one cost for another
Traditional General Obligation and Revenue Bonding:			
1) Direct operation of project			
— long-term contracts describing repayment	X		
— municipal utility pricing	?	X	
2) Grants to local governments			
— construction	?	X	
— purchase private bond insurance	X	X	
3) Loans to local governments	?	X	
4) State guarantee of local debt	?	X	
Bond Banks:		X	X
Regulation:			
1) Securities			
— removing any requirements to award underwriting contracts according to net interest cost	X		
— information/reporting requirements	X		?
— coordinating solicitation of bids of underwriters	X		?
2) Banking			
— reform qualification of instruments held in trust accounts	X		?
— allow banks to make secondary markets in bonds	X		
— allow banks to bid on all underwriting contracts	X		

Continued

TABLE 1–1 (Continued)

State Government Policy Options

	Effect of policy		
Policy	Reduces cost to govt.	Reassigns cost among users	Exchanges one cost for another
3) Water law			
— define rights in terms of consumptive use instead of diversion	X		?
— promote voluntary transfer with protection of third-party interests	X		?
Planning/Technical Assistance:	X		

X, Indicates likely outcome
?, indicates possibility; the questions in column one pertain to whether these policies affect the overall financial capability of the project; the questions in column three pertain to whether the overall savings exceed the administration costs.

project, enhance the local economic base, or bolster the ability of the borrower to withstand adverse changes in its economic, legal, or operating environment.

Building collateral is only part of the strategy for low cost finance. Informing potential investors of the project's economic strength is the other. *Marketing* collateral—disseminating information and finding the buyers most willing to purchase debt—is enhanced or inhibited by a state's policies and regulations.

This book is organized to provide a detailed analysis of water finance in the context of building and marketing collateral. The specific state and local policies examined are summarized in tables 1-1 and 1-2, respectively. These policies are analyzed according to their ability to: 1) reduce total financing costs to state and local governments; 2) reassign financial responsibility among different levels of government or different project users, without reducing total financing costs; and 3) exchange one type of cost for another, without reducing total financing costs. The judgments contained in these tables are based on four types of analysis: 1) application of general economic principles of financial markets; 2) empirical studies of those markets; 3) examination of the programs and practices of the

TABLE 1–2

Local Government Policy Options

Policy	Effect of policy		
	Reduces cost to govt.	Reassigns cost among users	Exchanges one cost for another
Traditional Bonding:			
1) Revenue vs. general obligation	?	X	
2) Tax increment/tax allocation		X	
Purchase Private Bond Insurance:	X		
User Fees:			
1) Connection charges	X	X	
2) Development fees	X		
3) Pricing according to:			
— flat rate		X	
— amount used	X		
4) Contacting			
— long-term with large users	X		?
5) Wastewater treatment			
— industrial and commercial be effluent charges	X		
6) Groundwater taxation with dedicated revenues to surface development	X		
Other Tax Revenues:			
1) Property tax		X	
2) Income tax		X	
3) Sales tax		X	
Private Sector Leasing/Ownership:	X		?
Planning and Financial Reporting:	X		?

X, Indicates likely outcome

?, indicates possibility; the questions in column one pertain to whether these policies affect the overall financial capacity of the project; the questions in column three pertain to whether the savings in overall costs exceed the cost of administration.

western states; and 4) review of recent financial innovations throughout the United States.

AN OVERVIEW OF THE BOOK

Chapter 2 describes the current state of water investment in the West, including the legal and institutional framework in which financing is conducted. Chapter 3 reviews the fundamental aspects of the municipal bond market, including different types of debt instruments, the role of bond ratings and underwriters, and the determinants of interest costs to municipalities and states. The traditional belief that general obligation bonds can be issued at lower cost than revenue bonds does not hold for water utilities. Nor does evidence support concern about saturation of the bond market with state or local government debt. Bond quality and timing of issuance with respect to general market conditions are the forces driving borrowing costs.

Chapter 4 examines the principles of water finance and the financial condition of western state and local governments. The discussion relates how different revenue sources for debt service—user-fees, taxes, and intergovernmental grants and loans—influence the financial collateral of state and municipal bonds.

Chapter 5 explores in detail the economic advantages of user fees as a revenue source for debt financing. It illustrates how user-fee financing need not conflict with equity goals, and describes how fee structures should be designed to reflect the different circumstances of agricultural, industrial, and residential water users. Coordinating the revenues collected from user fees with those raised by groundwater taxation and effluent fees can improve the quality of project financing, and represents a little used, though promising, source of additional revenues.

The next two chapters explore alternative state policies to support the building and marketing of financial collateral. Chapter 6 reviews fiscal and legal issues that may limit the development of effective financing policies, including tax and debt limitations, water law, and the regulation of the banking and security industries. The case for user-fee financing is strengthened by statutory and constitutional restrictions on state and local governmental finances. Policies that encourage more financial institutions—such as commercial banks—to compete in underwriting and the making of secondary markets for bonds would reduce the costs and increase the effectiveness of marketing state and municipal debt.

Chapter 7 investigates financial and administrative relations between state and local governments. The mechanisms discussed include bond banks, grants-in-aid and loan programs financed from dedicated state tax revenues, bond guarantees, and capital planning. States can offer technical assistance to local governments that will reduce overall financing cost, by correcting problems associated with poor dissemination of information, restriction of entry into marketing bonds, and the sporadic arrival of municipal bonds to the marketplace. Only grants to defray the cost of purchasing private bond insurance for high-risk bonds promise to reduce overall financing costs, because this insurance is cost-effective. All other means of aid—bond banks, grants, and loans—redistribute the cost of finance to state governments at the expense of higher overall financing costs.

Chapter 8 examines the potential role of the private sector as a partner in financing water projects because of tax advantages, enhanced operating efficiencies, or financing efficiencies. The case for privatization is found to be weak on tax grounds, especially as an alternative to paying high interest rates on public debt. However, private firms can offer efficiencies in operating and financing that can make this an attractive financing option. The transfer of ownership or management responsibility to private firms, however, raises questions about the proper role of regulation and other contractual mechanisms to ensure that a municipality does not create a private monopoly as it embraces these efficiencies.

Chapter 9 presents the major conclusions from the preceding chapters. It outlines how states can improve the prospects for low-cost financing of water investment, without incurring major financial commitments, by exerting leadership in selected areas of statutory and regulatory reform and by providing technical assistance to local water authorities. Most of the policies rely on the voluntary participation of local authorities and will assist those small communities that have been the focus of policy concern.

This book is intended for governors, their policy staffs, local governments, those in the private sector, and the academics who are concerned with water finance. Although the emphasis of the book is upon water finance in the West, the policies and programs, and the financing guidelines developed, can be applied to many types of public works in all regions of the country.

The task of developing an effective state water-financing strategy is not easy. Policies and programs that have endured for decades may have to be reversed. New planning and financing techniques may have to be designed and carried out. States must adopt and modify approaches to fit their own fiscal, economic, and cultural environment. These policies are not alchemists' formulas that produce low-cost from high-cost funds. But this book does provide policymakers with some basic principles to use in building a water-financing strategy and a menu of policies to serve as the ingredients of that strategy.

TEXT NOTES

1. Computed from data appearing in Western States Water Council (1981), table 16-4, p. 5.
2. Computed from data on federal, state, and local spending and intergovernmental grants in U.S. Department of Commerce, *U.S. Statistical Abstract* (1983), table 364, p. 209.
3. Computed from data on EPA waste-treatment facilities' construction grants and local governments' capital expenditures on water quality in U.S. Department of Commerce, *U.S. Statistical Abstract* (1983), table 472, p. 280, and table 364, p. 209, respectively.

CHAPTER 2

WATER INVESTMENT AND GOVERNMENTAL FINANCING IN THE WEST

In the last 25 years—a period during which irrigation has grown dramatically in the West—the U.S. Bureau of Reclamation (USBR) transformed the nature of water investment and finance. USBR funding not only increased invested capital per irrigated acre, but also reduced the role of private ownership in favor of government control of irrigation enterprises. Recent cuts in federal spending for water projects may reverse this trend.

Historical and institutional forces shaped the ways that water is financed in the West. This chapter describes those forces and reviews the debt levels of western states relative to other regions. The special character of western water supply and distribution necessitates distinctive approaches to water law and finance that must be considered when formulating financing strategies.

INSTITUTIONAL INNOVATION IN THE WEST

The 100th meridian separates our nation into two radically different hydrologic systems. To the east, rainfall averages over 40 inches per year. A diffuse system of rivers carries water from natural sources to industrial, residential, and agricultural users. Abundant rainfall throughout the year provides a steady flow to meet demands. Areas to the west—the most fertile agriculturally, the most advantageous sites for industry and residences, and the most conducive to future economic development—are not always adjacent to rivers and streams. The water supply fluctuates over time. Natural rainfall can vary by a factor of 10 within two months, but demand remains steady or even increases as rainfall declines. Phoenix, for example, averages 0.12 inch of rain during June and 1.22 inches in August.

These features of western water supply—sparse amounts located at great distances from users and occurring at inopportune times—influenced the development of western water institutions. The West's hydrology made obsolete earlier legal doctrines and necessitated the founding of large numbers of local organizations for coordinating water development. The geographical misplacement of western water supply away from water demand was the central problem addressed through the new legal institutions.

Eastern states adopted English, or riparian, tradition, under which water could be used only on the land adjacent to the body of water. The West, in contrast, developed the *Appropriative Doctrine* which allowed the separation of water use from the location of its natural supply. This institution provided the impetus for investment in the grand "plumbing system" of pipelines, canals, and aqueducts that are the lifelines of the West.

The development and operation of these systems required substantial capital investments. The balance between private and public investment shifted over the years in response to factors that are still influential—explicit allocation of water among users and the assignment of costs according to water use. A brief sketch of the historical evolution of irrigation finance highlights key policy issues.

Early western water development was dominated by private ownership. Individual partnerships and mutual irrigation companies financed water diversion and distribution among the members according to private contract (*see* Mead, 1907; and Hutchins, 1935). The philosophy of development and finance was that water users should pay for irrigation systems and that water rights should be expressly and unambiguously stated. State corporation laws established mutual irrigation companies as nonprofit entities, in which water rights and responsibilities for costs were prorated according to ownership of shares in the mutual.

With the passage of the Wright Act (1887) in California, local government entities with limited general taxation powers entered into water development. The act relaxed the strict connection between water use and responsibility to pay for water system costs. Local irrigation districts were empowered to raise revenues by any combination of water charges and property taxation chosen by its elected board of directors. Water rights were either prorated according to land ownership, or allocated according to discretionary powers of the board of directors—whose legal duty was to be "just and equitable."

Public irrigation districts were financial failures until the 1920s (*see* Brewer, 1961). Most of the Wright Act districts formed in California were dissolved within a few years of incorporation. Mutuals and partnerships remained the dominant source of irrigation development until the late 1920s and early 1930s. Then public ownership blossomed as it became a precondition of receiving U.S. Bureau of Reclamation (USBR) funding (Leshy, 1983), and, after World War II, the financial advantages of tax-exempt public district debt grew with higher federal personal income tax rates.

12

WATER SUPPLY, IRRIGATION, AND FORMAL ORGANIZATION

Western states differ in the magnitude of their water problems, their water use, their fee structures, and in their water organizations. Although the region as a whole is arid, annual rainfall varies considerably among states (*see* table 2-1). These "irrigation states" include all of the continental states west of the 100th meridian. Their annual rainfall is only 57 percent of the national average. Arizona, Nevada, and New Mexico average fewer than 10 inches of rain per year. Kansas, Nebraska, Oklahoma, and Oregon average more than 30 inches annually. Northern California receives 7 inches more rain per year than southern California. East Texas has almost 33 more inches of rain per year than west Texas. Western Washington's annual rainfall exceeds that of eastern Washington by 21 inches.

The most common misperception about western water practices is the belief that irrigation water is spread to every conceivable use without regard to cost or productivity. Although irrigation is important to western agriculture, less than 10 percent of total agricultural acreage is irrigated, including range land (*see* table 2-2 for most recent data available from U.S. Dept. Agriculture). Where natural

TABLE 2–1

Annual Precipitation (Inches per Year) in Western States

State	Rainfall	State	Rainfall
Arizona	7.05	Oklahoma	31.37
California		Oregon	37.61
Northern	18.38	South Dakota	24.72
Southern	11.39	Texas	
Colorado	15.51	East	40.25
Idaho	11.50	West	7.7
Kansas	30.58	Utah	15.17
Montana	14.99	Washington	
Nebraska	30.18	Eastern	17.42
Nevada	7.20	Western	38.79
New Mexico	7.77	Wyoming	14.65
North Dakota	16.66		
West average	19.50	U.S. average	33.86

Source: *U.S. Statistical Abstract* (1983), table 373, p. 216.

13

TABLE 2–2

Amount (Millions of Acres) and Growth in Acreage (Percent) in Western Agriculture by Irrigation Status, 1978

State	Total acreage		Irrigated acreage		
	Amount	Growth*	Amount	Growth*	Share of Total acreage
Arizona	38.7	1.2	1.2	2.8	3.1
California	33.5	−6.4	8.6	17.2	26.0
Colorado	35.5	−3.4	3.5	17.8	9.7
Idaho	14.9	3.1	3.5	24.0	23.6
Kansas/Oklahoma	82.1	−3.9	3.3	47.4	4.0
Montana	62.3	−1.0	2.1	12.5	3.3
Nebraska	46.3	0.9	5.7	69.0	12.3
Nevada	10.5	−2.2	0.3	−92.3	2.9
North Dakota	42.0	−2.6	0.1	80.5	0.3
New Mexico	48.3	3.2	0.9	9.5	1.9
Oregon	18.4	2.2	1.9	23.4	10.4
South Dakota	44.5	−2.3	0.3	83.2	0.8
Texas	137.5	−3.6	7.0	1.9	5.1
Utah	10.5	−7.3	1.2	14.5	11.3
Washington	17.0	−3.2	1.7	31.7	9.9
Wyoming	33.7	−5.1	1.7	10.1	5.0
West Average		−1.9		22.1	8.1

*1969 to 1978

Source: U.S. Department of Commerce, *Census of Agriculture*, Part 4, *Irrigation* 1978), table 1, pp. 146–147.

rainfall is low—Arizona, Nevada, New Mexico, and Texas—the share of total acreage irrigated is quite small. Where natural rainfall is more plentiful—California, Nebraska, Oregon, and Washington— irrigated agriculture represents a larger share of total agricultural acreage. Overall, western irrigated agriculture grew by 8.1 percent from 1969 to 1978, while total acreage in these states declined by 1.9 percent during the same period—primarily because of urban growth.[1] Those states with greater natural rainfall—the Dakotas, California, Idaho, Kansas, and Washington—exhibited the strongest growth in irrigated agriculture.

Another common misperception is that all irrigation projects in the West have been large scale. Although large organizations are important to western water development, overall only 56.4 percent of

irrigated acreage is served by formal organizations: mutual irrigation companies, public irrigation districts, USBR-operated projects,
and state and local governments (see table 2-3). Over time this share
has barely increased. Acreage served by these organizations grew by
only 1.6 percent between 1969 and 1978, while total irrigated
acreage in the West expanded by 22.1 percent.

States in which groundwater supplies a large share of total
water supply—Kansas, Oklahoma, Nebraska, Texas, and the Dakotas —have smaller shares of their irrigated acreage served by formal
organizations. The water supply of formal organizations is primarily
from surface sources, and, secondarily, from out-of-state sources
(see table 2-4). Only 1.9 percent of their supply originates from
groundwater. On average, western states receive 12.5 percent of their
water from out-of-state sources. Arizona exhibits the greatest depen-

TABLE 2–3

Irrigated Acreage (Millions of Acres) in Irrigation Organizations in the Western States, 1978

State	Acreage	Share of Irrigated acres	Growth*(%)
Arizona	0.6	50.6	−15.1
California	5.8	68.0	15.1
Colorado	2.7	78.2	− 5.6
Idaho	2.6	75.3	− 0.2
Kansas/Oklahoma	0.1	3.7	−16.2
Montana	1.7	80.1	7.4
Nebraska	0.8	14.1	− 0.7
Nevada	0.3	87.4	0.2
New Mexico	0.5	54.4	5.2
North Dakota	0.04	25.0	−16.6
Oregon	1.1	55.7	10.8
South Dakota	0.1	27.5	17.3
Texas	1.1	15.2	− 0.3
Utah	1.4	100.0	0.6
Washington	1.2	30.0	8.6
Wyoming	1.3	80.0	5.2
West Average		56.4	1.6

*1969 to 1978

Source: U.S. Department of Commerce, Census of Agriculture, Part 4, Irrigation
(1978), table 1, pp. 146–147.

TABLE 2—4

Sources of Water Supply for Irrigation Organizations

State	Share (%)			
	Surface	Ground	Other Organization	Imported from Other State
Arizona	52.0	10.5	31.1	6.4
California	67.2	1.3	31.0	0.5
Colorado	78.4	1.0	1.0	20.6
Idaho	54.3	2.3	39.2	4.2
Kansas/Oklahoma	56.6	0.0	30.4	13.0
Montana	87.0	0.1	12.8	0.1
Nebraska	59.7	0.2	17.4	22.7
Nevada	59.0	1.1	22.7	17.2
New Mexico	88.4	1.9	7.4	2.3
North Dakota	28.5	1.1	12.1	3.8
Oregon	75.2	1.2	22.8	0.8
South Dakota	83.0	1.1	12.1	3.8
Texas	88.1	0.3	8.5	3.1
Utah	72.0	5.4	21.0	1.6
Washington	54.1	2.7	2.7	43.2
Wyoming	72.0	0.2	27.6	0.2
West Average	67.2	1.9	18.7	12.5

Source: U.S. Department of Commerce, *Census of Agriculture*, Part 4, *Irrigation* (1978), chart 2, p. 143.

dence, relying on 64 percent of its water from out-of-state sources. Wyoming enjoys the smallest dependence of only 0.2 percent.

The growth of irrigated acreage was encouraged by direct USBR projects that also spurred the growth of public irrigation districts (*see* figures 2-1 and 2-2). Irrigated acreage served by private, mutual irrigation companies only increased from 6.6 million in 1920 to 9.0 million in 1978. Irrigated acreage served by public irrigation districts and USBR projects increased from 1.8 million and 1.3 million in 1920, to 10.8 million and 6.6 million in 1978, respectively, with most of this growth occurring since 1960. The steady growth in the share of irrigated acreage served by USBR projects and public irrigation districts occurred at the expense of declining acreage shares for mutuals and others, including commercial enterprises, state and local agencies, and the Bureau of Indian Affairs.

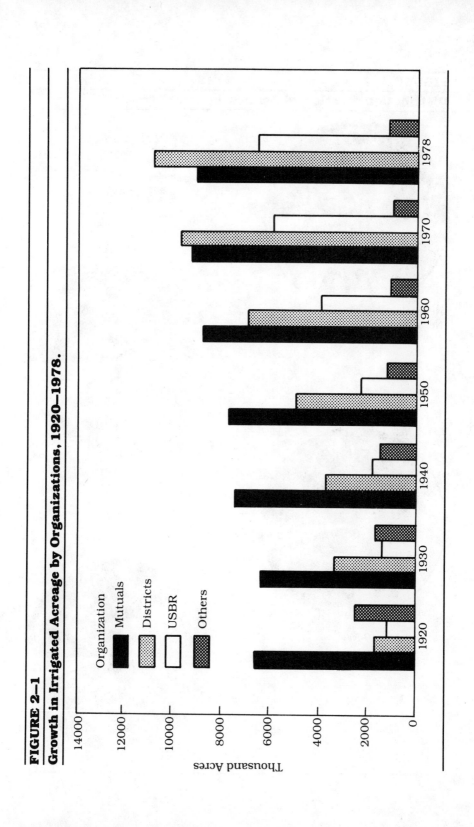

FIGURE 2–1

Growth in Irrigated Acreage by Organizations, 1920–1978.

FIGURE 2—2
Distribution of Irrigated Acreage by Time Periods

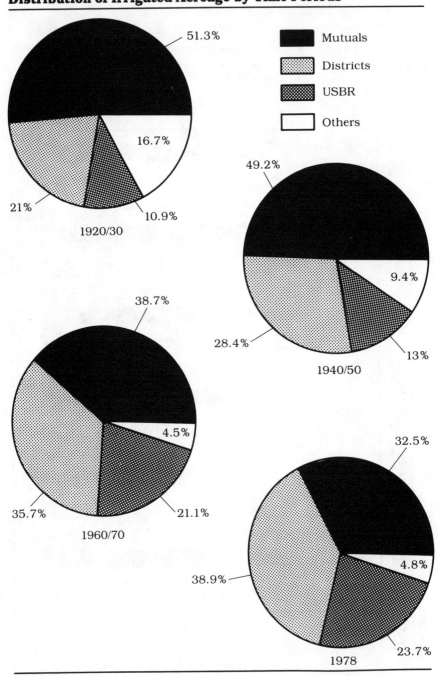

51.3%

Mutuals

Districts

USBR

Others

16.7%

21%

10.9%

1920/30

49.2%

9.4%

28.4%

13%

1940/50

38.7%

4.5%

35.7%

21.1%

1960/70

32.5%

4.8%

38.9%

23.7%

1978

TABLE 2–5

Distribution of Irrigated Acreage among Organizations

State	Fraction of total acreage served by USBR projects	Acreage share by organization				
		Mutuals	District	USBR operated	State/Local government	Other
Arizona	53.0	14.8	66.2	0.0	0.0	19.1
California	40.2	13.2	83.5	1.3	0.8	1.1
Colorado	7.3	89.4	9.1	0.0	0.0	1.4
Idaho	79.9	61.9	29.5	0.0	0.0	8.5
Kansas/Oklahoma	77.0	0.0	77.0	0.0	0.0	23.0
Montana	17.3	61.1	24.9	0.7	3.0	10.3
Nebraska	45.6	7.5	90.8	0.0	0.0	1.8
Nevada	40.6	50.6	42.2	0.0	0.0	7.2
North Dakota	68.3	0.0	91.2	0.0	0.0	8.8
New Mexico	41.5	39.9	32.4	17.1	0.0	10.6
Oregon	45.6	35.9	60.6	2.2	0.0	1.4
South Dakota	76.4	16.3	83.8	0.0	0.0	0.0
Texas	30.1	1.5	71.3	4.5	14.0	8.7
Utah	8.0	85.4	6.0	0.2	0.2	8.2
Washington	67.6	10.6	77.4	0.0	0.0	12.0
Wyoming	17.6	38.3	30.9	0.1	0.0	30.6
West Average	44.7	32.9	54.8	1.6	1.1	9.5

Source: U.S. Department of Commerce, *Census of Agriculture*, Part 4, *Irrigation* (1978), table 15, pp. 192–196.

Western states differ in their reliance on government agencies for irrigation development. The importance of USBR projects varies considerably among the western states (*see* table 2-5). Formal organizations in Colorado, Utah, Montana, and Wyoming depend less on USBR investments than organizations in Idaho, Kansas/Oklahoma, North and South Dakota, and Washington. Consequently, the potential effect of cuts in federal funding will differ among western states.

Overall, public irrigation districts are the predominant organizational form in the West, servicing 54.8 percent of the acres irrigated by formal organizations.[2] Arizona, California, Kansas/Oklahoma, North and South Dakota, Texas, and Washington rely quite heavily on public ownership. Private ownership—through mutual irrigation companies—is also important, servicing 32.9 percent of the acreage irrigated by formal organizations. Colorado, Idaho, Montana, and Utah are the bastions of private ownership.

USBR projects, on the other hand, by statutory requirements, promote public ownership at the expense of private ownership. States with larger shares of irrigated acreage serviced by USBR projects do not rely as heavily on mutual irrigation companies,[3] and rely instead on public irrigation districts.[4] USBR projects also are associated with relatively intensive water use (*see* table 2-6). They convey 55.3 percent of the water to only 44.7 percent of the irrigated acreage. Both public irrigation districts and private mutual irrigation companies convey smaller shares of water than their share of irrigated acreage.

TABLE 2—6

Distribution of Conveyed Water by Irrigation Organizations, 1978

State	Fraction of water from USBR projects	Water share by organization				
		Mutuals	District	USBR	State	Other
Arizona	65.0	7.3	47.9	24.8	0.0	20.0
California	46.0	10.5	41.7	27.6	7.0	13.2
Colorado	28.8	79.2	14.8	3.4	0.3	3.0
Idaho	52.2	35.2	19.6	40.4	0.0	4.8
Kansas/Oklahoma	75.8	0.0	60.8	14.9	0.0	24.2
Montana	60.2	31.3	13.8	50.4	1.4	3.1
Nebraska	35.6	4.3	82.9	10.1	0.0	2.7
Nevada	58.1	36.6	59.0	0.0	0.0	4.4
North Dakota	77.1	0.0	83.1	0.0	0.0	16.9
New Mexico	64.3	19.4	32.7	37.6	0.0	10.4
Oregon	63.8	22.7	48.2	15.5	0.0	13.5
South Dakota	83.7	10.9	74.8	14.3	0.0	0.0
Texas	14.7	2.0	54.3	3.1	30.9	9.6
Utah	18.8	80.1	10.6	0.6	1.0	7.6
Washington	81.8	3.5	41.9	45.2	0.0	9.4
Wyoming	58.9	18.1	30.2	39.5	0.0	12.2
West Average	55.3	22.5	44.8	20.5	2.5	9.6

Source: U.S. Department of Commerce, *Census of Agriculture*, Part 4, *Irrigation* (1978), table 15, pp. 192–196.

TABLE 2–7

**Water Use (per Irrigated Acres) and Revenues Collected
(per Acre Foot of Water Used), 1978**

State	Water use (gal.)	Water revenues ($)
Arizona	4.57	7.01
California	2.97	8.69
Colorado	2.03	2.45
Idaho	4.54	1.77
Kansas/Oklahoma	1.13	9.96
Montana	2.26	1.90
Nebraska	1.63	5.64
Nevada	3.68	2.25
New Mexico	2.24	4.34
North Dakota	1.71	7.17
Oregon	2.81	2.93
South Dakota	1.51	3.97
Texas	2.28	9.11
Utah	2.60	2.75
Washington	3.70	4.89
Wyoming	2.54	1.54
West Average	2.64	4.77

Source: U.S. Department of Commerce, *Census of Agriculture*, Part 4, *Irrigation* (1978), table 28, pp. 248.

DETERMINANTS OF WATER USE

Differences in water use are due not only to rainfall variation but to factors such as price and farm size. For example, a 10 percent increase in the price of water produces a 2 percent reduction in water use, whereas a 10 percent increase in farm size is associated with a 2 percent reduction in water use per irrigated acre.[5] Price and farm size explain almost 70 percent of the differences in water use among states.

On average, western states diverted 2.64 acre-feet of water per irrigated acre in 1978. But usage varied from more than 3 acre-feet in Arizona, Idaho, Nevada, and Washington, to fewer than 2 acre-feet in Kansas, Oklahoma, Nebraska, and North and South Dakota (*see* table 2-7). Organizations that distribute water collected, on

TABLE 2–8

Distribution (Percent) of Irrigated Acreage by Method of Irrigation, 1978

	Irrigation method			
	Furrow/ ditch	Flooding	Sprinkler	Other
Arizona	52.0	46.7	1.3	0.0
California	45.5	35.5	17.1	2.0
Colorado	54.2	37.0	8.8	0.1
Idaho	46.2	26.6	26.8	0.4
Kansas/Oklahoma	79.7	18.8	1.6	0.0
Montana	25.4	54.6	18.5	1.5
Nebraska	84.7	11.8	3.0	0.4
Nevada	27.0	70.8	2.1	0.1
New Mexico	63.1	30.1	6.8	0.0
North Dakota	40.4	53.2	6.5	0.0
Oregon	17.4	46.7	35.9	0.0
South Dakota	24.7	66.5	8.8	0.0
Texas	51.8	46.2	1.6	0.4
Utah	37.2	48.7	14.1	0.1
Washington	41.4	2.6	55.9	0.1
Wyoming	43.1	49.4	7.2	0.3
West Average	45.9	40.3	13.5	0.3

Source: U.S. Department of Commerce, *Census of Agriculture*, Part 4, *Irrigation* (1978), table 10, pp. 176.

average, $4.80 per acre-foot of water delivered in 1978. Costs were highest in Kansas and Oklahoma ($9.96), Texas ($9.11), California ($8.69), and Arizona ($7.01) and lowest in Idaho ($1.77) and Wyoming ($1.54).

Irrigation practices also affect water use, and their types vary among western states (*see* table 2-8). The furrow-and-ditch method is the most prevalent form, irrigating 45.9 percent of irrigated acreage. Flooding techniques irrigate another 40.3 percent. Sprinkler techniques irrigate only 13.5 percent. Chapter 5 discusses how the financial incentives for adopting various irrigation techniques depend on the method of financing water investment.

WATER INVESTMENT IN THE WEST

Irrigation is capital intensive. Costs for construction of conveyance facilities and acquisition of right-of-way and water rights are incurred many years before the project begins operation. The historical pattern of invested capital illustrates the dominant role played by federal funding in financing past western water investment in the past (*see* figures 2-3 and 2-4).

Irrigation investments in the last 25 years have been financed almost exclusively through public irrigation districts and the USBR. Invested capital in irrigation districts almost doubled from $1.4 billion in 1960 to $2.7 billion by 1978—measured in inflation-adjusted 1972 dollars. Invested capital financed by USBR projects increased from $2.3 billion to $4.1 billion over the same period. By 1978, 79.8 percent of invested capital in western irrigation enterpises was financed through these two sources.

However, there is considerable variation among western states in the level of investment and in the importance of the different formal organizations. Table 2-9 reports net investment by western states from 1970 to 1978. New investment during this eight-year period equaled $93.37 per irrigated acre. North Dakota, Arizona, and California were high-investment states, spending $5,754.00, $495.36, and $206.87 per irrigated acre, respectively.[6]

USBR projects accounted for 54 percent of western water investment over the past decade. In North Dakota, Kansas, and Oklahoma, all new investment, and, in Arizona 75 percent of new investment, was through USBR projects. On the other hand, only 16 percent of the water investment in Montana and Washington was accounted for by the USBR. The larger the share of a state's water investment financed through USBR, the greater the level of new investment per irrigated acre.[7]

The bureau also has been an important source of debt finance for western water development (*see* table 2-10). Western states' total debt outstanding for irrigation development was $140.90 per irrigated acre in 1978, 66.7 percent of which was owed to the bureau. This debt involves contracts through which irrigators repay the capital and operating costs incurred by USBR projects.

WESTERN STATE AND LOCAL GOVERNMENTS' DEBT

Prudent evaluation of water-financing alternatives in response to fewer federal funds requires an understanding of the overall debt

FIGURE 2–3

Invested Capital by Formal Organizations, 1920–1978 ($1972)

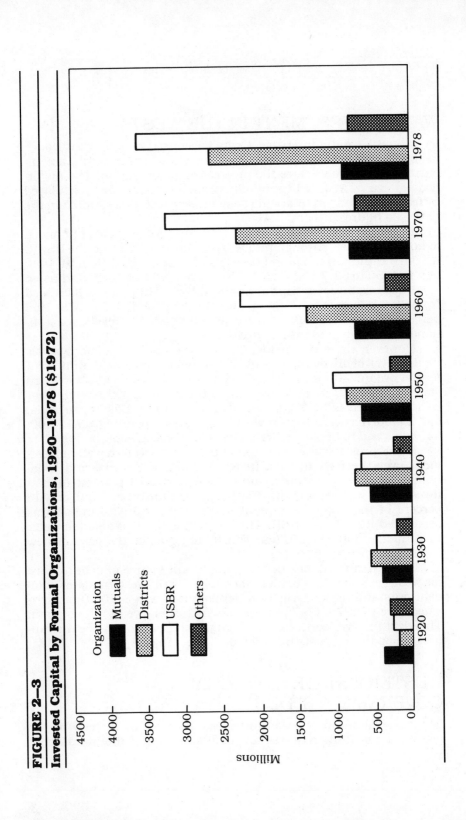

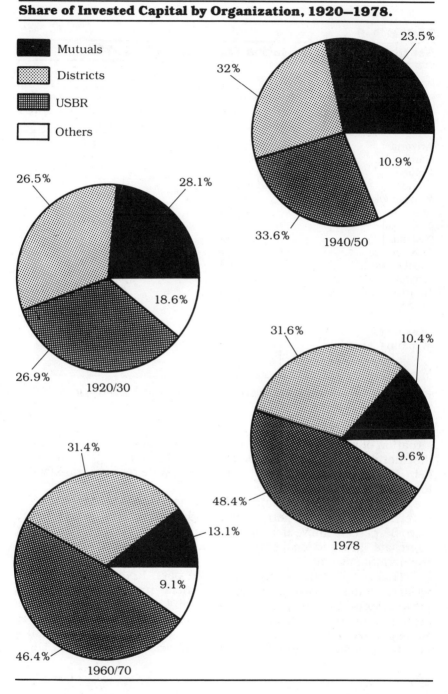

FIGURE 2—4

Share of Invested Capital by Organization, 1920—1978.

- Mutuals
- Districts
- USBR
- Others

23.5%

32%

10.9%

33.6%   1940/50

26.5%   28.1%

18.6%

26.9%   1920/30

31.6%   10.4%

9.6%

48.4%   1978

31.4%

13.1%

9.1%

46.4%   1960/70

TABLE 2—9

Net Investment in Irrigation Facilities, 1970-1978

State	Investment per irrigated acre ($/acre)	Share in USBR projects (%)
Arizona	495.36	94.7
California	206.87	78.2
Colorado	25.93	55.0
Idaho	43.52	77.5
Kansas/Oklahoma	90.27	100.0
Montana	42.18	16.8
Nebraska	29.08	20.1
Nevada	12.38	15.2
New Mexico	103.55	74.7
North Dakota	5,754.23	99.9
Oregon	114.30	66.7
South Dakota	2.95	54.0
Texas	57.09	35.2
Utah	70.90	36.9
Washington	30.80	16.1
Wyoming	75.35	72.7
West Average	93.37	54.0

Source: U.S. Department of Commerce, *Census of Agriculture*, Part 4, *Irrigation* (1978), table 22, pp. 224–226.

situation of western state and local governments. Western states are distinctive in the relative role of state versus local governmental debt. This partly reflects the greater use of state revenue transfers to local governments.

Compared to other state and local governments, western state governments have 55 percent less and western local governments have 35 percent more debt outstanding (*see* table 2-11).[8] However, aggregate state and local governmental debt in western states equals the national average.

This regional difference results, in part, from the tradition in western states of placing greater financial responsibility on local governments. But the greater reliance on local debt is offset by the large role of intergovernmental revenue transfers (see chapter 4). State governmental revenues transferred to local governments substitute for reduced state borrowing to finance public works. These transfers have a modest effect on combined amount of state and local debt outstanding.[9] In contrast, federal grants to state governments increase the debt of state governments, and federal grants to local governments increase those governments' debt. Federal grants normally contain obligations for the recipient to match federal funds, and those requirements necessitate borrowing.

Western states also differ from nonwestern states in the nature of their outstanding debt (see table 2-12). At both the state and local levels of government, western states have smaller fractions of their long-term debt (maturity exceeding one year) in bonds backed by the full faith and credit of the issuing government. They rely more heavily on limited obligation or revenue bonds. The debt of western state and local governments is longer term than that of the nation as a whole. The growth rate of state debt for western states has been similar to

TABLE 2–10

Total Debt Outstanding and Owed to USBR, 1978

| State | Total debt outstanding | | Share owed to USBR |
	Per acre	Per acre foot of water	
Arizona	297.58	36.46	53.5
California	236.02	57.35	39.4
Colorado	77.45	13.07	79.9
Idaho	67.41	8.99	87.0
Kansas/Oklahoma	186.12	69.69	100.0
Montana	41.40	10.98	43.9
Nebraska	93.15	51.67	96.1
Nevada	63.95	6.51	9.1
New Mexico	128.17	24.60	76.9
North Dakota	*	*	*
Oregon	148.33	27.90	66.0
South Dakota	53.69	19.87	68.1
Texas	128.93	30.67	63.5
Utah	332.95	80.77	83.1
Washington	132.95	24.10	64.2
Wyoming	84.85	15.45	70.8
West Average	140.90	31.90	66.7

Source: U.S. Department of Commerce, Census of Agriculture, Part 4, Irrigation (1978), table 26, pp. 236.

27

TABLE 2—11

Per-Capita State and Local Government Debt (Dollars), 1980-1981

State	Debt outstanding		
	State	Local	Combined
Arizona	51	1,951	1,966
California	380	730	1,110
Colorado	247	1,294	1,541
Idaho	401	429	830
Kansas	178	1,507	1,685
Montana	385	1,132	1,517
Nebraska	157	2,862	3,019
Nevada	693	1,055	1,748
New Mexico	585	1,483	2,067
North Dakota	325	927	1,252
Oklahoma	573	704	1,276
Oregon	2,241	929	3,170
South Dakota	1,003	631	1,634
Texas	186	1,396	1,582
Utah	396	1,090	1,486
Washington	434	2,771	3,205
Wyoming	959	2,279	3,238
West average	540	1,360	1,900
U.S. average	784	1,127	1,911

Source: U.S. Department of Commerce, *Governmental Finances in 1980-1981*, table 19, pp. 56–61.

states in other regions, but western local governments' debt grew at almost twice the rate of local governmental debt nationwide.

CONCLUSIONS

The historical record of western water development is one of innovation and adaptation to the region's geographical and economic circumstances. The *appropriative doctrine* replaced the legal institutions of the East. Meager rainfall compelled the development of supplies from distant sources. Individuals, private organizations, and local governments were early leaders and sources of sustained investment in irrigation. The pattern of investment is economically rational—counter to popular characterization: water use is smaller where costs are high.

Federal funding, injected through USBR projects, has been an important source of financing for water investment. Bureau funding not only increased invested capital per irrigated acre, but also transformed the relative roles of private and public ownership of irrigation enterprises. Federal funding cuts return financing responsibility to the original institutions in western states.

At the most general level, this shift in policy will require greater

TABLE 2–12

Composition and Growth (Percent) of State and Local Government Debt for Western States, 1980-1981

State	Fraction of total debt long-term		Share of long-term debt full faith		New Issuance of Debt relative to total	
	State	Local	State	Local	State	Local
Arizona	100.0	95.7	0.0	34.1	32.8	11.3
California	98.6	98.0	69.8	43.9	4.4	3.7
Colorado	98.7	99.0	0.0	41.8	33.6	14.0
Idaho	100.0	83.8	0.2	61.8	13.6	4.0
Kansas	100.0	94.8	6.6	29.9	−4.8	17.6
Montana	100.0	99.1	2.0	19.6	−2.1	41.2
Nebraska	100.0	94.1	0.0	15.3	19.1	1.9
Nevada	100.0	99.9	18.8	63.1	4.8	11.5
New Mexico	99.3	99.2	3.1	16.3	6.9	24.8
North Dakota	96.9	99.6	4.9	30.2	−7.1	2.1
Oklahoma	99.8	97.7	9.8	47.0	11.3	10.5
Oregon	100.0	96.3	93.2	57.0	17.5	5.6
South Dakota	99.9	99.9	0.0	21.6	6.1	2.4
Texas	100.0	98.7	33.1	46.5	7.2	7.1
Utah	100.0	99.9	15.3	35.2	7.2	46.0
Washington	99.9	99.0	78.7	16.6	9.6	13.7
Wyoming	100.0	99.7	0.0	29.7	19.4	−29.0
West average	99.5	97.2	19.7	35.9	10.6	11.1
U.S. average	98.4	93.8	30.9	48.0	10.3	6.5

*1969 to 1978

Source: U.S. Department of Commerce, *Governmental Finances in 1980-1981*, table 19, pp. 55–61.

financing through the municipal bond market. Whatever the allocation of financial responsibility between state and local governments, private investors will become the source of funds previously obtained from the USBR. How much will be forthcoming from private investors, and at what interest rates, will depend on the revenues standing behind the borrower's repayment obligations.

Western states' aggregate debt levels are comparable to those prevailing in other regions. Given the West's tradition of placing greater financial responsibility on local governments—the debt levels of which have been accelerating faster than national rates—it is not clear how western governments can replace federal funding without significant increases in financing costs. Therefore, the next five chapters provide the framework for addressing these issues. Chapter 3 examines the workings of the municipal bond market and the factors that affect the cost of public capital investment. That examination is followed by, in the next four chapters, a discussion of the strategies available for meeting these market forces on the best possible terms.

TEXT NOTES

1. U.S. Department of Commerce, *Census of Agriculture, Part 4, Irrigation* (1980), table 1, pp. 146-147.

2. The averages for western states in figure 2-2 differ from those given in table 2-5 because the former takes the share of western acreage in the various alternatives and the latter computes those shares by states and then averages over the 17 western states. The different results indicate that states with smaller totals of irrigated acreage have greater shares served by irrigation districts and USBR projects than do states with larger amounts of irrigated acreage.

3. The correlation between the share of acreage served by USBR projects and the share of acreage in mutual irrigation companies is −0.60.

4. The correlation between the share of acreage served by USBR projects and the share of acreage in irrigation districts is +0.65.

5. Regression analysis explaining the variation among states in their water use per acre by per unit revenues and average farm size yields the following coefficients and t-statistics (reported in parentheses): Water use = 2.122 (3.00) − 0.226 (−1.46) revenue/acre-foot + 0.780 (4.99) farm size. R^2 = 0.687. Standard deviation: Dependent variable = 0.622; Residual = 0.373.

   All variables are measured in natural logarithms. The per-unit-revenue variable is statistically significant at the 8 percent level (one-tailed test). The farm-size variable is statistically significant at the 0.0002 level (one-tailed test).

6. North Dakota's absurdly high invested capital per irrigated acre is explained by the substantial investment projects still in progress. The costs of these projects are included in the Commerce Department's data on invested capital, while the expected expansion in irrigation acreage awaits their completion.

7. Regression analysis of investment per acre versus the share of investment financed through USBR yielded the following results: Investment = 4.64 (10.60) + 0.874 (2.06) USBR share. $R^2 = 0.245$.

   Both variables are measured in natural logarithms. The analysis excludes North Dakota, whose inclusion would have strengthened the effect of the share of investment financed through the USBR and new investment per irrigated acre.

8. Regression analysis of state and local government debt per capita yields the results used in the text's discussion. The estimated coefficients and t-statistics (reported in parentheses) are:

Explanatory Variable	State Debt Per Capita	Local Debt Per Capita
Constant	−21.73 (−3.37)	1.24 (0.27)
Population	−0.046 (−0.34)	−0.033 (−0.36)
Income	2.00 (2.91)	0.35 (0.76)
Western region	−0.55 (−2.76)	0.35 (2.59)
Federal money to state	1.96 (4.12)	−0.20 (−0.63)
Federal money to local	0.22 (0.60)	0.25 (1.01)
State money to local	−0.34 (−1.57)	0.45 (3.06)
Alaska	−0.47 (−0.57)	1.46 (2.64)
R^2	0.619	0.589
Standard deviation:		
Dependent variable	0.859	0.551
Residual	0.573	0.382

With the exception of the western-region and Alaska variables, all other variables are measured in natural logarithms.

9. The findings in note 8 indicate that a 10 percent increase in state revenue transfers to local governments would reduce state per-capita debt by 3.4 percent and increase local per-capita debt by 4.5 percent. Applying these percentages to average western per-capita state and local debt outstanding ($540 and $1,360, respectively) implies that state debt would decline by $18.36 and local debt would increase by $61.20. So, combined state and local debt would increase by $42.84, or by 2.25 percent. Therefore, a 10 percent increase in state revenue transfers to local governments increases total state and local debt by 2.25.

CHAPTER 3

THE MUNICIPAL BOND MARKET AND THE COST OF CAPITAL TO STATE AND LOCAL GOVERNMENTS

THE MUNICIPAL BOND MARKET is the major mechanism through which states, municipalities, and their political subdivisions borrow money. The volume of money raised in any year usually accounts for 20 percent to 25 percent of state and local governments' spending.[1] This process is aided by thousands of specialized financial intermediaries—rating agencies, underwriters, insurance institutions, and brokers—whose task it is to compile and disseminate the complex information needed by the buyers and sellers of bonds.

How effectively does the market perform? How well is information about the vast number of issues coordinated and delivered among this community of borrowers and investors? Is the market for municipal debt likely to be saturated by the growing volume of public debt issued to meet increased demands for public investment? If so, will this impose additional costs for financing water investment? This chapter answers these questions by analyzing historical developments in the municipal bond market and examining the traditional mechanisms—yield differentials, bond ratings, and bidding practices—used to develop and transmit information about the collateral underlying bond issues. This discussion provides the background for subsequent analysis of state government policies affecting western water finance and identifies the important factors that determine the cost of capital.

The first section describes the basic borrowing transaction as a process in which the borrower builds and markets collateral. The next section describes recent trends in outstanding debt levels and new issues. The third section reviews municipal interest rates, differentials between yields on municipal and corporate bonds, and differentials between yields on municipal bonds of various risk classes. The fourth section discusses how bond yields depend upon bond ratings and the disposition of bond proceeds. The fifth section examines the role played by underwriters and how the selection of and competition among underwriters can affect the cost of raising money. The sixth section summarizes what is known about how these factors determine the cost of borrowing money. The final section shows how the postmortem on the largest default in the history of municipal bonds—The Washington Public Power Supply System—forced the investment-banking community to extend their analyses into the underlying economics of the financed project.

BUILDING AND MARKETING COLLATERAL

Debt finance represents a deceptively simple exchange: one party receives money in return for the promise to repay in the future. *Collateral* is the security that underwrites the ability to execute that promise: the more secure the future repayment, the more cheaply money can be borrowed. However, despite its importance, collateral is an elusive concept. It is difficult, if not impossible, to measure objectively.

Much of the activity in the bond market centers on structuring a government's promise to repay private investors. *Building collateral* involves enhancing the borrower's ability to repay. This can be done by strengthening the financial health of the project being financed and by making the borrower better able to withstand unexpected and adverse changes in future economic, fiscal, and other conditions. *Marketing collateral* involves disseminating information about the borrower and the project to be financed to potential investors. Borrowers must compete with the large number of other jurisdictions in the market.

These two functions—building and marketing collateral—are central to the development of a successful water-financing strategy.

RECENT TRENDS IN MUNICIPAL DEBT AND NEW BOND ISSUES

The 1960s and 1970s witnessed sweeping changes in the municipal bond market—a sixfold increase in the number of issues, growth in the relative importance of revenue bonds in the tax-exempt market, and shifts in the ownership of municipal debt.

Municipal Debt: Magnitude and Ownership

The debt of state and local governments represents a quarter of total governmental debt in the United States. This share increased to 30 percent in the mid-1970s, but financing of recent federal deficits has reduced the share to its former level.[2] Although the share has been relatively stable, the amount has grown. Overall, state and local outstanding debt increased by 158 percent between 1970 and 1981.

State governmental debt increased 223 percent, while local governments' debt increased by 131 percent. Local governments remain the major source of debt, although their share of total municipal debt declined from 70.8 percent to 63.4 percent over the last decade.

Commercial banks and households purchase and hold the largest share of state and municipal debt. Although their shares have declined slightly during the 1970s, commercial banks hold about 45 percent and households around 24 percent of municipal debt today. The share of debt held by insurance companies has grown from 17 percent during the 1970s to almost 25 percent. All of these sectors have absorbed the increasing amounts of state and local governmental debt (see figure 3-1).

Because the interest is exempt from federal income taxation, municipal bond ownership is concentrated among high-income households.[3] Households with marginal federal income tax rates below 20 percent own less than 5 percent, whereas those with marginal federal income tax rates above 50 percent own almost 70 percent of the municipal debt held by individuals.

New Issues of Municipal Debt: Types and Uses

Municipal bonds may be divided into two categories—general obligation bonds and revenue bonds. General obligation bonds are long-term issues backed by the full faith and credit and taxing power of the jurisdiction issuing the bond. Revenue bonds are long-term bonds issued to finance a revenue-generating project and rely solely on project revenues for repayment. However, in recent years, this simple categorization has blurred. A new hybrid, double-barreled bonds, has the jurisdiction's taxing power stand behind the revenues raised by the project.

In recent years the bond market has changed in two dramatic and interrelated ways. First is the method of repayment. Short-term issues have grown, and hybrid bonds, moral obligation double-barreled bonds, have proliferated. This has restructured how governments use their ability to incur debt by invoking their general taxation powers. Second, the reasons for issuing bonds have changed. The tax-exempt market has been used increasingly to finance private projects—through the issue of pollution-control bonds, mortgage revenue bonds, and health-care revenue bonds.

Long-term and short-term debt. The volume of long-term debt outstanding in 1980 soared to three times the volume outstanding in 1970, which was, in turn, two and a half times the volume in 1960 (see table 3-1). The issuance of short-term debt also

FIGURE 3–1
Ownership of Outstanding State and Local Debt.

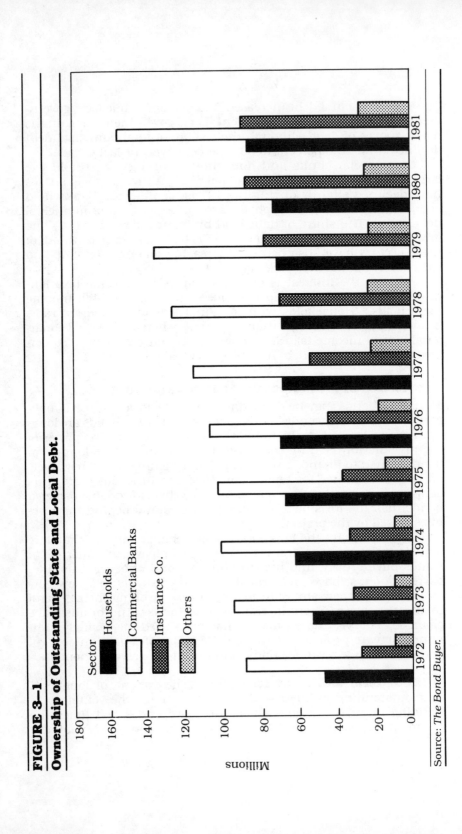

Source:: *The Bond Buyer.*

Table 3—1

New Issues of State and Municipal Debt, 1955-1982

Year	Debt type			
	Long term		Short term	
	Volume (millions)	Percentage of general obligation	Volume (millions)	Ratio to long term
1955	5,977	71.0	2,593	0.434
1960	7,230	69.6	4,006	0.554
1965	11,084	67.2	6,537	0.590
1970	17,761	66.4	17,880	1.007
1975	29,326	51.2	28,973	0.988
1980	47,133	34.6	26,449	0.561
1981	45,323	30.7	34,333	0.756
1982	74,877	30.8	42,915	0.573

Source: *Moody's Municipal and Government Manual,* special supplement section, p. a6.

has been growing, but not as rapidly. The ratio of short-to-long-term debt issues recently declined to the level prevailing in the late 1960s, although the levels of both debt issues were at historic highs. Issuing short-term bonds was one way states and municipalities could reduce the costs of debt finance when interest rates were at record levels in the early 1980's, because short-term bond issuance allowed for refinancing when rates fell.

Distribution by type of government. The distribution of debt issuance has evolved steadily by type of government (*see* table 3-2). During the 1970s, state governments' share of total long-term activity declined by 50 percent. Counties' share grew by 56 percent, whereas that of school districts and special districts declined by 33 percent and 55 percent, respectively. Statutory authorities displayed the strongest growth, more than doubling their share during the 1970s. Municipalities share of debt issuance grew in the 1960s and declined during the 1970s.

Purposes for issuing debt. The purposes for which debt is incurred also have changed (table 3-3). The traditional public purposes of debt (water and sewer, transportation, and education) have given way to pollution-control, industrial-development, and public power bonds.[4] These newer purposes rely more on revenue bonding

TABLE 3–2

Municipal Borrowing by Government Entities

Authority	% borrowed in:				
	1966	1970	1974	1978	1980-1981
States	21.0	22.0	15.9	10.0	11.0
Counties	6.6	9.1	8.7	10.3	10.3
Municipalities	20.9	26.3	27.0	20.3	18.0
School districts	14.2	11.8	9.2	5.4	4.0
Special districts	6.9	6.4	5.3	2.3	3.1
Statutory authorities	30.4	24.4	33.9	51.7	53.6

Source: Public Securities Association, *Fundamentals of Municipal Bonds*
(New York: Public Securities Association, 1998l), p. 51.

than do traditional purposes. Therefore, the changing public purpose of governmental expenditure is partly responsible for the declining reliance on general obligation bonds.

INTEREST RATES ON MUNICIPAL DEBT

Much of the present pessimism about the ability of states to issue more debt for public works without paying higher interest rates is based upon three misconceptions about the municipal bond market:[5] 1) interest rates for municipal bonds have risen because New York City's financial problems in 1975, Cleveland's bankruptcy in 1978, and the recent default of the Washington Public Power Supply System raised concerns about default for all municipalities; 2) the differential between yields on tax-exempt and taxable debt has narrowed sharply and is unlikely to return to former levels; and 3) differentials among yields on municipal bonds of different risk classes have widened.

If these observations were true, they would indicate that the market was on the verge of saturation—that is, it would not be possible to increase the volume of state and local debt without substantially increasing interest rates. However, the evidence shows no factual support for any of these beliefs.

The Level of Municipal Bond Interest Rates

Interest rates on municipal bonds reached record levels in recent years. Most of this increase, and most of the major fluctuations in municipal bond rates, is attributable to changes in overall economic conditions and not to factors that are peculiar to the tax-exempt market.

Overall economic conditions influence the bond market in two ways. First, cyclical downturns widen the yield differentials between U.S. government bonds and other, more risky bonds, and upturns narrow these differentials (Kidwell and Koch, 1982). Second, apart from these cyclical effects, the risk premium on municipal bonds—the amount their yields exceed the rates on U.S. Treasury notes—rises as overall interest rates increase (Yawitz, 1978).[6] These two relations exist because recession and high interest rates weaken the ability of state and local governments to service their outstanding debt in the face of other competing financial obligations.[7]

Table 3-4 shows the predicted yields from historical relations prevailing for the past 27 years for four categories of municipal bonds under different growth rates of real gross national product (GNP) and different rates on Treasury notes.[8] The data indicate that a decline in the growth rate of real GNP from 2 percent to −2 percent is associated with an increase in the yield on AAA-rated bonds by 61

Table 3—3

Tax-Exempt Long-Term Borrowing (Percent) by Purpose,

| Year | Purpose | | | | | |
	Water & sewer	Public power	Pollution Control	Transpor-tation	Education	Industrial revenue bonds
1970	13.3	6.0	*	17.7	27.6	*
1971	12.9	5.2	3.6	17.3	21.3	*
1972	5.5	5.1	1.7	7.2	12.2	*
1973	8.0	5.9	6.3	6.7	9.7	*
1974	8.5	3.8	6.4	6.4	15.7	*
1975	7.5	8.8	7.2	7.2	15.3	4.2
1976	8.5	7.6	5.4	9.6	15.0	4.2
1977	7.1	10.3	5.6	6.2	10.9	4.9
1978	6.7	12.1	5.6	7.3	10.4	7.3
1979	6.4	11.1	4.3	4.9	10.5	14.6
1980	5.0	8.8	4.0	4.5	7.9	14.4
1981	6.1	13.2	9.2	7.3	9.4	21.2

*, Indicates data not available.
Source: Vaughan (1983), table 17, p. 91.

TABLE 3—4

Yields on Municipal Bonds and Market Conditions

Bond rating	Growth rate in real GNP	Yield on 10-year Treasury bill at:			
		6%	8%	10%	12%
AAA	4	4.60	6.08	7.55	9.03
	2	4.91	6.38	7.86	9.33
	−2	5.52	6.99	8.47	9.54
	−4	5.82	7.30	8.77	10.25
AA	4	4.81	6.33	7.85	9.38
	2	5.13	6.65	8.17	9.69
	−2	5.77	7.29	8.81	10.33
	−4	6.09	7.61	9.13	10.65
A	4	5.07	6.59	8.11	9.63
	2	5.44	6.96	8.48	10.00
	−2	6.17	7.69	9.21	10.73
	−4	6.53	8.06	9.58	11.09
BAA	4	5.41	6.97	8.52	10.08
	2	5.82	7.37	8.93	10.49
	−2	6.63	8.18	9.74	11.30
	−4	7.03	8.59	10.15	11.70

Source: See text.

basis points—1 basis point is equal to 1/100 of a percentage point. An increase in the yield on 10-year U.S. Treasury notes from 8 percent to 10 percent is associated with an increase in AAA yields of 295 basis points.[9]

Between 1955 and 1982, these two aspects of overall economic conditions explain over 90 percent of the variation in year-end municipal bond yields. They exerted as powerful an influence at the end of the period as they did at the beginning—there is no evidence of any change in behavior of the market. Figure 3-2 illustrates this absence of change by showing the actual and predicted yields on AAA- and BAA-rated bonds based on the historical relations prevailing from 1955 to 1982. Because no evidence exists that the well-publicized fiscal problems experienced by New York City and a handful of other municipalities raised the interest rates for other municipal borrowers (Kidwell and Trezcinka, 1982), a strong economic recovery

FIGURE 3–2A

Actual and Predicted Yields on AAA Municipal Bonds.

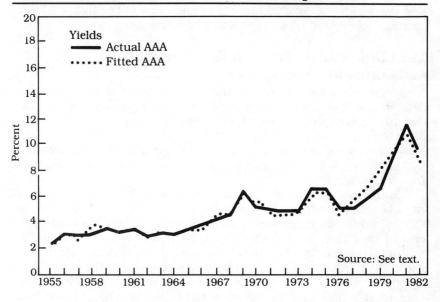

FIGURE 3–2B

Actual and Predicted Yields on BAA Municipal Bonds.

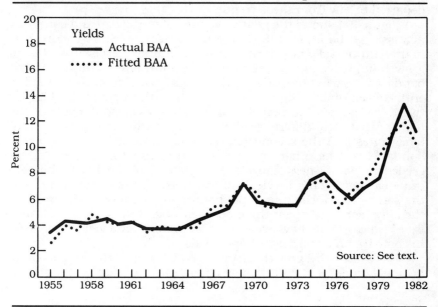

and lower rates of inflation will alleviate many of the financial difficulties experienced by state and local governments.

Yield Differentials Between Tax-Exempt and Corporate Debt

Many observers are concerned that the expansion of new municipal debt issues has eroded the interest rate differentials between tax-exempt and corporate debt (Congressional Budget Office, 1979; Johnson, 1982; and Peterson, 1979). However, evidence, reviewed below, indicates that neither the overall growth of municipal debt nor the growth of municipals relative to taxable debt has influenced the yield differential.

Municipal bond interest rates are lower than corporate bond rates because the interest payments on the former are exempt from federal, and sometimes state, income taxes. Figure 3-3 reports the end of year (December) yield differentials between outstanding municipal and taxable corporate bonds outstanding by utilities for the highest (AAA) and lowest (BAA) investment-grade bonds rated by Moodys.[10] Yield differentials are expressed as: 1) the difference between yields on corporate and municipal bonds; and 2) the ratio of municipal to corporate bond yields. Both measures indicate similar trends. Municipal yields have fallen relative to corporate yields, evidenced by the rising differential in yields and the falling ratio of yields. The differentials in 1981 and, to a lesser extent in 1980, departed briefly from these trends.

Figure 3-4 shows the relative volume of municipal and corporate new issues of bonds for 1955 to 1982. The last two years were unusual in that municipal new issues exceeded corporate new issues—due to growth in issues of pollution-control and industrial-development bonds. Comparing these data with the pattern of interest rate differentials over time in figure 3-3 shows that the year of the *highest* relative volume of municipal issues (1982) was also the year of the *highest* historical differences between corporate and municipal interest rates and the second *lowest* ratio of municipal to corporate bond yields. The other years in which municipal new issues exceeded corporate new issues (1959, 1973, 1977 to 1979) show no unusual movements in yield differentials. Those concerned about the saturation of the municipal bond market concentrate on 1981, the only year in the past three decades when municipal new issues exceeded corporate new issues and municipal bond yields increased in comparison to corporate bond yields.

Fears that the growth of municipal debt relative to corporate debt will erode yield differentials ignore the importance of arbitrage

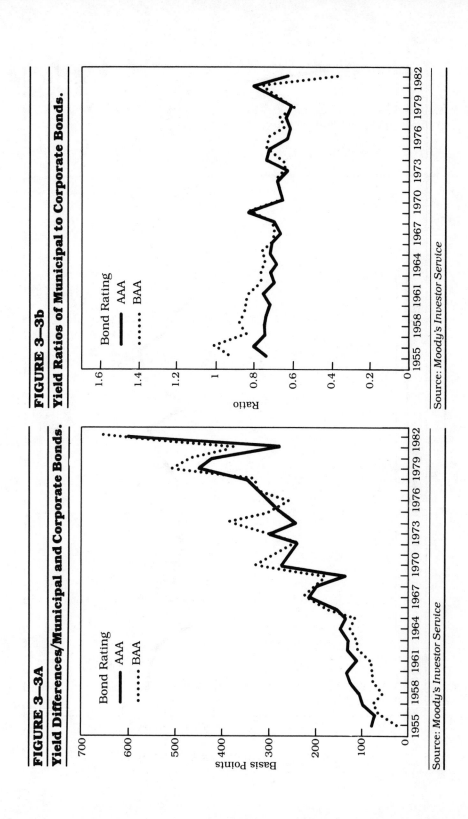

FIGURE 3–3A

Yield Differences/Municipal and Corporate Bonds.

Source: *Moody's Investor Service*

FIGURE 3–3b

Yield Ratios of Municipal to Corporate Bonds.

Source: *Moody's Investor Service*

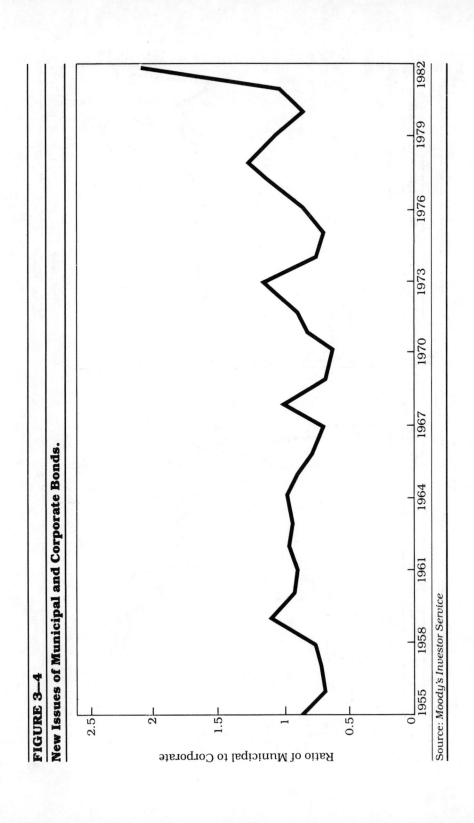

FIGURE 3—4

New Issues of Municipal and Corporate Bonds.

Source: *Moody's Investor Service*

activities by the largest owner of municipal debt—commercial banks. By rapidly changing the volume of tax-exempt issues that they hold, banks and corporations can shift enormous volumes of investment funds between the tax-exempt and the taxable debt markets (see Miller, 1977, and Fama, 1977).

Because of this arbitrage, yield differentials between municipal and corporate bonds are not affected systematically by the volume of new state and local debt issues or the amount of debt outstanding relative to corporate debt. For all maturities and bond ratings, yields on municipal debt follow corporate debt yields, with no systematic effect from increasing or decreasing state and municipal share of total issuance of new bonds (Trezcinka, 1982).[11] One study estimates that a $1 billion increase in state and local debt increases relative municipal yields by only one-tenth of a basis point.[12] The link between the level of municipal debt and municipal bond yields is tenuous in theory and fact.[13]

The yield differential between corporate and municipal bonds depends on the level of corporate rates and on the state of the economy (see table 3-5).[14] If the growth rate of real GNP falls from 2 percent to −2 percent, the yield differential on AAA and BAA bonds narrows by 29 and 39 basis points, respectively. The yield differential widens when the level of corporate interest rates increases. There was, indeed, a narrowing of the yield differential during 1981 for AAA and BAA bonds that cannot be explained by changes in the level of interest rates or the state of the national economy. The phenomenon may be a result of the adjustment of the market to large changes in corporate and personal income tax rates enacted that year. However, the departure was short-lived, and yield differentials have since returned to their historic levels (see Figure 3-5). Saturation of the municipal bond market, per se, is not a significant problem confronting debt financing of water projects.

Yield Differentials Between Municipal Bonds of Different Risk Classes

Many water projects—both water supply and wastewater treatment—are financed by agencies with little credit experience or a poor credit rating. While low-rated bonds traditionally command higher yields, no recent developments place them at a further disadvantage. Between 1955 and 1982, the yield on BAA-rated bonds exceeded that on AAA, AA, and A-rated bonds by 85.8, 64, and 36 basis points, respectively. The variability in the relative yield differentials has changed little over time.[15] Figure 3-6 reports differen-

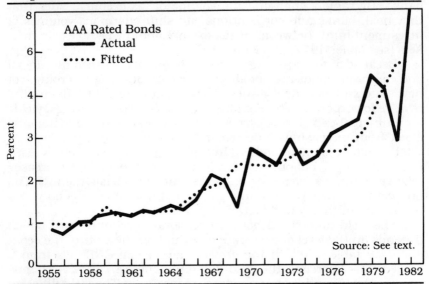

FIGURE 3–5A

Actual and Predicted Yield Differentials of Municipal and Corporate Bonds.

AAA Rated Bonds
—— Actual
...... Fitted

Source: See text.

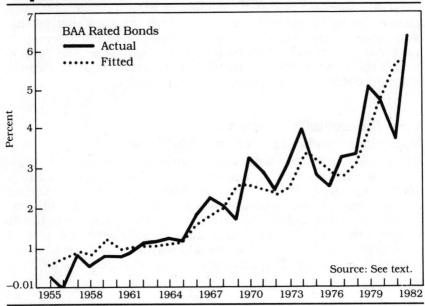

FIGURE 3–5B

Actual and Predicted Yield Differentials of Municipal and Corporate Bonds.

BAA Rated Bonds
—— Actual
...... Fitted

Source: See text.

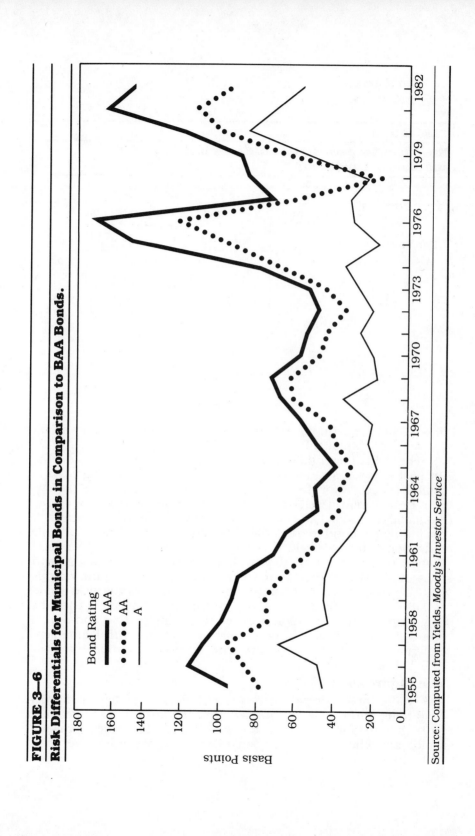

FIGURE 3–6

Risk Differentials for Municipal Bonds in Comparison to BAA Bonds.

Bond Rating

AAA

AA

A

Basis Points

1955 1958 1961 1964 1967 1970 1973 1976 1979 1982

180 160 140 120 100 80 60 40 20 0

Source: Computed from Yields, *Moody's Investor Service*

TABLE 3–5

**Municipal/Corporate Yield Differentials
and Market Conditions**

Bond rating	Growth rate in real GNP	Yield on comparably rated corporate bond at:			
		8%	10%	12%	14%
AAA	4	2.58	3.24	3.90	4.57
	2	2.43	3.09	3.76	4.42
	−2	2.14	2.80	3.47	4.13
	−4	1.99	2.65	3.32	3.98
BAA	4	2.32	3.09	3.86	4.63
	2	2.14	2.91	3.68	4.45
	−2	1.77	2.54	3.31	4.08
	−4	1.59	2.36	3.13	3.89

Source: See text.

tials in yields on the lowest investment-grade bond (BAA) and on various higher-quality bonds.

The yield differentials exceeded their long-term averages during the past four years causing some concern about increasing costs of capital, especially for the lower-quality bonds (Johnson, 1982). However, these recent developments in the bond markets reflect overall economic conditions and do not reflect any fundamental changes in the municipal bond market. Table 3-6 shows how overall economic conditions effected yield differentials over the past 27 years.[16] Higher interest rates on 10-year Treasury notes and lower growth rates in real GNP widened the yield differentials among the various risk classes of municipal bonds. The movements in the yield differentials during the last four years are completely consistent with the long-term historical relation between those differentials and overall economic conditions. A strong economic recovery with falling general interest rates will find a narrowing of these yield differentials.

The Importance of Timing

The studies of municipal interest rates indicate that overall market conditions at the time of issuance drive the issuer's cost of capital for both high- and low-quality bonds. When the economy is growing rapidly and when inflation is low, yields on new issues are lower than during recessions or periods of high inflation. Prudent timing of a bond issue can cut the cost of debt finance by as much as 5 or 6 percentage points. Integrated planning of operating and financial demands is an important aspect of the general services provided by underwriters, whose functions are discussed later in this chapter.

RATING BONDS

To finance a project at the lowest possible cost, state and local governments must be able to persuade potential investors of the underlying creditworthiness of their bond issue. The rating earned from one of the two rating agencies is one of the most important ways of transmitting such information to the market.

Assessing bond quality is difficult. It involves predicting the tax and expenditure policies of the issuing government many years into the future, and the sheer number of bond issues—there are more than 1.5 million outstanding—makes it difficult for investors to obtain and process information. Investors are aided in this task by the rating process.

A bond rating is an independent assessment of the creditworthi-

TABLE 3—6

Risk Yield Differentials and Market Conditions

Bond rating	Growth rate in real GNP	Yield on 10-year Treasury bill at:			
		6%	8%	10%	12%
AAA	4	0.76	0.91	1.06	1.21
	2	0.96	1.11	1.26	1.41
	−2	1.36	1.51	1.66	1.81
	−4	1.56	1.71	1.86	2.01
AA	4	0.57	0.64	0.71	0.77
	2	0.70	0.77	0.84	0.90
	−2	0.96	1.03	1.10	1.17
	−4	1.09	1.16	1.23	1.30
A	4	0.34	0.40	0.45	0.51
	2	0.37	0.43	0.49	0.54
	−2	0.44	0.50	0.55	0.61
	−4	0.47	0.53	0.59	0.64

Source: See text.

ness of a proposed bond issue. It tells the issuer how the market-place perceives risk, and how different forms of collateral—revenue streams, management plans, legal covenants—influence this perception. The two major agencies providing ratings are Standard & Poors Corporation (S&P) and Moody's Investors Service, Inc.

Ratings consider the municipality's credit risk and its bond's marketability. This requires the rating agencies to assess the economic and financial strength of the issuing government and its willingness to retire its debt. Ratings are made primarily at the time the bonds are issued.[17] They may be reviewed either at the time of a subsequent new issue by the same government, or, less frequently, when economic or political developments change the government's financial capacity. Large issues are more likely to be rated than small issues—(see table 3-7). This does not imply any inherent disadvantages of small-scale borrowing. Most small issues are undertaken to purchase a specific piece of equipment and are held to maturity by commercial banks. These bonds do not enter national capital markets and are distinct from the larger issues used to finance large capital projects, which enter into the national municipal bond market.[18]

The four investment grade ratings used by the two agencies are: 1) AAA—capacity to pay interest and principal extremely strong; 2) AA—capacity to pay interest and principal very strong; 3) A—strong repayment capacity, more susceptible to adverse effects of changes in economic circumstances, and 4) BBB (BAA in Moody's system)—adequate capacity, even more susceptible to adverse effects of

---

TABLE 3—7

Percentage of Bonds Rated by Size of Issue, 1970

Size of issue	% rated	
(×$1,000)	Dollar volume	Number of issues
< 250	43.5	41.0
250 – 500	58.6	57.6
501 – 1,000	67.4	65.7
1,001 – 5,000	88.7	87.2
5,001 – 20,000	91.5	90.6
> 20,000	90.6	90.8
Overall	88.8	69.4

Source: Twentieth Century Task Force on Municipal Finance, *The Rating Game*, table 7, p. 41.

changes in economic circumstances. The two agencies rate bonds similarly 70 percent of the time. In 90 percent of the remaining cases, S&P gives a higher rating than Moody's (*see* Twentieth Century Fund 1974, p. 43).

The Rating Process

Rating involves analyzing *four aspects of debt assessment* (*see* Lamb and Rappaport, 1980): 1) *the nature of debt*—provisions of repayment and protection afforded by relative positions of obligations in event of bankruptcy or reorganization; 2) the *economic base of the jurisdiction*; 3) the *financial policies of the issuing government*; and 4) the *administrative policies of the issuing government.*

In recent years, this process has been complicated by the growing use of tax bases other than property taxes, the growth of intergovernmental transfers, and the increasing frequency of overlapping debt.[19] Because revenue bonds rely on the revenues generated by the proposed project, their rating analysis concentrates on the revenues dedicated to their repayment, rather than on the jurisdiction's taxing powers. In general, rating revenue bonds requires more detailed investigation than rating general obligation bonds, because the latter can rely on a review of the overall creditworthiness of the issuer. It does not have to examine the details of the projects that will be financed by the bond proceeds.

Moody's and Standard & Poors differ slightly in their rating methodologies. Moody's places more emphasis on debt analysis and Standard & Poors considers economic base as the most significant factor. In both cases, the agencies strive to be forward looking about the financial prospects of the issuing entity repaying the principal and interest promised at the time the bonds are sold.

There are *five ingredients of debt analysis* that have a significant bearing on a bond's eventual rating:[20] 1) *debt policy*—uses, purposes, and type of instrument; 2) *debt structures*—plans for debt retirement, including the relation between the rate of its retirement and its purpose; 3) *debt burden*—gross and net debt, including the degree of overlapping debt; 4) *debt history and trend*—includes the community's intent to refund instead of retire its maturing bonds and/or funding operating deficits by issuing debt; and 5) *prospective borrowing*—authorized but unissued debt as well as the future debt needs of the community.

In general, a community's rating is higher the closer its debt structure is to the useful life of its capital stock and the less likely the community is to issue further debt that might reduce its ability to meet its existing debt obligations. Both moral and statutory obligations are included in this analysis (Lamb and Rappaport, 1980, p. 101).

Analysis of debt is not conducted separately from analysis of the community's economic base. Debt levels per se do not indicate a problem unless they are high relative to the underlying financial capacity of the jurisdiction. The six most important *aspects of the economic base* considered by Standard & Poors are: 1) *income levels and growth*—relative to the community's region and the nation as a whole; 2) *employment mix*—a diversified employment base is better than reliance on a few basic industries; 3) *educational levels*—higher educational levels are preferred; 4) *age distribution of the population*— the greater the share of the population in the "dependency years" (under 18 and over 65 years of age), the smaller the perceived financial capacity; 5) *building activity*—the rate of new construction is viewed as an indicator of future growth; and 6) *age and composition of the housing stock*—deterioration is viewed as an indicator of less commitment to the community's future. These are all aspects of a jurisdiction's financial capacity and willingness to honor future repayment obligations.

The ratio of debt to market value of property is commonly used to combine the debt and economic base analyses. Property values are a good indicator of the economic value of services provided by the local government (*see* Tiebout, 1956; and Oates, 1972). Property values are higher in communities with more attractive combinations of public services and tax rates because such areas are more desirable places to live. So, a low debt-to-property-value ratio signifies a favorable combination of low future tax obligations (to service and retire the debt) and an attractive residential environment. Bonds with high ratings tend to have a low ratio of debt to assessed property values: AAA-rated bonds have an average ratio of debt to assessed value of 0.028; AA, 0.102; A, 0.150; and BAA, 0.360 (Carleton and Lerner, 1969, p. 75).

High bond ratings also are associated with a low ratio of net direct debt to assessed valuation, a low aggregate level of overlapping debt, a large property tax base, high median family income, and a low percentage of taxes uncollected (Rubinfeld, 1973). From the perspective of bond ratings, debt levels matter *primarily* relative to the size of the community's economic base.

The third aspect of rating analysis—*financial policies*—focuses on four areas of prudent fiscal management: 1) How sensitive is the revenue structure to future changes in economic conditions? 2) Have revenues and expenditures been in balance over the years? 3) How much reliance is placed on federal or state aid (reliance on intergovernmental aid is viewed as a potential liability, because if an important element of revenues is under the control of "outsiders" whose agendas may change, then that may place unexpected future financial burdens on the community.) and 4) Are revenue sources sufficiently diversified?

Revenue bonding requires stronger covenants than general obligation bonds because the collateral behind the bond must be built entirely from the financial capacity of the project. In general, three covenants are offered: 1) *debt service reserve*—a fund capable of covering the maximum annual debt service (interest payments plus debt retirement) incurred during the life of the bond; 2) *rate covenant*—an obligation that the pledged revenues will cover a specified percentage (usually 120 percent for water and sewer bonds) of operating, maintenance, and debt service costs; or 3) *replacement and renewal or maintenance fund*[21]—this fund sets aside proceeds to maintain and replace capital facilities.

For revenue bonds issued to finance water investment, *four project characteristics* are important in assessing quality (Lamb and Rappaport, 1980, pp. 62-64): 1) *the nature of the demand for the service*—a growth trend and little sensitivity to cyclical fluctuations are desired; 2) engineer's appraisal of the *soundness of physical plant*—facilities with *explicit* maintenance strategies and concern by management to avoid deterioration of capital are preferred; 3) *legal protection in covenants*—especially of concern is protecting the bond's priority in event of subsequent issuance of additional revenue bonds; and 4) *security of water supply*—is the water right guaranteed within the region or dependent upon the continued cooperation of outsiders? These are *forward looking* assessments of the strength of the "market" for the project's services.

Rating agencies also consider how much revenue can be raised by the authority relative to project costs. Table 3-8 reports the median values of common indices used in assessing bond quality for financing various municipal services. Projects have greater perceived bond quality when they boast larger net takedown, interest and debt-service coverage, and interest and debt-service safety margins. If a project's revenue and operating policies were to reduce these indices, the municipality would find its perceived bond quality deteriorating.

The final element in the rating analysis focuses on the *jurisdiction's planning process*. An explicit plan that forecasts the fiscal resources devoted to the project and the economic conditions of the community allows the marketplace to assess how well the issuer can meet its long-term obligations. A state or local government with foresight, a sound planning process backed by good information, and a clear implementation strategy strengthens the element of trust in-

TABLE 3—8

Financial Medians of Municipal Enterprises, 1982

	Municipal enterprise				
Characteristic*	Water	Sewer	Airport	Electricity Generation	Hospital
Net take-down (%)	38.7	39.2	48.2	11.0	26.0
Interest coverage (multiple)	4.3	3.6	4.2	4.2	na
Debt service coverage (multiple)	2.4	2.4	2.3	2.6	1.0
Debt service safety margin (multiple)	21.7	21.2	28.9	15.9	7.9

*Definitions — Net take-down: net revenues (gross revenues less operating and maintenance expenses) divided by system gross revenues. Interest coverage: net revenues available for debt service divided by interest for year. Debt service coverage: net revenues available for debt service divided by principal and interest requirements. Debt service safety margin: net revenues less current debt service divided by system gross revenues. na, not available.

Source: *Moody's Investor Service*

herent in the debt transaction. Financing problems are suspected when the jurisdiction appears to be poorly managed and short-sighted.[22] The consequence is higher financing costs.

Changes in an Issuer's Financial Status

Evaluation of an issuer's creditworthiness does not cease after a bond is issued. If the market judges that the economic and social conditions prevailing at the time of issue have changed markedly, the issuer's rating will be reassessed. The symptoms of economic or fiscal difficulties are cash-management problems including increasing amounts of unpaid current obligations, an increase in the ratio of debt to assessed property values, greater reliance on short-term borrowing, growing use of long-term bond proceeds to finance current expenditures, and an increasing amount of unpaid short-term debt at year's end. There are no hard and fast rules that define what level these indicators must reach to constitute danger signals, because the signals must be weighed against earlier expectations of the municipality's fiscal and economic performance.

Indicators of the underlying deterioration of a jurisdiction's fiscal and economic condition used by rating agencies as *red flags* include the following. For *revenues*—1) decreasing level or growth rate of the value of taxable property; 2) increasing ratios of unpaid taxes to taxes due; 3) increasing tax rates; 4) declining number or value of building permits; and 5) more frequent budget deficits resulting from unanticipated declines in revenues. For *expenditures*— 1) a growth in excess of current expenditures over current *local* revenue; 2) an elevation of excess of current expenditures over current total revenue; 3) increased real government expenditures; 4) more frequent excess of expenditures over approved budget levels; and 5) increasing unfunded pension liabilities.

A reduction in rating increases the cost of future borrowing. The market anticipates the change in ratings to some extent by requiring larger yields to purchase bonds from municipalities whose ratings were subsequently lowered. Yet the announcement of the rating change itself affects yields (Jantscher, 1970). The implication for water financing is clear. The market and rating agencies examine financial practices, planning processes, and management procedures. Borrowers who do not conduct these in a prudent fashion will suffer higher borrowing costs.

UNDERWRITING

Investment bankers and commercial banks provide important services to the municipal bond market. Through their underwriting activities, banks coordinate the bond market—matching buyers to sellers, designing financing plans, and disseminating information about the creditworthiness of municipalities. Competition among underwriters usually leads to higher-quality services and lower underwriting fees. State and local governments must use the services provided by underwriters effectively if they are to minimize the costs of issuing bonds.

The Function of Underwriters

Underwriters provide three services: advice and counsel, risk-bearing, and marketing of debt. The advice-and-counsel service familiarizes issuers with market conditions, so that they can secure the best possible terms for their issue, and also offers issuers technical assistance necessary to put together the financing plan. Risk-bearing enables the borrower to raise money without the speculation inherent in the sale of bonds. The underwriter purchases the bonds from the issuing government at a prearranged price, resells them on the open market, and keeps the proceeds.

The underwriter's commission from the risk-bearing service is the difference between the price paid the borrower and the revenue received from the sale of the bonds, called the underwriter's spread. This transaction guarantees states and municipalities revenues, even if market conditions change between the time underwriters purchase the bonds and the time they resell them to investors.[23] Because they participate infrequently in the market, states and municipalities cannot market bonds as effectively as underwriters, who provide similar services to many bond-issuing entities.

By conventional antitrust standards, the underwriting markets for both general obligation and revenue bonds are competitive—that is, the market should not be dominated by a small group. In 1979, the degree of concentration was so low that a merger between any of the top 10 underwriting firms would not have violated Department of Justice guidelines.[24] However, the underwriting market for revenue bonds is approximately twice as concentrated as that for general obligation bonds, although its level is not alarmingly high. The difference in concentration between the two markets is explained in part by the way the securities industry is regulated by the Glass-Stegall Act (*see* chapter 6).

An expanded volume of new issues can be accommodated with no reduction in the degree of competition among underwriters. The rapid growth in the 1970s was accompanied by a decline in market concentration—by 1979 it had fallen to 20 percent of its 1969 level.

Underwriting Fees

Underwriter's fees, or spreads, vary according to issue size, type of bond, and the public purpose to which funds are applied. Table 3-9 reports information on spreads and seems to suggest three findings: 1) Costs do not grow proportionally to issue size,[25] as evidenced by the spread per $1,000 being smaller the larger the size of issue; 2) general obligation bonds have lower underwriting costs than revenue bonds; and 3) general obligation bonds exhibit greater scale economies than revenue bonds, as evidenced by the differential in underwriting costs growing with issue size.

It should not be concluded, however, that general obligation bonds are necessarily a cheaper mode of financing than revenue bonds. The nature of underwriting services differs between general obligation and revenue bonds: Risk assessment involves the *general* creditworthiness of the municipality for the former and the economic viability of the specific project for the latter. Therefore, under-

TABLE 3—9

Underwriting Spreads (Dollars per \$1,000 Par Value of Bond) for 1979 by Size of Issue

Size of issue (×\$1,000)	General obligation	Revenue	Amount revenue exceeds general obligation
< 500	19.72	16.40	−3.32
500 − 999	16.76	19.49	2.73
1,000 − 1,999	14.33	20.28	5.95
2,000 − 2,999	13.39	19.05	5.66
3,000 − 4,999	12.32	20.21	7.89
5,000 − 9,999	12.70	19.53	6.83
10,000 − 24,999	12.46	19.19	6.73
25,000 − 49,999	10.11	19.83	9.72
> 50,000	9.88	17.46	7.58

Source: Fischer, Forbes, and Peterson (1980), table 5, p. 11.

writing costs are higher for revenue bonds because the *scale* of services is more extensive.

Underwriting fees also depend on the purpose and quality of the bond (*see* table 3-10). Underwriting spreads are greater the lower the bond's rating, for both general obligation and revenue bonds. More traditional revenue bonds—such as those for water and sewer and power projects—exhibit lower spreads than those for newer purposes, such as housing and hospitals.

Underwriting spreads are determined by the issue size, the bond quality, the number of underwriters bidding, and whether the bond is general obligation or revenue backed. One study found that, although average underwriting spreads for revenue bonds were \$2.64 above those of general obligation bonds,[26] after allowing for differences in bond characteristics, the underwriting costs of revenue bonds were only 48 cents per \$1,000 of par value more expensive than general obligation bonds (Kessel, 1971).[27]

The number of bidders and bond quality have more influence on underwriting costs than does issue size. Table 3-11 shows the implied savings in underwriting spreads from increasing: 1) issue size above \$500,000; and 2) the number of bidders above three. Increasing issue size from \$500,000 to \$5 million reduces spreads by a meager 14 cents per \$1,000, whereas doubling the number of bidders reduces underwriting spreads by \$1.18 per \$1,000. Increasing

TABLE 3–10

Mean Understanding Spread
(Dollars per $1,000 Par Value of Bond)
for 1979 by Bond Purpose

Purpose	Rating category		
	AA	A	BAA
Water/sewer	11.45	15.92	21.93
Power	14.48	18.61	na*
Housing	19.46	23.76	27.95
Hospitals	20.73	21.55	27.41

*na, Not applicable.

Source: Fischer, Forbes, and Peterson (1980), table 6, p. 12.

the bond's quality from a Standard & Poors BBB rating to AAA reduces underwriting spreads by $3.00.[28] Every dollar saved on underwriting costs is equivalent to the municipality receiving an extra dollar from the sale of its bonds without *any* additional interest payment or debt-retirement obligation.

TABLE 3–11

How Issue Size and Number of Bidders Affect Spreads

Issue size (×$1,000)	$1,000	$2,000	$3,000	$4,000	$5,000
Savings[a]	0.016	0.047	0.078	0.109	0.140
Number of bidders	Four	Five	Six	Seven	
Savings[b]	0.489	0.868	1.178	1.440	

[a] Dollars per $1,000 par value of bonds issued from increasing issue size from $500,000 to scale indicated by entry in table.

[b] Dollars per $1,000 par value of bonds issued from increasing number of bidders from three to number indicated by entry in table.

Source: Computed from Kessel (1971), table 5.

TOTAL BORROWING COST

A state's or municipality's borrowing cost is how much money it can raise in exchange for its repayment promise—the level of coupon payments and specified schedule of debt retirement. The greater the amount of money raised for a given promise, the lower the borrowing cost.[29] What determines borrowing costs is revealed by examining general market trends and by analyzing the yields on individual bond issues.

The examination shows how a variety of factors affect the yield paid by a municipality over the life of its bond. Table 3-12 shows the value to a municipality of reducing the yield on bonds of different maturity[30]—a savings of 10 basis points on a 20-year bond enables the issuing government to raise an additional $9.82 per $1,000 par value of its bonds if the prevailing market yield is 8 percent. Generally, the value of yield reduction is greater for longer-term bonds and when interest rates are low.

Lessons from General Market Trends

It is commonly believed that general obligation bonds command lower yields than revenue bonds (Heins, 1962; Sorenson, 1980; Swenson, 1974; and Van Horne, 1978). The usual explanation is that the underlying taxation power that backs general obligation issues is subject to smaller fluctuations than the operating revenues backing revenue bonds. Table 3-13 shows the average differential between 10-year, AA-rated revenue and general obligation bonds for 1966 to 1979. This differential has varied considerably over time—

TABLE 3—12

The Economic Value of Savings Basis Points (Dollars per $1,000 Par Value)

Maturity	Basis points*		
	10	40	70
10	6.71/5.65	26.84/22.60	46.87/39.55
15	8.56/6.81	34.23/27.24	59.92/47.68
20	9.82/7.47	39.27/29.88	68.73/52.29
25	10.67/7.84	42.70/31.37	74.72/54.90
30	11.26/8.06	45.03/32.22	78.80/56.39

* Entry above and below "/" indicates savings per $1,000 par value of bond at 8 percent and 12 percent market interest rates, respectively.

TABLE 3–13

Average Reoffering Yield on 10-year, AA-Rated Bonds (1966–1979)

Year	General obligation	Revenue	Revenue less general obligation (basis points)
1966	3.62	3.85	23
1967	3.61	3.79	18
1968	4.00	4.14	14
1969	5.18	5.26	8
1970	5.28	5.32	4
1971	4.36	4.38	2
1972	4.29	4.34	5
1973	4.52	4.59	7
1974	5.23	5.68	45
1975	5.63	6.23	60
1976	5.11	5.46	35
1977	4.50	4.72	16
1978	5.05	5.32	27
1979	5.54	6.04	50

Source: Forbes, Fischer, and Petersen (1981), table 13, p. 175.

widening during cyclical downturns and narrowing during upturns (Swensen, 1974). Overall economic conditions and the secular growth in the relative share of revenue bonds explain more than 70 percent of the annual movements in the yield differential.[31] An increase in the growth rate of real GNP from −2.0 percent to 4.0 percent reduces the yield differential by 26 basis points, whereas an increase in the share of revenue bonds in the tax-exempt market from 30 percent to 70 percent (which occurred between 1966 and 1979) increases the yield differential by 44 basis points.

The increased yield differential attributable to the shifting composition of new issues may reflect two forces: the extension of debt into new areas, or the market's difficulty in absorbing increased quantities of revenue bonds relative to general obligation bonds. The aggregate data in table 3-13 do not allow separation of these influences.

Table 3-14 provides more recent information on yield differentials between 20-year general obligation and revenue bonds of different quality. The yield differential averages 30 basis points.[32] Yields on AAA, AA, and A bonds are lower than those on BAA bonds by 71, 40, and 19 basis points respectively. For both types of bonds, improving bond quality significantly reduces a borrower's cost of capital.

Lessons from Individual Bond Yields

Examining interest rates for categories of bonds masks important variations among yields for individual bonds. The effect of bond ratings, for example, reveals the *tendency* for AA bonds to have higher yields than AAA bonds. This statement does not imply that all AA bonds have larger yields than all AAA bonds. Many dimensions of bonds combine to determine the yield necessary for successfully marketing a municipality's debt.

Bond Ratings. Many studies have found that higher ratings lead to lower yields (Kessel, 1971; Twentieth Century Fund, 1974; and Kidwell and Koch, 1982). In comparison to BAA-rated bonds, AAA , AA , and A-rated bonds command smaller yields of 62, 47, and 25 basis points, respectively. There is no evidence of any long-term changes in the relation between bond quality and bond yields.[33]

Number of Bidders. Increasing the number of bidders for the underwriting contract from one to two saves 10 basis points, and increasing the number of bidders from two to four saves another 10

TABLE 3—14

Yields on New Issues of 20-Year Municipal Bonds

Year and type of issue	Bond rating			
	AAA	AA	A	BAA
Revenue bond				
1978	5.67	6.00	6.24	6.33
1979	6.04	6.42	6.47	6.62
1980	7.72	8.22	8.38	*
1981	10.67	11.25	11.86	11.93
General obligation				
1978	5.52	5.69	5.92	6.17
1979	6.02	6.05	6.27	6.53
1980	7.56	7.78	7.92	8.02
1981	10.67	10.93	10.97	11.47

* Not sufficient number of issues for source to compute a meaningful average.

Source: Starr and Forbes (1982), table 2, p. 454.

basis points (Kessel, 1971; Kidwell and Koch, 1982; and Cagan, 1978). Competition among underwriters is as important for lowering bond yields as it is for reducing underwriter's spreads.[34]

General Obligation Versus Revenue Bonding. Much of the observed differences in yields are due to differences in the number of bidders, maturity and call provisions (see below), and not to the differences in the types of revenues backing the bond. One study found that almost 50 percent of the apparent yield differential between revenue and general obligation bonds is explained by differences in other bond characteristics (Kessel, 1971). General obligation bonds receive an average of two more bids than revenue bonds for their underwriting contracts. General obligation bonds are sold on a sole-source basis 6 percent of the time, whereas revenue bonds are 33 percent of the time. General obligation bonds contain call provisions 33 percent of the time, and revenue bonds, 93 percent of the time. So, the high cost of revenue bonds is the consequence of *decisions* by the issuing government related to the special characteristics of the bond.

Call Provisions. This is a provision of the bond contract that allows the issuing government to retire the debt before maturity at a specified price and time. This provision is not free to issuing governments and will be reflected in the original yields.[35] The advantage of a call provision is that it allows flexibility in retiring debt early. Rather than repurchasing bonds on the open market, the call provision places a ceiling on the price paid to investors (Kidwell, 1977).

Issue Size. "Bigger is better" is a common theme emphasized in discussion of municipal finance (Lamb and Rappaport, 1981). The evidence is, at best, mixed. Kidwell and Koch (1982) found that *larger issues* paid slightly *higher* yields than smaller ones, after controlling for other important characteristics of the bond issue. Kessel (1971) did find some evidence supporting the "bigger is better" theme, although its quantitative significance was minor. His results indicate that increasing the scale by $10 million reduces the bond yield by 1.4 basis points. Widely held beliefs to the contrary, the size of the issue does not significantly affect interest costs.

THE LARGEST DEFAULT IN THE HISTORY OF MUNICIPAL BONDS

The Washington Public Power Supply System (WPPSS) has declared the largest default in municipal bond history when it missed its interest payments on $2.25 billion of the $8.30 billion of bonds it sold for financing nuclear power generation in the Pacific Northwest. The state of Washington Supreme Court ruled that bond convenants in this case were invalid, because the utilities participating in the financing overstepped their legal authority when they obligated themselves to service WPPSS's debt. This episode provides an important lesson for prudent municipal finance, even though lawsuits remain and attempts at federal financial assistance spring anew (*Business Week*, February 7, 1983).

Despite the attention devoted to legal and political issues, the fundamental cause of the WPPSS default was economic. The ill-fated projects were based on the unquestioned conventional wisdom that electricity demand would grow at 6 percent to 10 percent (Carlson, 1983). Those projections were the backbone of the financial projections indicating that there was sufficient financial capacity to repay the borrowed funds. Furthermore, there was the presumed backing of the Bonneville Power Administration.

Unfortunately for investors, growth of demand for electricity during the 1970s was far below projections. Problems in meeting bond obligations encouraged borrowers to pursue legal means of escaping repayment. In the future, bond analysts can be expected to focus more attention on the underlying economics of the project (Carlson, 1983). Even legally sound contracts offer little protection for investors if they are based on repayment obligations beyond the utility's customers' ability-to-pay.

Despite its size, the WPPSS default did not create problems for municipal borrowing generally. As with the New York crisis, the bond market did not project the financial problems of one group onto the entire market. Municipal borrowers in the Pacific Northwest, of course, recently have faced higher borrowing costs and even difficulties in marketing their bonds. The state of Washington's Supreme Court decision has raised fears about the general legal environment in the affected states.

CONCLUSIONS

Four conclusions place the policy concerns about financing water investment into proper perspective: 1) *quality*, and not quantity of debt per se, is the primary determinant of an issue's cost of capital; 2) *timing* debt issuance to coincide with a strong overall economy will reduce financing costs for both high- and low-quality debt; 3) a bond's quality depends on its maturity, provisions of repayment, rating, the way in which the issuer selects the underwriter, and the economic repayment capacity created by the project; and 4) ratings disseminate information on preceived credit quality to the marketplace, and are not an independent factor determining the borrowing costs of states and municipalities.

These conclusions do not support the current pessimism over the prospects of financing increased infrastructure investment. State and local governments need not face increased financing cost simply because many municipalities are issuing more debt. Financing costs will be affected by the quality of the issuer's debt instrument, which depends on the underlying financial strength of the project or the jurisdiction, or both.

Many of the concerns about the municipal bond market, the fears of increasing risk differentials and yields relative to the corporate sector, are either without factual support or represent short-term deviations from long-term, enduring market forces. The market does not appear to be on the verge of saturation with state and local governmental debt. Bond quality and timing of issuance relative to overall health of the economy are the significant questions for determining the financing costs facing municipalities.

Quality refers to the collateral behind the repayment promise. Financial strength and resilience to adverse changes in future economic and political conditions lead to better ratings and lower borrowing costs. The competitive structure of the market for underwriting services means that a strong financial product can be distributed to investors at a reasonable cost. Successful financing policy centers upon improving an issue's quality and marketing the issue at the lowest possible cost. The experience of WPPSS illustrates forcefully and tragically that project financing cannot be divorced from the underlying project economics. The next two chapters explore how well alternative revenue bases meet these prescriptions.

TEXT NOTES

1. Peterson (1974), p. 20. Issuance of long-term debt, of course, represents an even higher proportion of state and local governmental capital spending, equaling 59.5 percent of state and local capital expenditures in 1970 and increasing to 118.7 percent by 1977. Vaughan (1983), table 12, p. 78.

2. More detailed data on the time pattern can be found in Vaughan (1983), table 11, pp. 76-77.

3. *See* Lamb and Rappaport (1980), pp. 30-32, for an exemplary discussion.

4. The purpose categories not included in the table are hospital bonds (share of which increased from 0.4 percent in 1971 to 5.4 percent by 1981), housing (share increased from 0.2 percent in 1970 to 5.9 percent by 1981), and other miscellaneous uses of funds.

5. An excellent statement of these points can be found in Johnson (1982), pp. 52-54. He offers a concise statement of the remedy of controlling volume of debt as a means of mitigating the perceived saturation of the bond market.

6. The risk premium must be viewed in the context of the tax deductibility of interest earned from municipal bonds. Although municipal bonds commonly yield less than Treasury bills, the differential is less than the tax benefits of municipal bonds. In other words, the yield on municipal bonds exceeds any reasonable estimate of the after-tax yield of Treasury bills. See Yawitz (1978), p. 480.

7. During cyclical downturns, tax or operating revenues of municipalities decline relative to finanical obligations. As interest rates increase, future financing costs are expected to be higher relative a given repayment capacity. In either case, the perceived probability of default is increased and requires a greater risk premium on municipal bonds. See Yawitz (1978), pp. 476-477.

8. Regression analysis reveals the following relations between the yield on municipal bonds with the yield on 10-year Treasury notes (Rtrea), and the growth rate in real gross national product (RGNP). The tables and figures in the text are based on these equations. The estimated coefficients and t-statistics (reported in parentheses) are:

Explanatory Variable	AAA	AA	A	BAA
Constant	0.788 (2.39)	0.879 (2.55)	1.239 (2.96)	1.553 (3.59)
Rtrea	0.738 (19.25)	0.761 (18.92)	0.761 (15.58)	0.778 (15.44)
RGNP	−0.153 (−3.70)	−0.160 (−3.70)	−0.183 (−3.49)	−0.203 (−3.74)
R^2	0.952	0.951	0.931	0.931
Durbin-Watson Statistic	1.39	1.557	1.407	1.470
Standard deviation Dependent Variable	2.264	2.342	2.398	2.475
Residual	0.513	0.549	0.654	0.676

9. The rising risk premium occurs from the municipal bond yield increasing by more than the amount predicted from the differences in tax treatment of municipal and U.S. Treasury bonds. If the risk premium remains constant, municipal yields increase by a fraction of the Treasury yield (that fraction being one minus the marginal income tax rate of investors in Treasury bills). The predicted rates in table 3-5 increase much faster than indicated by reasonable values for the marginal tax rate. See Yawitz (1978) for a complete discussion of the relationship among the tax treatment of bonds, risk premia, and observed differentials in interest rates.

10. The finance literature commonly invokes yields on utilities as the most relevant corporate bond yield for comparison with municipalities. In principle, one aspires to compare activities with the same degree of risk. In fact, this is impossible. The presumption is that utilities engage in the most similar activity in the corporate sector to the activities conducted by state and local governments.

11. Despite common bond ratings, municipalities and utilities may represent different financial risks to bondholders. Trezcinka (1980) allows for this possibility in his empirical work by using a statistical technique that allows the magnitude of this risk difference to vary over time. Trezcinka argues that municipalities represent *greater* risks than corporate ownership for bondholders, and this fact has not been accounted for in other studies. Chapters 6 and 7 return to the finance literature's arguments in support of Trezcinka's proposition, for they have a bearing on some of the roles for affirmative action by state governments in the financing of water development.

12. This estimate is taken from Kormendi and Nagle (1981), table A.3, p. 142. I have taken the results from the appendix instead of the results preferred by the authors, because table A.3 uses the specification more in accordance with the theory developed by Miller (1977) and Fama (1977). Kormendi and Nagle did not account for the varying nature of the risk differential between corporate and municipal bonds as did Trezcinka (1980). This difference in methodology does not seem to be the source of confusion on the primary issue raised here: the absence of an effect of the volume of municipal debt on yields of municipal bonds.

13. Readers familiar with the Peterson (1979) study may be puzzled about how Kormendi and Nagle (1981) came to the opposite conclusion. The differences in results are reconciled by the authors, relating to inappropriate measurement of the debt-outstanding variable. Once corrected, Peterson's data also show *no effects* of debt outstanding on municipal bond yields (*see* Kormendi and Nagle, 1981, pp. 127-129).

14. Regression analysis reveals the following relations of the yield differential between corporate and municipal bonds with the yield on comparably rated corporate bonds (Rcorp) and the growth rate in real gross national product (RGNP). The tables and figures in the text are based on these equations. The estimated coefficients and t-statistics (reported in parentheses) are:

Explanatory Variable	AAA	BAA
Constant	−0.45	−1.01
	(−1.10)	(−2.38)
Rcorp	0.35	0.39
	(9.27)	(10.76)
RGNP	0.05	0.04
	(0.93)	(0.74)
R^2	0.802	0.854
Durbin-Watson Statistic	2.28	2.00
Standard deviation		
Dependent Variable	1.298	1.571
Residual	0.577	0.625

15. The coefficient of variation of the yield differentials (the ratio of the standard deviation to the mean multiplied by 100) is 42.31, 43.28, and 48.89 for the differential yield of BAA-rated bonds with AAA, AA, and A-rated bonds, respectively. These data indicate that the yield differentials between risk classes are being subjected to common forces exerting the same proportionate effect on their magnitudes.

16. Regression analysis reveals the following relations among the yield differentials between RBAA-rated and higher-rated municipal bonds and the differential in the previous year [Dif(-1)], the yield on 10-year U.S. Treasury notes (Rtrea), and the growth rate in real gross national product (RGNP). The table in the text is based on these equations. The estimated coefficients and t-statistics (reported in parentheses) are:

Explanatory Variable	AAA	AA	A
Constant	0.313	0.283	0.097
	(1.86)	(1.58)	(0.94)
Dif (−1)	0.500	0.029	0.011
	(3.19)	(4.37)	(3.37)
Rtrea	0.017	0.029	0.011
	(1.10)	(1.67)	(1.15)
RGNP	−0.033	−0.040	−0.007
	(−1.87)	(−2.09)	(−0.59)
R^2	0.519	0.654	0.515
Durbin-Watson Statistic	1.93	2.13	2.12
Standard deviation			
Dependent Variable	0.277	0.363	0.176
Residual	0.204	0.227	0.130

17. *See* Twentieth Century Task Force 1974 on Municipal Bond Credit Ratings, *The Rating Game*, for a more detailed discussion of the rating system.

18. *See* Lamb and Rappaport (1980), p. 25.

19. *See* Lamb and Rappaport (1980), chapter 3.

20. *See* Lamb and Rappaport (1980), p. 58.

21. The Internal Revenue Service limits to 15 percent the portion of proceeds from bond sales that can be collected in the replacement and renewal fund. Limiting interest rate arbitrage by municipalities (where they borrow at the tax-exempt rate and invest their replacement and renewal fund at taxable rates; that is, nevertheless exempt from federal taxation) is the motivation of this IRS ruling. This ruling, of course, does not preclude a municipality from loaning revenues raised by user fees at the higher taxable interest rate.

22. The problem is analogous to the one concerning a policy allowing *voluntary* disclosure of student grades. A potential employer wonders why a student exercises his right of privacy. Is it because of his poor grade-point average or his moral commitment to privacy? The temptation is to consider the former explanation more likely than the latter one.

    Another example involves criminal law. The fifth amendment protects an individual from answering questions that may provide incriminating evidence against himself. In theory, exercising this right should not be viewed as an indication of guilt. Yet many trial lawyers distinguish between the theory and the practice of the law.

23. Fluctuations in bond prices absorbed by underwriters, of course, need not always portend loss. Market conditions could change so that the municipality's bonds are more valuable than originally anticipated. This would occur, for example, if

the general level of interest rates declined between the time the bid was accepted and the time the bonds were resold to investors.

24. Using data from Forbes, Fischer, and Peterson (1981, tables 18 and 20, pp. 181-182), the Herfindahl indices of concentration for these markets are:

Year	General Obligation	Revenue
1979	0.055	0.010
1969	0.116	0.019

This index is defined as the sum of squared market shares of firms participating in the market. Its inverse is sometimes intrepreted as the number of equal-sized firms competing in the industry (*see* Stigler, 1968, chapter 4). Generally, merger activity is currently viewed as not threatening to competition so long as the Herfindahl is below 0.17 (*see* U.S. Department of Justice, *Merger Guidelines*).

25. When costs per unit decline with increasing scale of activity, the cost conditions are said to exhibit *economies of scale.*

26. Kessel (1971) examined the underwriting spreads for 9,420 municipal bonds issued between 1959 and 1967 (Cagan, 1978, has shown that Kessel's results are applicable to the 1970s). The spreads in Kessel's data are less than those reported in table 3-9. Part of this difference could be attributed to the changing nature of bond issues, as hospital and housing bonds with spreads generally higher than the more traditional water-and-sewer and power bonds grow. Yet the spreads between those traditional purpose bonds and general obligation bonds are generally greater in 1979 than the $2.79 differential observed by Kessel. This apparent increase in underwriter's spreads cannot be attributed to inflation, because underwriters' spreads are expressed relative to $1,000 par value of bonds (inflation increases both the numerator and the denominator by the same amount).

27. Computed from Kessel (1971), table 4. After controlling for bond quality, issue size, number of bidders, and other considerations, Kessel estimates that underwriting spreads for revenue bonds still exceed those for general obligation bonds by 48 cents per $1,000: with the coefficient for the dummy variable signifying whether the bond was general obligation or revenue. This amount equals only 18 percent of the gross differential: $2.79.

28. Kessel also estimates the effects of number of bidders, bond quality, and issue size on underwriting costs separately for general obligation and revenue bonds. Using those results does not change the fundamental conclusions. The most striking difference would be that the savings in underwriting costs from increasing the number of bidders would be 25 percent greater than that indicated in table 3-11. The effect of bond quality is another important difference between general obligation and revenue bonds: increasing bond quality has about a $1.00 per $1,000 par-value-of-bond greater effect for revenue than it does for general obligation bonds. Issue size still remains of secondary importance (*see* Kessel, 1971, table 5).

29. A municipality's cost of capital has two parts: 1) the coupon rate the market requires to hold its bond, referred to as the yield to maturity; and 2) the fee paid the underwriter as the difference between the amount the market pays for the bond and the proceeds received by the issuing government.

   The preceding section discussed the determinants of underwriters' spreads.

The information below indicates that the vast majority of debt financing involves the first portion of cost, the determinants of which are discussed below.

30. The table computes how much more investors would pay for the same coupon stream if the true underlying risk were reduced by an amount the value of which is indicated by the reduction in basis points.

31. The following relation explains the annual variation in the yield differential: Differential = 158.87 (3.13) − 5.19 (-1.39) Rtrea − 4.85 (−3.31) RGNP − 151.55 (−3.36) GOB, where Rtrea = yield on 10-year treasury note; RGNP = growth rate in real gross national product; and GOB = share of new issues that were general obligation bonds. R^2 = 0.684. Durbin-Watson statistic = 1.90. Standard deviation: dependent variable = 18.60; Residual = 11.92.

32. The following regression explains the yields reported in the table: Yield = 11.69 (14.5) − 0.30 (−5.4) GO − 0.711 (−8.8) AAA − 0.402 (−5.0) AA − 0.191 (−2.4) A − 5.27 (−68) Y1 − 4.92 (−63) Y2 − 0.321 (−40) Y3, where GO means general obligation, Y1 signifies 1978, Y2 signifies 1979, and Y3 signifies 1980.

    The coefficients measure how the yields on various rated bonds differ from those on BAA-rated revenue bonds in 1981. The negative coefficients for the year variables indicate that interest rates were higher in 1981 than they were in the other years. The negative coefficients for the ratings indicate that the yield on higher-rated bonds are lower than those on BAA-rated revenue bonds. The negative coefficent on the GO variable measures that a GO bond had a 30-basis-point-lower yield than a comparably rated revenue bond over the four years represented in the table. R^2 = 0.996. Standard deviation: dependent variable = 2.18; residual = 0.154.

33. As discussed in the third section ("Interest Rates on Municipal Debt"), the levels of risk class differentials are affected by the level of interest rates and fluctuations in aggregate economic activity. These effects represent short-term deviations from the longer-term steady differentials indicated by the evidence cited in the text. Financing policy, of course, may wish to distinguish between financing problems resulting from temporary and long-term trends. If so, the best evidence suggests that the market continues to value bond quality in the same manner as it always has.

34. See chapter 6 for a discussion of why the number of bidders matters. The economic explanation possesses implications for how state security regulation and information-reporting policies can reduce financing costs for state and local governments.

35. Kidwell and Koch (1982) estimate that adding this provision increases the required yield that municipalities must pay by 11 basis points. Kessel (1971) found that placing a 10-year call provision on a 20-year bond increases the required yield by 5 basis points. Cagan (1978) estimates the cost of that provision to be almost 9 basis points.

CHAPTER 4

BUILDING COLLATERAL FOR WESTERN WATER INVESTMENT

The revenues required to finance debt can be raised from many sources—user fees, intergovernmental grants, and taxes on property, income, and sales. The choice of revenue source affects the cost of borrowing, because these sources provide different levels of collateral. This chapter examines how these alternative sources affect financing cost by using two criteria: 1) How effectively does the revenue source channel a project's benefits into revenue streams to service debt? 2) How durable are the revenue streams in the face of adverse changes in future economic and political conditions? Are the risks of a revenue shortfall related to the project itself or to other events?

This chapter is divided into five sections. The first reviews revenue collections by western state and local governments and water authorities. The second section explains why a project's financial capacity cannot be defined simply in terms of its ability to raise revenue. The third and fourth sections explain the connection between alternative revenue sources and project benefits and costs. The final section analyzes the resilience of revenue sources in the face of adverse economic and political events.

THE REVENUE STRUCTURE OF WESTERN STATES

Water investment can be financed by general tax revenues or by the revenues raised by the water organizations empowered to build, operate, and finance the facilities. Traditionally, financial capacity is measured by a government's ability to raise revenue relative to its population base or its residents' income.[1] Western states are already at the national average in their levels of tax collections, and they transfer more revenue from state to local governments than non-western states. If western states use general revenue sources to finance additional water development, then their tax rates must be further raised, placing them above the national average. The alternative is to finance water projects with revenues connected to the direct benefits of the project.

Western water organizations—municipal water utilities and irrigation districts—traditionally rely on water fees as their primary source of revenue. Tax revenues raised by special taxation powers are an important, although secondary, source of financing. Unlike the East, user fees are used widely to back water investment in the West.

State and Local Government Revenue Collections in the West

The extent to which western state and local governments can shoulder increased financial responsibility for water investment depends on the answers to three questions: 1) Do western states have unduly low tax collection efforts that can be increased to finance water investment? 2) Can state/local revenue transfers be increased to channel low-cost funds to local governments? and 3) Are existing revenue sources suitable for water investments in the future? These questions are addressed by comparing general features of western state and local governmental tax collections with national norms.

State governments in the West have distinctive revenue systems compared to nationwide norms. In 1981, western states collected per capita revenues of $1,258—$130 less than the national average (*see* table 4-1). Federal grants provided 27.4 percent of the West's total revenues (about the national average). Western states rely slightly more on sales and other taxes, and nontax revenues than the national average. They also rely considerably less on income taxation (both corporate and personal) than nonwestern states.[2]

Local governments in the West also have distinctive revenue systems (*see* table 4-2). In 1981, revenues averaged $1,117 per resident—$62 above the national average, and western local governments received 7.7 percent and 33.0 percent of their revenues from federal and state governments, respectively. Compared to the national average, western local governments are less dependent on federal revenues and equally dependent on state revenues.

Western local governments also are distinctive in how they raise revenues. They rely less on taxes than local governments nationally, raising only 59.8 percent compared to the national average of 75.2 percent. No western local government raises revenue via income taxation, whereas local income taxation accounts for 2.5 percent of all local governmental tax collections nationally. Western local governments show a mild preference for property and sales taxation relative to the national norm for local governments.

These simple comparisons do not take account of how per-capita income, population, and intergovernmental aid affect revenue-raising activity.[3] Do differences in these factors among states mask

TABLE 4–1

Per Capita and Distribution by Sources of Revenues of Western State Governments, 1980–1981.

State	Total revenues ($)[a]	Revenues from federal govt. (%)	Share of state taxes collected	Distribution of state tax collection			
				Income	Sales	Property	Other[b]
Arizona	1,013	20.3	0.813	0.275	0.451	0.069	0.205
California	1,371	26.0	0.854	0.455	0.354	0.035	0.156
Colorado	1,001	29.2	0.706	0.374	0.367	0.003	0.256
Idaho	1,045	30.8	0.786	0.440	0.270	0.001	0.289
Kansas	998	26.6	0.804	0.406	0.327	0.014	0.256
Montana	1,332	35.9	0.692	0.428	0.000	0.051	0.522
Nebraska	931	26.8	0.753	0.318	0.350	0.004	0.328
Nevada	1,106	29.1	0.821	0.000	0.394	0.045	0.561
New Mexico	1,889	18.9	0.591	0.106	0.437	0.009	0.448
North Dakota	1,627	22.9	0.550	0.230	0.287	0.006	0.478
Oklahoma	1,227	22.0	0.771	0.279	0.171	0.000	0.550
Oregon	1,258	22.7	0.671	0.772	0.000	0.000	0.278
South Dakota	1,031	36.5	0.645	0.012	0.531	0.000	0.457
Texas	967	22.9	0.770	0.000	0.366	0.002	0.632
Utah	1,144	31.8	0.745	0.395	0.412	0.000	0.193
Washington	1,271	29.4	0.843	0.000	0.549	0.168	0.282
Wyoming	2,145	29.1	0.656	0.000	0.420	0.055	0.524
West average	1,258	27.4	0.733	0.261	0.334	0.027	0.377
U.S. average	1,387	27.7	0.763	0.329	0.311	0.020	0.340

[a]Nontax revenue includes: current charges for education, hospitals, miscellaneous earnings, insurance trust revenues, utility revenues, and liquor store revenues.
[b]Other taxes include: motor fuels, motor vehicle licenses, severance, and miscellaneous.

Source: U.S. Department of Commerce, Bureau of the Census, *Governmental Finances in 1980–1981*, table 5, pp. 18–26, and table 28, p. 96.

substantial divergency of western states from the national norm? The data suggest four important findings.[4]

First, western states are not more dependent on federal revenues than states in other regions. They have adequate mechanisms to finance needed public services and facilities. Proposed

TABLE 4-2

Per Capita and Distribution of Sources of Revenues
of Western and Local Governments, 1980–1981

State	Total revenues	Revenues from federal govt. (%)	Revenues from state (%)	Share of local taxes collected (%)	Distribution of (%) local tax collections		
					Sales	Property	Other[b]
Arizona	1,142	9.6	38.7	60.1	17.6	76.0	6.5
California	1,525	7.5	46.9	56.5	16.7	69.7	13.6
Colorado	1,208	6.0	29.3	67.0	24.4	68.7	6.9
Idaho	815	8.4	38.5	55.4	0.0	96.4	3.6
Kansas	1,013	6.6	25.7	60.5	3.4	91.4	5.2
Montana	1,037	8.2	23.9	72.4	0.0	97.3	2.7
Nebraska	1,076	7.1	22.2	60.7	6.0	89.5	4.5
Nevada	1,298	4.1	29.3	53.1	8.7	63.8	27.5
New Mexico	944	11.0	50.7	53.9	14.8	72.2	13.7
North Dakota	959	7.3	37.0	55.2	0.0	96.7	3.3
Oklahoma	844	8.8	36.3	58.6	34.2	59.9	5.9
Oregon	1,227	10.3	27.6	65.1	0.0	90.7	9.3
South Dakota	855	10.7	23.2	74.1	7.5	87.8	4.7
Texas	959	7.4	27.8	62.2	10.3	83.6	6.9
Utah	891	6.2	37.0	65.4	16.1	77.3	6.7
Washington	1,164	7.6	40.4	46.4	14.3	61.7	24.0
Wyoming	2,039	4.4	26.5	50.0	11.2	86.7	2.1
West average	1,117	7.7	33.0	59.8	10.9	80.5	8.6
U.S. average	1,040	8.9	33.0	75.2	8.0	79.9	9.6

[a] Nontax revenue includes: current charges for education, hospitals, miscellaneous earnings, insurance trust rewvenues, and utility revenues, and liquor store revenues.

[b] Other taxes include: motor fuels, motor vehicle licenses, severance and miscellaneous.

Source: U.S. Department of Commerce, Bureau of the Census, *Governmental Finances in 1980–1981*, table 5, pp. 18–26, and table 28, p. 96.

reductions in federal funding for water projects simply reinforce the general tendency for western states to receive lower per-capita federal grants.[5]

Second, revenue collections by western state governments are not low by national standards.[6] Therefore, any new water projects must be financed from *additional* state or local revenues generated by the projects.

Third, western state governments transfer about 30 percent more of their revenues to their local governments than do comparable non-western state governments.[7] Any additional state grants to local governments would increase further the above-average dependence of localities on state funding.

Fourth, western local governments raise about 10 percent more revenues per capita than do comparable nonwestern states.[8] Local governments in the West should attempt to finance additional water investments from the *expansion* of revenue bases, rather than from further taxation of existing ones.

Revenue Sources of Public Water Organizations

The vast majority of municipal water utilities and public irrigation districts have been financed with no state or federal assistance.[9] The little state aid that has been given, such as in Oklahoma, Texas, and Utah, has been in programs targeted toward small and poor communities. Although there are little systematic data summarizing the finances of these organizations, the state comptroller of California provides data for the state's special districts—which include a variety of agricultural and municipal water organizations (*see* table 4-3).[10]

Water organizations in California raise 55 percent of their revenue from water charges and fees—a marked contrast from financing practices in eastern states, where water often remains unmetered. This share is about the same for agricultural, municipal and industrial, and water-wholesaling organizations.

Property taxes and assessments account for another 25 percent of revenues. Agricultural organizations rely more heavily on property taxation than do other water organizations. The Metropolitian Water District—a cooperative effort by 34 municipalities for transporting water into southern California—depends slightly less on water charges and more on property taxes than most other water organizations in California.

There are no direct data on the relative importance of user fees and general tax revenues of municipal water utilities in the West. However, there is some indirect evidence. Table 4-4 shows the share of total long-term debt of municipal water utilities that was in the form of general obligation bonds. Assuming that general revenues back general obligation debt and operating revenues (user fees) back non-general obligation debt, then states whose utilities have relatively greater shares of general obligation debt probably rely more on

TABLE 4-3

Revenue Sources for California Public Water Organizations, 1975–1976

Type of organization	Source of revenue (%)			Total Revenue (millions)
	Water charges and fees	Taxes and assessments	Other	
Agricultural				
Irrigation	57	26	17	79.6
California water	57	22	21	56.9
Water storage	78	10	12	24.7
Water conservation	27	62	11	5.1
Municipal and industrial				
Municipal utility	72	13	15	42.2
County water	56	18	26	101.8
County waterworks	55	27	18	14.6
Community service	56	18	26	11.9
Water wholesalers				
Metropolitan water district	52	35	13	154.5
Water agency or authority	46	21	33	106.1
Muncipal water	61	21	18	126.9
Statewide	55	24	21	760.0

Source: Phelps, Moore, and Graubard (1978), table 2, p. 12.

taxation and less on water charges than states with smaller shares. These data imply that western organizations rely less on their taxation powers than do municipal water systems for the nation as a whole. On average, 28.1 percent of western long-term water debt was backed by taxation. In contrast, 35.2 percent of municipal water debt nationally was backed by general taxation.[11] Only four western states—Nevada, Colorado, South Dakota, and Oregon—had a higher fraction of their debt backed by taxation than the national average.

Future Water Investment

This review of western finances shows that financing water investment requires judicious decision making. Western states already exert average tax collection efforts and an above-average reliance on state/local revenue transfers—two of the most important financial characteristics affecting bond quality. Western bond quality can be diminished by water financing that increases state/local governmental transfers and/or places more demand on original tax bases than it generates in new ones.

CAPACITY TO FINANCE WATER INVESTMENT

A state or local government can reduce the cost of debt finance by exhibiting both the willingness and ability to repay its debt.[12] Willingness and ability to pay depend not only on the present financial standing of a jurisdiction, but on events after the loan is made. Decisionmakers, therefore, must be *forward looking* in assessing financial capacity.

Increased borrowing does not necessarily make a jurisdiction less creditworthy. If the project sufficiently expands the jurisdiction's ability to raise revenues, then ability to repay is increased. High taxes or high water prices are not bad per se, nor are low taxes

---

TABLE 4—4

Share (Percent) of Municipal Utilities' Long-Term Debt in General Obligation, 1976–1977

State	Share	State	Share
Arizona	21.9	Okalhoma	34.8
California	19.4	Oregon	46.4
Colorado	77.0	South Dakota	64.7
Idaho	9.1	Texas	10.4
Kansas	2.5	Utah	17.3
Montana	2.1	Washington	5.7
Nebraska	7.6	Wyoming	30.4
Nevada	91.2		
New Mexico	19.5	West average	28.1
North Dakota	16.7	U.S. average	35.2

Source: Computed from U.S. Department of Commerce, Bureau of the Census, *Census of Governments, 1977*, table 15, pp. 31–34.

or low water prices always preferable. The following hypothetical example illustrates this point.

Water Investment in Arid County

Arid County houses a typical community in the Southwest. Originally settled as an agricultural community, Arid County has developed a diversified agricultural base of orchards and field crops—wheat, cotton, alfalfa, and speciality crops. It has a growing metropolitan area, Arid City, which supports its surrounding agricultural areas with industrial and commercial enterprises—manufacture of farm machinery and transportation of agricultural products to processing centers on the West Coast. The city's water supply is provided by the Arid County Municipal Water District (ACMWD).

Arid County can grow if additional water is transported into the area. Currently, only 20 percent of the county's irrigable acreage is irrigated. The remaining acreage is dry-farmed. Many industries have expressed interest in locating new plants in Arid County, provided that sufficient public services (including water) are supplied by the local government. Among the interested parties are steel-castings producers, microcomputer chip manufacturers, and poultry processors.

Two distinctive features affect any investment in expanding ACMWD's system capacity.[13] First, construction costs will be incurred several years before additional water will be available. Water rights must be acquired, right-of-way for conveyance established, and distribution systems laid in. Some of these costs may be contracted up to 10 years before the delivery of additional water. Second, considerable uncertainty surrounds the potential value of additional water to be distributed to newly irrigated acreage and new residential, commercial, and industrial users. Decisions about capacity expansion are made in anticipation of *future* uses, the worth of which is currently unknown and cannot be accurately predicted.

Three financing options are available to Arid County. First, ACMWD could shoulder the financial responsibility by exercising its powers to raise water rates, impose property taxes, or issue bonds. Second, Arid City could finance the investment from its general tax revenues and general obligation bonds. Finally, ACMWD could lobby its state government for grants-in-aid. These options do not result in equal financing costs.

The Advantages of Debt Finance

Regardless of the source of funds, debt financing is preferable to pay-as-you-go financing. It smooths out repayment obligations over the life of the project and allows future project benefits to be applied to meet up-front capital costs. Pay-as-you-go financing, on the other hand, requires an uneven flow of funds, and the demand for funds will not match the county's ability to pay. High revenues must be raised by levying surcharges on water or tax rates during construction, when the bulk of capital costs are incurred. Lower revenues are needed after completion, when the additional water is delivered, which increases ACMWD's ability to raise revenues and boost the county's tax yields without resorting to surcharges. Fluctuating tax rates—inevitable under pay-as-you-go financing—are more costly and less efficient than steady tax rates as ways of raising revenues.[14]

Debt financing creates a smooth flow of revenue over time, allowing the same total amount of revenue to be raised with more economic efficiency (Barro, 1979). The least-cost strategy is not to levy a "temporary sales tax surcharge" but to impose a smaller, but permanent, increase in sales tax over the life of the water project. The savings could be substantial. For example, the City of Arid can reduce the economic inefficiency by 44 percent by financing a water project with debt. Debt financing would entail an increase in the sales tax from the current 3 percent to 4 percent, a modest 1 percent hike, for 20 years, whereas pay-as-you-go financing would increase the sales tax 3 percent, from 3 percent to 6 percent, for 5 years.[15] The benefits of debt financing accrue regardless of the revenue source that ACMWD chooses.

The economic advantages of debt finance can be maximized by making the term of bond financing the same as the useful life of the project. This policy spreads the repayment obligation over all future users of the project and allows the *smallest* permanent increase in water or tax rates consistent with servicing debt obligations.[16] It also avoids political problems with pay-as-you-go financing, under which the temporary surcharges have current residents paying for services provided to future residents. Moderating increases in tax collections is important for protecting bond quality of western local governments, which have been shown to be above national norms in their tax collection efforts.

How the Benefits and Costs of a Project Influence Financial Capacity

Project-financing costs depend heavily on the purposes for which the funds are borrowed. What will the project ultimately contribute to the community's economic base? How long will the project be useful? The underlying financial risk that bondholders must bear depends on the link between the project's ultimate revenues and costs and the repayment obligation. Since bondholders pay careful attention to the level of risk associated with a project, risk affects the interest rate paid on the bonds issued for the project.

Bondholders use four considerations when judging whether the planned repayment base is sufficient to meet principal and interest obligations: 1) the level of benefits generated by the project; 2) how effectively revenue raising relates to those benefits; 3) the amount of uncertainty about the benefits; and 4) the costs incurred by the project. The continuing example of Arid County illustrates how these forces affect financing cost.

Arid County must decide how much to expand system capacity. Future benefits and costs associated with its water system are uncertain. How much more agricultural income can be generated by switching from dry-farming to irrigation? How much water will new businesses demand and at what price? How many more households will be established in Arid County? What will construction costs be?

The value of Arid County's expanded water capacity depends on the growth of population, income, and economic activity. If growth meets or exceeds the planners' expectations, then the water project may provide benefits in excess of costs (net benefits). If, however, planners were overly optimistic and growth fails to reach predicted levels, then expensive excess capacity may result, leaving Arid County's citizens worse off.

Whatever ACMWD's ultimate investment decision, four general policy considerations influence the financial risk associated with the project:

First, managing the project to capture the greatest net benefits enhances the project's financial repayment capacity. Finding the highest valued uses for the project's water "increases" the gains from the investment.

Second, using the project's benefits as a revenue base strengthens repayment capacity. The benefits realized from the expanded capacity include the value of additional agricultural, industrial, and municipal uses of water. These gains can be pledged as security to bondholders only if they are the revenue base behind the repayment promise.

Third, reducing the uncertainty about future repayment capacity reduces risks. General obligation bonds issued by growing areas and by areas dependent on one major employer or industry carry higher interest rates than those issued by established and diversified areas (Hastie, 1972), because investments in growing areas are inherently more risky.[17]

Fourth, perceived risk will be lower, the higher the level of potential benefits is, relative to projected costs. Benefits in excess of costs provide a cushion against adverse future events.

ALTERNATIVE REVENUE BASES AND FINANCIAL CAPACITY

The additional water delivered by ACMWD can increase the city of Arid's revenue bases by: 1) inducing existing citizens and firms to expand activities that generate additional tax or user-fee revenues; or, 2) attracting new residents and firms, increasing the number of commercial and residential taxpayers. Different revenue sources will affect the growth of the county's economic base in different ways.

A properly designed user-fee system makes revenue collections dependent on the intensity of water use—people use more water when they receive more value from its use. Making people pay for the water they receive generates revenues at the lowest possible economic cost. Water is used only if its value in use exceeds its costs. Alfalfa acreage in Arid County will expand only if the extra income earned from irrigating rather than dry-farming exceeds the costs of developing and transporting irrigation water. A car wash will expand its operation and purchase more water from ACMWD only if its customers are willing to pay the price of extra water. The benefits from increased agricultural, commercial, residential, and industrial activities are naturally harnessed to back the debt incurred.

General tax revenues are a much less efficient means of financing the project. Instead of user fees, the county will have to raise general tax rates. But because water can now be consumed at a zero cost, total consumption will increase, requiring further subsidies from the municipality's revenues. Also, the cost of supplying the additional water will divert consumer and business expenditures from other goods and services taxed by the municipality.[18]

Over time, the municipality will experience fiscal problems. Firms and households that are relatively heavy water users will move into Arid County. However, their water consumption will be subsidized by all taxpayers, so the growth of firms and households that are not heavy water consumers will be lower than if all customers paid for what they used. The city of Arid would have more water-intensive steel-casting and poultry-processing plants and fewer microcomputer firms. Overall, the tax base will grow more slowly than if water had been properly priced.

The same problems occur if the water project were financed by a grant from the state. Localities in the state as a whole must pay for this program. Those localities which receive more in grants than they pay in added taxes will attract additional growth. But the others will suffer reduced growth.

This inherent inequity explains why preferential tax treatment to selected firms or industries does not lead to increased growth (*see* Vaughan, 1979; and Kieschnick, 1981). One group's tax preference is another's tax burden. The growth in the favored group will be more than offset by the decline of others, and the cross-subsidizing level of government—be it city, county, or state—will suffer an overall decline in its tax base.

ALTERNATIVE REVENUE BASES AND PROJECT COSTS

Project costs are not under the sole control of the water authority. Individual decisions on water use also shape system expense. For example, the amount of water delivered depends on plumbing and landscaping designs in residences and recylcing decisions in the industrial sector. The water authority's treatment costs are affected by how much water treatment industry undertakes before discharging its wastes.

As discussed above, a project's financial capacity depends on servicing only those water demands with benefits of use exceeding the costs imposed on the system. Devising effective means of communicating to water users how their decisions affect system cost is an important aspect of effective system management.

The full costs of providing water to a user include both capital and operating costs and may vary among customers. For example, residential water use leads to different treatment costs than industrial use—and not all industrial uses require the same treatment costs. Also, the fraction of "diverted" water that is actually consumed varies among users (*see* chapter 5).

Including capital costs may appear obvious, but many debates over utility pricing are precisely over this point.[19] The argument for excluding capital costs arises from the notion that costs are a *forward looking* concept and capital costs are incurred in the past. Once the facility is built, the incremental cost of service involves only operation, maintenance, and depreciation. Requiring users to pay for more than these incremental costs is viewed as unduly restrictive.

This argument is flawed on two grounds. First, it is the future expansion costs, not the original construction costs, that determine the appropriate price of water. If water users are not charged for the costs of expanding the system, water supplies will not be adequate to satisfy the demands of all users. The water authority will have less revenue to finance new capacity. Second, incurred capital costs are a legal obligation of the borrowing jurisdiction and must be financed.

Considering reuse possibilities in the definition of user costs represents a departure from standard practices. For example, the Bureau of Reclamation defines project costs in terms of water *diverted,* rather than water consumed. This leads to an inappropriate attribution of costs if some of the diverted water returns to a surface water source or percolates into a groundwater reservoir. These return flows are part of the water supply for other users (*see* chapter 5). Not all of the diverted water is at the expense of the consumption of others.

User-fee financing is more effective than tax financing in communicating information about costs to water consumers. For example, fee structures can be designed that provide incentives to treat waste on site when it is cheaper to do so than it would be for the water authority (*see* chapter 5). In contrast, sales or property tax financing of water investment would impose financial liabilities on consumers that had little, if any, relation to how their water-use decisions affected system costs. More waste-treatment responsibility and greater water demands would be imposed on the authority and would increase the amount of required debt financing. This extension of debt relative to the area's economic base guarantees a reduction in financial collateral and an increase in borrowing costs.

SENSITIVITY OF REVENUE BASES TO ADVERSE FUTURE EVENTS

User fees also compare favorably with other forms of revenue generation in two important ways: 1) User fees do not combine risks of project financing with other nonproject-related risks; and 2) revenues generated by user fees are not inordinately sensitive to fluctuations in the community's income. The former advantage implies that bondholders do not bear risks related to other municipal activities when financing water projects. The latter means that water bondholders are assured that the project's finances will not be compromised during a downturn in the economy.

User fees do suffer the important risk that the anticipated demand that stimulated project investment will not materialize. If the population and income growth expectations used in planning are reasonably accurate, however, user fees can raise sufficient revenues to service the debt. Studies of water demand indicate that water use is relatively insensitive to business-cycle fluctuations, so general economy-wide fluctuations have little bearing on the repayment capacity of water investment secured by user fees.

General taxation, on the other hand, suffers from three disadvantages. First, as with user fees, the risk of inaccurate forecasts of population and income growth can reduce the jurisdiction's debt-service capacity. Second, competing nonwater uses place independent demands on tax revenues. When the city of Cleveland faced its recent financial crisis, it chose to use its dwindling tax revenues for police and fire services and not to give bondholders priority. The promise behind bond covenants was less compelling than other municipal demands.

The third problem with state and local taxes is their sensitivity to fluctuations in the overall economy. Evidence, presented in chapter 3, shows that investors require greater differential yields to hold higher-risk bonds during downturns in the economy, because bonds backed by these revenue sources are more likely to experience financial difficulties at precisely the time the bond market requires greater yields for absorbing risk.[20] Because they are financed from general taxation powers, intergovernmental transfers also are not a resilient revenue base. Government transfers reassign the revenue responsibility, but do not reduce the overall financing commitment.

The substitution of state for local governmental financial responsibility would probably *increase* the overall sensitivity of the bond's revenue backing to adverse future events for three reasons. First, state governments rely more on taxation bases with greater sensitivity to fluctuations in the general economy than local governments do. Western state governments raise almost 60 percent of their tax revenues from income and sales taxes, whereas western local governments only raise 10 percent of their revenues from sales taxes (*see* tables 4-1 and 4-2). So, intergovernmental transfers substitute more cyclically sensitive sales and income taxation for less cyclically sensitive user fees and property taxation.

Second, most intergovernmental grants require a match that increases the adverse consequences of changes in the local government's own tax base. Every dollar of reduced local revenue can jeopardize the matching portion of state transfers,[21] and decrease total local revenues by even more than a dollar (Lamb and Rappaport, 1980, chapter 3).

Finally, unless intergovernmental transfers are guaranteed for the life of the bond, future legislatures may reduce transfers in times of fiscal crisis. During a late 1950s fiscal crisis in Michigan, the cost of capital to municipalities increased by 17 basis points, based on the market's anticipation of cutbacks in transfers to local governments. Combined with state governments' greater sensitivity to business cycles, transfer programs do not promise a means of reducing the overall risk for financing water investment.[22]

CONCLUSIONS

User fees offer the most promising opportunity for building collateral for debt financing. They can tailor revenue responsibility to project costs, and are reasonably resilient to adverse changes in future economic and political circumstances. Reliance on general taxation powers and intergovernmental transfers between state and local governments tends to reduce tax bases and increase the riskiness of debt offered. However, user fees are often difficult to implement for political reasons. The next chapter reviews these concerns and describes how user-fee schedules can be designed to achieve low-cost financing without sacrificing important political objectives.

TEXT NOTES

1. *See* Maxwell and Aronson (1977), pp. 38-40, and Advisory Commission on Intergovernmental Relations (1971).

2. These aggregate data mask considerable variations among the states. Wyoming, New Mexico, and North Dakota raise more than $1,600 per resident, compared with Nebraska, Texas, and Kansas, which raise less than $1,000. South Dakota, Montana, Utah, and Idaho receive more than 30 percent of their revenues from the federal government, whereas New Mexico, Arizona, Oklahoma, Oregon, and North Dakota receive less than 25 percent from federal sources.

   The western states also differ with respect to their revenue structures. Nevada, Texas, Washington, and Wyoming raise no revenues through income taxes; Idaho, Montana, Kansas, and Utah raise at least 40 percent of their revenues through income taxes. Washington, South Dakota, Arizona, New Mexico, and Wyoming raise 40 percent of their revenues through sales taxes; Montana, Oregon, Oklahoma, Idaho, and North Dakota, less than 30 percent.

3. Hyman (1981) and Musgrave and Musgrave (1975) provide concise reviews of the studies of how these factors affect revenue structures.

4. The discussion in the text relies on the findings from a regression study of the determinants of the 50 states' fiscal structures. The dependent variables are measured as the natural logarithm of per-capita revenues. The estimated coefficients and t-statistics (reported in parentheses) are:

	Dependent Variable				
Explanatory variable	Federal money to states	Federal money to locals	State money to locals	State revenue collection	Local revenue collection
Constant	3.287 (1.64)	−3.636 (−1.59)	−5.672 (−1.43)	− 10.222 (−4.06)	−8.416 (−4.12)
Population	−0.184 (−5.80)	0.023 (0.63)	0.308 (3.79)	−0.001 (−0.02)	−0.022 (−0.67)
Income	0.437 (1.98)	0.869 (3.43)	0.367 (0.82)	1.172 (4.15)	1.480 (5.96)
Western region	−0.085 (−1.26)	−0.073 (−0.95)	0.295 (−2.24)	−0.013 (−0.16)	0.096 (1.38)
Federal money to states	—— ——	—— ——	0.96 (3.37)	1.093 (6.05)	—— ——
Federal money to locals	—— ——	—— ——	—— ——	—— ——	0.066 (0.50)
State money to locals	—— ——	—— ——	—— ——	—— ——	0.193 (2.75)
R^2	0.439	0.231	0.327	0.677	0.632
Standard deviation					
Dependent variable	0.278	0.272	0.486	0.444	0.334
Residual	0.215	0.246	0.416	0.264	0.214

With the exception of the Western-region variable, all explanatory variables are measured in natural logarithms. The region variable equals one for western states and zero for nonwestern states. Multiplying its coefficient by 100 yields an estimate, in percent, of how western and nonwestern states differ in their fiscal structure independent of state differences in population, income, and the other revenue transfers indicated by the other explanatory variables.

5. Federal revenues transferred to western state and local governments were, respectively, 8.5 percent and 7.3 percent less than those received by nonwestern states with comparable income and population. (See the coefficients for the western-region variables in the equations for federal revenue transfers in note 3).

6. Western states raise the same amount of revenue as nonwestern states of comparable income, population, and federal revenues received by itself and its local governments. (See the coefficients for the western-region variables in the equations explaining state and local revenue collections in note 3.)

7. Western state governments transfer 30 percent more revenues to their local governments than nonwestern states of comparable population, income, and federal revenues received by the state and its local governments. (See the coefficients for the western-region variables in the equations explaining state revenue transfers to local governments in note 3).

8. Western local governments raise 10 percent more revenue than nonwestern local governments in states with comparable population, income, and revenues received from federal and state governments (see note 3).

9. Local organizations had obtained outside financing by dealing directly with the federal government.

10. The representativeness of California water institutions is exemplified by the a standard water law casebook (Trelease, 1974). He divides water institutions into two basic models: California and Colorado.

11. The numbers in the text are the averages across states and not total general obligation debt for the states divided by total long-term debt for the states.

12. *See* discussion of the purposes of bond ratings and their effects on borrowing costs in chapter 3.

13. The example abstracts from many important real-world issues: multiple benefits from projects, seasonality of use and value of services, and economies of scale (average costs of services decline with the scale of investment). Chapter 5 examines these issues.

14. The economic explanation for the higher costs incurred because of fluctuating tax rates is complex (*see* Barro, 1979). They can be understood with reference to the hypothetical example. Two problems would occur if Arid County decided to forgo the benefits of debt finance and were to finance a water project either by increasing its sales tax rate from 3 percent to 6 percent or by increasing user charges the necessary amount during the construction period.

    First, the higher sales tax reduces economic efficiency because the revenues raised are less than the income sacrificed by the residents (*see* Harberger, 1971). Residents not only pay more money to the government, but they lose as they adjust their behavior to the higher taxes. For example, because the county has a higher sales tax, some residents will shop in adjacent counties to avoid the tax—at least for some purchases. The longer trip is an additional, if voluntary, cost of the tax hike.

    Residents also change their consumption patterns in response to the higher tax rates. They purchase fewer taxed goods—clothing, meals in restaurants, and video games—and more of those goods and services that are exempt from the sales tax—shelter and food at home. (Smith, 1978) analyzed the 1971-72 Consumer Expenditure Survey and found that food at home and restaurant expenditures are quite sensitive to their relative prices. For example, Smith found that raising restaurant prices by 6 percent through an increase in sales tax rates while exempting groceries would reduce restaurant expenditures by 30 percent and increase food at home expenditures by about 28 percent.

    These adjustments are economically inefficient because people are responding to false signals about the true cost of providing goods and services. Harberger (1971) presents a classic explanation. The inefficiency from taxation is created by the divergence between the cost to the individual and the cost to society of producing the taxed good (consumption, income, savings, or gasoline). The cost to the consumer provides an inaccurate signal about the resource cost of the activity. The person restricts his activity by an inappropriate amount. This inefficiency from increasing tax rates grows with the level of tax rates, because the noise in the signal becomes increasingly muddled.

15. The savings from debt finance can be illustrated by the following example. Suppose that a city considers financing a $9 million, 20-year project that takes 5 years to construct by increasing its rate of sales taxation above its current level of 3 percent. The relation between the sales tax rate, t, and total expenditures, E, is given by the following equation (where the implied price elasticity is -0.75): (*) $E = 433.334 - 333.334*(1+t)$.

Two financing options are available: 1) finance the $9 million by increasing the sales tax for the 5 years and dedicate the additional revenues to pay project construction; or 2) finance the $9 million by issuing a 20-year bond at 8 percent.

Computations not reported here show that the economic inefficiency from the increased sales taxation has the following present values for these options: 1) $1.94 million, for the temporary surcharge of adding a 3 percent tax rate onto the original 3 percent rate; or 2) $1.09 million, for the permanent increase in the sales tax rate from 3 percent to 4 percent that would be required to raise additional revenues for meeting the bond's principal and interest obligations. Hence, debt financing has a 44 percent lower capitalized efficiency loss than pay-as-you-go financing.

16. Extending the bond's term beyond the useful life of the project would diminish the advantages of debt finance, because it would violate the fundamental principle of bond quality that the life of the bond should not exceed the life of the project—see chapter 3.

17. Project uncertainty can be reduced. For example, a more diversified economic base is less risky than a concentrated one because the former is influenced by more independent forces. This spreads the risk and reduces the chance of a major economic recession. If the local economy is dependent on only one employer or on one industry, there is a much higher chance of a major economic catastrophe (Hastie, 1972). There is no implied fiscal imprudence on the part of the growing communities. Limiting financing risks is sometimes "too expensive" in terms of sacrificed uses made available by the investment.

18. Chapter 5 reports evidence indicating that lowering user fees by 50 percent could easily induce a 40 percent increase in the demand for water. Water users cut back on their use of other goods and services.

19. Kahn (1971) provides an excellent general treatment of the problem.

20. Property taxation is not as sensitive to economic fluctuations as the other forms of taxation. Yet delinquency rates on tax payments are higher in recessions than during economic booms.

21. Chapter 7 reviews evidence indicating that revenue transfers from higher levels of governments increase the revenues collected by lower levels of government.

22. If the transfers were guaranteed by state governments, then those programs would become a future obligation of states and an additional claim on future revenues. Chapter 7 discusses how this transaction transfers the bond risk from local to state governments.

CHAPTER 5

DESIGNING USER FEES FOR EFFICIENT WATER USE AND LOW-COST EQUITABLE FINANCING

USER FEES are an efficient and equitable means for financing water projects. User fees promote efficient allocation of water because they require the user to weigh the benefits of the water in any particular use against the costs. In addition, the market information generated by the sale of water provides officials with meaningful information from which to make investment decisions. User fees are also an equitable way to distribute scarce water supplies, in that those who receive the benefits from the water are the same people who pay for it.

Designing an efficient schedule of user fees involves estimating the costs associated with supplying different users. Cost may be explicit—expenditures on materials and labor—or implicit—the increase in pumping costs that results as additional water is drawn from a common aquifer, or the endangerment of another's life and property from developing additional water supply. The critical policy question in imposing user fees is whether the gains from pricing water efficiently conflict with other social objectives, such as making water available at affordable prices.

This chapter establishes *six practical rules for designing a user-fee structure* to build financial collateral and promote efficient and equitable allocation of water among competing uses.

Rule 1: Pricing schedules should reflect the true economic cost of water, including the delivery and treatment costs as well as the value of potential reuse.

Rule 2: Pricing schedules should allocate connection costs directly to new customers.

Rule 3: Two-part tariffs (a service charge plus a price independent of quantity) are efficient and equitable. Declining block pricing (water rates that decline with quantity used) and increasing block pricing (water rates that increase with quantity used) are inefficient.

Rule 4: Taxing groundwater extraction can control the overdraft problem and finance conjunctive use of groundwater with surface water supplies.

Rule 5: Charging effluent fees for wastes discharged into a jurisdiction's water supply will reduce publicly incurred costs for maintaining and restoring water quality.

Rule 6: Charging water users for dam safety, property owners for flood control, and hydroelectric power users the competitive price for electricity is economically efficient.

Rules 4 and 5, it should be noted, identify revenue sources not frequently used in financing water investment which could expand the fiscal resources available for debt financing of water investment.

THE ADVANTAGES AND DISADVANTAGES OF USER FEES

User fees are becoming increasingly popular among states and municipalities. Boston, Philadelphia, and Baltimore have recently imposed sewer- and water-user fees to finance capital construction (Chester, 1982). Though user fees are becoming increasingly acceptable as a source of financing, they are still controversial and are not fully understood. How user fees promote efficient resource allocation and build financial collateral must be weighed against metering of costs, forgoing of general obligation bonding, and possible sacrificing of equity goals. The evidence reviewed below suggests that efficient water pricing need not conflict with equity considerations nor entail significant costs because of metering and revenue bond financing.

The Case for User Fees: Efficiency in Resource Use

Properly structured user fees encourage efficient use, management, and design of water systems. User fees require consumers to consider the cost of water and thereby discourage the use of water when its value is less than the cost of service. User fees also provide managers with more complete information about consumer demand for water. This information gives a rational basis for water system design and investment decisions. Bond quality, in turn, improves because the borrower's economic base grows relative to its level of debt.

Consumers can reduce their water use in response to higher prices in two ways. First, they invest in equipment that captures and transmits water to its place of use more effectively. For example, households can reduce the size of shower heads or the capacity of toilet systems (Stone, 1978). Companies can recycle water and allow multiple applications of the same water. Farmers can line ditches and install drip-irrigation techniques so that the same volume of water can be applied to crops with a smaller amount of water diversion. People or firms will make these changes only if they save more in reduced water bills than they pay out to install these new devices.

Second, consumers can use water for different purposes. When

Tucson increased its water rates in the 1970s, many households altered their landscaping by replacing water-intensive lawns with indigenous plants suitable for the arid environment. Farmers can change to crop patterns requiring less water. They might shift from water-intensive alfalfa and cotton crops to less water-intensive ones.

Several studies have found that water consumption is quite responsive to price (*see* table 5-1 for a summary of studies of municipal water use). The evidence indicates that, in all regions in the United States and in other countries, residential, commercial, and industrial water uses are responsive to water pricing—measured by the elasticity of water demand (the ratio of the proportionate reduction in water use to a proportionate increase in water price):

In-house residential demand is the least responsive to water price, but is still sensitive. A 10 percent increase in price reduces residential water use by 3.5 percent to 6 percent.

Outdoor residential use (including gardening and car washing) is considerably more responsive to price. A 10 percent increase in price reduces this form of water use by 7 percent to 14 percent.

Industrial water uses are even more price responsive than residential uses. Total western waterworks systems show greater price responsiveness than residential demand alone (compare Morgan, 1973, with Bain et al., 1966, or Conley, 1967). A 10 percent increase in water price reduces residential use by 2.5 percent to 4.5 percent and total use—residential plus industrial—by 11 percent.

The water-conservation potential from imposing user fees on municipal and industrial water users will be an important consideration for future western water investment. Much of the anticipated western growth involves continued urbanization and transference of resources out of agriculture. While historically accounting for less than 10 percent of consumptive water use, municipal and industrial uses will become increasingly important.

Agricultural users are also price responsive (Phelps, Moore, and Graubard, 1978, pp. 61-63). Many studies of California's irrigation conclude that water use in the San Joaquin, Imperial, and Sacramento valleys could decline by 20 percent to 40 percent in the face of a 10 percent increase in water price (Schelhorse, et al., 1974). These estimates may apply to potential water conservation elsewhere in the West, because the San Joaquin and Imperial valleys capture the aridity of the Southwest, and the Sacramento Valley mirrors circumstances found in the Northwest.

The potential for water conservation varies by crop. Perennials—such as orchards, trees, and vines—are less price responsive than annual crops—such as alfalfa and other field crops (Smith, 1983).

TABLE 5–1

Studies of the Effect of Price on Municipal Water Use

Investigator	Price elasticity*	Water system
Bain et al. (1966)	−1.10	41 Waterworks in California
Clark & Goddard (1977)	−0.63	22 Waterworks in Ohio
Conley (1967)	−1.07	24 Waterworks in southern California
DeRooy (1974)	−0.35 to −0.89	30 U.S. waterworks: industrial users
Elliot & Seagraves (1972)	−0.70	33 U.S. cities: industrial users
Ethridge (1970)	−0.40	5 Poultry-dressing plants
Flack (1965)	−0.12 to −1.0	54 Western waterworks
Gallagher & Robinson (1977)	−0.24 to −0.89	Residential use in Australia
Gardner & Schick (1964)	−0.77	43 waterworks in Utah
Gottleib (1963)	−0.66 to −1.24	Waterworks in Kansas
Grima (1970)	−0.93	91 U.S. waterwork systems
Hanke (1970)	−0.59	Residential in-house use, Boulder, Colorado
	−1.39	Residential outdoor use, Boulder, Colorado
Herrington (1972)	−1.16 to −1.58	Industrial use in England
Howe & Linaweaver (1967)	−0.70	10 Western waterworks
Metcalf (1926)	−0.65	29 U.S. waterworks
Morgan (1973)	−0.25 to −0.45	Residential use in southern California
Rees (1969)	−0.96 to −6.7	Industrial water use in England
Renshaw (1958)	−0.45	36 U.S. waterworks
Ridge (1972)	−0.30 to −0.60	U.S. brewing & fluid milk plants
Seidel & Bauman (1957)	−0.12 to −1.0	U.S. waterworks
Turndovsky (1969)	−0.05 to −0.40	19 Massachusetts waterworks
Ware & North (1967)	−0.61 to −0.67	Waterworks in Georgia
Wong et al. (1953)	−0.01 to −0.72	Waterworks in Illinois
Wong (1972)	−0.02 to −0.28	Chicago, Illinois, waterworks
Young (1973)	−0.41 to −0.60	Tucson, Arizona

* Measures ratio of the percent change in water use to the percent change in water price.

Source: Hanke (1978), table 1, p. 488.

Higher water prices also would cause farmers to alter their crop choice, switching from more to less water-intensive crops (Hedges, 1974). These shifts in crop patterns would reduce further water use in agriculture.

Adopting water pricing in place of tax financing improves financial collateral of water investment for two reasons. First, reduced water consumption saves more in costs than benefits sacrificed, because subsidized water pricing extends water use with value less than the costs of service. Second, user-fee financing increases the share of consumption by residential users, because higher prices generate proportionately greater reductions in water use by industrial and agricultural users than for residential users. The revenue streams of such projects would experience less **cyclical volatility** because industrial users' cutback on consumption during recessions would be more than residential users' cutback. Debt repayment will be jeopardized less by downturns in the economy.

Skeptics who question the efficacy of user fees do so because they do not believe that the demand for water is as responsive to price changes as the studies indicate. Their skepticism stems from observations that during droughts water prices soar while water use hardly falls. Also, during experiments with price increases, declines in consumption seem temporary.

These phenomena do not contradict the findings of demand studies. Consumers do not respond immediately to an increase in price. They need time to determine whether the price increase is permanent or temporary, and may decide to wait until their equipment is obsolete before replacing it with more water-conserving devices. For these reasons, demand for water is always more responsive to sustained price increases in the long run than in the short run.

Inflation also has overtaken recent one-time increases in water prices. Price elasticity studies measure the response of demand to **real** constant-dollar price increases, not to increases in nominal prices. A water utility that doubled its price in the mid-1970s would find that well over half of the price increase has been "repealed." The prices of other goods and services have increased by over 60 percent during that time, so the real price of water has been declining by 5 percent to 10 percent each year since the increase in the nominal price of water. The "temporary" nature of cuts in water use do not refute these demand studies. They are, in fact, predicted by them.

The Case for User Fees: Improved Planning

As water use nears system capacity, political pressure builds to expand the system. How much additional capacity is demanded depends partly on how revenues are raised. A system of user fees improves the prospect that only those demands with value in excess of the cost to supply will enter into the political process.

User fees inspire a more rational balance between private and public investment in water facilities. In the late 1950s, 75 percent of New York City's water users were unmetered (DeHaven, 1963). Users allowed their plumbing systems to fall into serious disrepair because there was no financial reward for fixing leaks. The resulting demands on the water authority—partly due to increased water use, and partly due to leaking water into sewers—led to pressure for the development of new water supplies.

In response, New York water authorities devised the Cannonsville project to transport additional water into New York City. Yet studies indicated that fixing leaks in private systems would have saved as much water as that project delivered and at a fraction of the cost! If New York City's water supply had been metered at that time, the water authority would have faced lower demands for water and delayed for many years, if not abandoned, additional development projects (DeHaven, 1963).

User-fee financing also seems to provide a better fiscal environment for engaging in timely maintenance and repair. Cities and water authorities that finance capital and operating expenses from user fees maintain their infrastructure better than those that rely on general tax revenues (Pagano and Moore, 1981, and U.S. Department of Commerce, 1980). User fees insulate water maintenance from competing political claims on general tax revenues. Timely repair and maintenance lowers capital-financing costs. The bond market views poorly maintained systems as potential sources of cost overruns during the life of the system (Lamb and Rappaport, 1980). This increases perceived financial risks for bondholders and translates into higher interest rates paid by the borrower.

The Case Against User Fees: Metering Costs

Even though user fees may be cost-effective in theory, the value of improved resource allocation may be less than the cost of installing the meters required for administering a user-fee system. This does not seem to apply to the West. In fact, the West has a long history of metering. Starting with mutual irrigation companies in the 19th century, water use has been metered to ensure that members used only the water that they owned (Smith, 1983). Metering also has been used by municipalities in the West, although revenues from water prices are usually supplemented by some general tax revenues.[1] The gains in allocative efficiency also exceed the cost of metering in the East, even though system-development costs, which partly determine the savings from metering, are much lower.

The Case Against User Fees: Sacrificing General Obligation Bonding

The revenues generated by a user-fee system are often used to back a revenue bond, the proceeds from which are used to finance construction. A system that is subsidized heavily from general tax revenues will have to rely on general obligation bonds unless construction is paid for out of general revenues. It is often alleged that general obligation bonds can be marketed at lower interest rates than revenue bonds, and simple comparisons of yields would seem to support this view.[2] However, general obligation debt cannot be extended indefinitely. States and localities must husband their general obligation credit by using it only for projects that have less attractive alternative means of financing (Lamb and Rappaport, 1980, p. 207). This viewpoint is especially relevant for western states, because they are more likely to face tax, spending, and debt limitations than states in other regions (*see* chapter 6), and local government debt in the West is growing much faster than it is nationwide.

The interest rate differential between general obligation and revenue bonds is much narrower when allowance is made for differences in bond quality and other factors (*see* chapter 3). The spread is narrowest for bonds issued to finance sewer and water projects. Using general obligation bonds for water project financing requires other public purposes to turn to revenue bonds, which will incur an even greater differential cost.

Revenue bonding can be an even cheaper means of financing water investment than general obligation bonding. The Twentieth Century Fund Task Force on Municipal Bond Credit Ratings (p. 80) reports that "in cases where a basic utility has the same service area as a municipality, it is usually given the same rating as the area's general obligation debt." In fact, water bonds are often so highly regarded that they can even command a higher rating than the municipality's general obligation bonds (Lamb and Rappaport, 1980, p. 208).

There are *no differences* between market yields of general obligation and water, sewer, and electric revenue bonds of comparable rating that receive the same number of underwriting bids (Benson, 1980). States and localities can minimize their total interest costs if they use their general-obligation-bonding capacity for those public purposes that cannot be backed by user fees.[3]

The Case Against User Fees: Equity Considerations

Critics oppose user fees on the grounds that they impose an inequitable burden on farmers, low-income consumers, and small businesses. They believe that water systems should be financed out of general tax revenues to ensure that all customers can afford it. Such critics are prepared to sacrifice efficiency in the pursuit of equity. However, efficiency and equity are not necessarily in conflict. In fact, an efficient fee structure usually entails price differentials that favor those about whom the equity concern is raised. Those concerned about equity may wish to dispute the size of the differential but need not object to user fees per se.

Providing water at no charge does not obviate the need to raise revenues. Someone must pay for the project. Using general revenues rather than user fees improves equity only if the gains from reduced water prices are greater than the burdens of increased general taxation for the targeted beneficiary group. Economic analysis of who gains and loses from using tax financing in place of user fees questions the effectiveness of this policy in achieving equity goals.

Consider the plight of a municipal water utility. It has thousands of customers—residential (rich and poor), industrial, commercial, agricultural, and tax-exempt. Which of these customers will benefit from reduced user fees and increased property taxes? An increase in sales taxes is likely to be much more regressive than an increase in property taxes and so would not be used for equity purposes (Hyman, 1981).

A comprehensive study of who gains and loses by reducing user fees and increasing property taxation was conducted by examining the pattern of water consumption among residential, commercial, industrial, and tax-exempt customers in San Diego in 1971 (Neuner, Popp, and Sebold, 1977). This water system delivered 52.7 million cubic feet of water and raised $18.8 million exclusively by user fees.[4] The authors matched the municipal utility's account files with the city's property-tax-assessment roles to find water use and property tax obligations for individual parcels of land. The authors studied 94.7 percent of all accounts who used 94.4 percent of the water and owned 84.9 percent of the assessed property value in the city of San Diego's service area.

Table 5-2 shows the estimated distribution of water use, water bills, and assessed valuation of property by key customer categories. Residential users consume 59.8 percent of the system's water and pay 67.7 percent of system revenues. The next largest user category includes government agencies, undeveloped land, and tax-exempt organizations (schools, churches, etc.), which use 24.5 percent of the water and pay 18.4 percent of the revenues. Agricultural users account for less than 1 percent of water use and revenues. The pricing structure follows a common pattern found in the West—per-unit revenues are greatest for residential users (40.1 cents per 100 cubic feet), lower for commercial and industrial users (31.6 cents), and even lower for agricultural users (27.7 cents).

Table 5-3 reports annual net gains and losses that would result from a shift from full user-fee funding (the actual practice at the time of the study) to a 25.8 percent subsidy supported by an increase in the property tax.[5] The data in the table show that there are two offsetting effects. Everyone's water bill is reduced while their property taxes increase—by 32.13 cents per $100 of assessed value. The "initial" row in the table shows the net result of these two effects for different user categories. Commercial and industrial users lose, while agricultural, residential, government agencies, tax-exempt organizations, and undeveloped land gain.

However, these initial effects are augmented by the effects of increased water consumption caused by the decline in price (labeled "adjustment" in table 5-3). The utility expands the quantity of water supplied,[6] and each user gains from additional water use because that water provides services with a value that exceeds the subsidized price. The expanded system capacity requires a further increase in property taxes. The extent to which customers gain or lose from these adjustments depends on the value of the additional water relative to the additional property taxes they must pay. The data indicate that, with the exception of agriculture, all water users are worse off from the adjustment.[7] For the system as a whole, the annual cost of the waste resulting from excessive water use is $379,017, or 8.3 percent of the initial reduction in water bills.

The total effects of the subsidy policy indicate how poorly water subsidization achieves its equity goals. For every $1 reduction in their water bills, households pay 91 cents in higher property taxes. About 95 percent of the remaining 9 cents of net gain is absorbed by losses incurred by financing "excess" water use.[8] Residential customers lose relative to industrial and commercial users because they value the additional water less and so do not increase their consumption as much.[9]

The pattern of net gains and losses among households residing in 22 areas shows a mixed record in improving equity (see figure 5-1). Fifteen of the 22 areas experience net gains. An area gains more (or loses less) from water subsidization the lower its median family income (consistent with common perceptions of equity goals) and the smaller the share of households headed by the elderly (inconsis-

TABLE 5–2

Water Use and Bills and Propety Values in
San Diego, California

Category	Share of water use (%)	Share of water bill (%)	Share of Assessed valuation (%)	Average revenue (S/100 cu. ft.)
Residential	59.81	67.69	61.52	0.401
Commercial/industrial	14.95	13.33	26.64	0.316
Agricultural	0.71	0.56	0.08	0.277
Other*	24.53	18.42	11.76	0.266
System totals	52,570 (1,000 cu. ft.)	18.80 (millions)	1,678 (millions)	

* Includes government agencies, undeveloped land, and tax-exempt water users.

Source: Computed from Neuner, Popp, and Sebold (1977), table 1, p. 42.

tent with common perceptions of equity goals). The absolute size of these numbers show that even the large 25.8 percent subsidy was worth only an $8 gain per customer in the residential area enjoying the highest benefits (median family income of $5,000 and 5 percent of households headed by an elderly person). In the area suffering the greatest net losses, the costs are only $7.42 per customer (median family income of $15,000 and 20 percent of households headed by elderly persons).[10]

Subsidizing water increases, not reduces, business costs. Commercial and industrial customers would suffer net losses averaging 29.3 percent of their original water bill—or about $100 per metered connection.[11] The increased costs from tax financing to those businesses that are relatively small water users more than offsets the benefits enjoyed by other businesses. Overall, user-fee financing will not drive out businesses.

Water subsidies do help agriculture. The only sector to benefit overall, farmers' gains average about 28.3 percent of their original bill—or about $683 per metered connection. As with residential, commercial, and industrial users, all farmers are not treated equally (Smith, 1983).[12] Crops using little water relative to assessed property valuation—some types of orchards, and probably grains—lose. Crops using large amounts of water relative to assessed property valuation—specialty crops, alfalfa—gain.

For the nation as a whole, it seems doubtful that water subsidization in the West has reduced U.S. food prices (Phelps, Moore, and
Graubard, 1978, pp. 46-48). Lower water prices would place down-
ward pressure on the prices of water-intensive crops, but upward
pressure on the prices of crops that use less water. But these pressures need not affect U.S. food prices. International competition and
U.S. price-support and acreage-allotment policies determine U.S.
food prices, and these forces need not be affected by how water
subsidization influences the composition of U.S. farm output.

TABLE 5–3

Annual Net Gains from a 25.8 Percent Water Subsidy

Category	Dollar gain	Net gain (dollars) per meter	Net gain as (%) of water bill
Residential			
Initial	282,204	1.95	2.35
Adjustment	−266,445	−1.84	−2.22
Total	15,759	0.11	0.13
Commercial/ industrial			
Initial	−609,171	−88.48	−25.76
Adjustment	−83,836	−12.18	−3.55
Total	−693,007	−100.66	−29.31
Agriculture			
Intial	21,989	536.33	22.21
Adjustment	6,008	146.55	6.01
Total	27,997	682.88	28.28
Other*			
Initial	304,978	125.56	9.33
Adjustment	−34,744	−14.30	−1.06
Total	270,234	111.26	8.27
System			
Initial	0	0.00	0.00
Adjustment	−379,017	−2.46	−2.14
Total	−379,107	−2.46	−2.14

* Includes government agencies, undeveloped land, and tax-exempt water users.

Source: Computed from data in Neuner, Popp, and Sebold (1977), table 1, p. 42.

FIGURE 5–1

Distribution of Residential Gains from Water Subsidy.

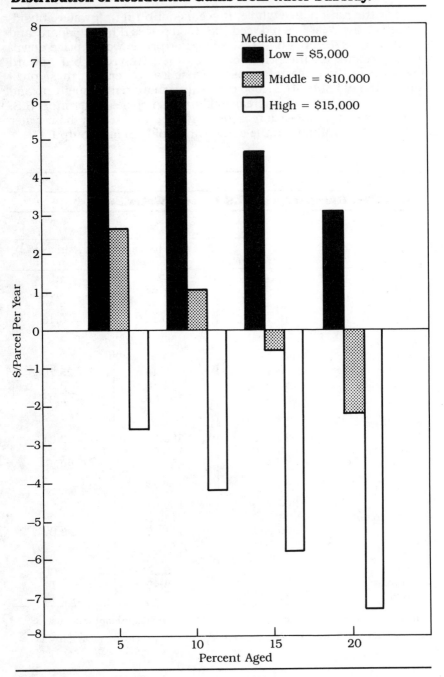

ESTIMATING TRUE SUPPLY COSTS

The price that customers pay for water should reflect the full cost of servicing their account. Estimating true costs is not easy. It should not be done by simply apportioning expenses over the volume of water supplied. This section describes three important issues: the composition of historical versus replacement costs for acquisition, purification, and transmission; the degree of scale economies;[13] and the possibility of reuse.

Replacement versus Historical Cost

The cost of replacing a facility is often much greater than the cost incurred when it was built. This is the result of overall inflation and real changes in land values, construction costs, and the value of water rights. Prices should reflect replacement costs, not the "book value" of past investment.

Table 5-4 shows the component costs of water plant investment for the city of Dallas. This municipal waterworks has been a strong advocate of user fees. Its sources of water are large-scale diversion projects (Graeser, 1978). Transmission and distribution facilities within the city are the most significant investments. Acquisition and transportation of water to the city account for 30 percent of total water investment. Investment in purification facilities is the next most important item.

TABLE 5—4

Water Plant Investment for Dallas, Texas, by Function

Function	Original cost Amount (× $1,000)	%	Replacement cost Amount (× $1,000)	%
Raw water & transportation	90.1	29	248.8	30
Purification	31.4	10	86.0	10
Transmission/distribution	167.6	54	550.0	55
Meters	10.9	4	16.1	2
Fire hydrants	5.5	2	14.7	2
Engineering, administration, & other	4.2	1	5.7	1
Total	309.8		821.0	

Source: Graseser (1978), table 3, p. 493.

Total replacement cost is 2.65 times the original construction cost. Costs of all categories of investment have increased. If the water authority were to use historical rather than replacement costs in setting prices, it would not generate sufficient funds to repair and replace the system as it wears out. The result would be a deterioration in the quality of services, which could trigger a red flag for the municipal bond market (see chapter 3).

Economies of Scale

Many water systems enjoy economies of scale—that is, their costs per gallon fall as the total number of gallons supplied increases. The data presented in figure 5-2 indicate that average costs (per gallon) to meet the standards of the Safe Drinking Water Act are over four times greater for small utilities than for the large ones.

Efficiency requires user fees to be set equal to the marginal, not the average, cost of supplying water. The marginal costs are those incurred by increasing the quantity of water supplied from its current level. Because average costs are declining, the marginal cost is less than the average cost. Setting the price equal to marginal costs generates total revenues that are less than total costs. The data in figure 5-2 indicate that large utilities would lose 9 cents and the smallest ones 68 cents per 1,000 gallons supplied—22.1 percent and 39 percent of the typical costs in each system, respectively—if water prices are set equal to marginal costs. To continue operating, these systems must obtain other revenues—either by requiring all users to pay a fixed annual charge on top of the per-gallon charge, or by subsidizing from general tax revenues (see below).

However, not all the components of a water system enjoy economies of scale, nor do scale economies continue indefinitely. If a utility extends its service area to exploit scale economies, average costs will eventually begin to increase as the size grows. As the service area grows, the increase in average transmission costs offset scale economies in other parts of the utility's operations (Clark et al., 1978).

Some water-development and transportation projects exhibit diseconomies of scale—average costs rising as the size of the system increases. In its planned diversion projects, the state of California estimates that marginal costs will exceed average costs as the system reaches its planned capacity (see table 5-5, in which marginal costs exceed average costs by over 300 percent for Los Vaqueros, 175 percent for Colusa, and 110 percent for Glenn). Marginal costs exceed average costs by 240 percent for the Peripheral Canal—whose bond issue was defeated in elections in 1982. When diseconomies of scale are experienced, efficient pricing generates net revenues, not losses.

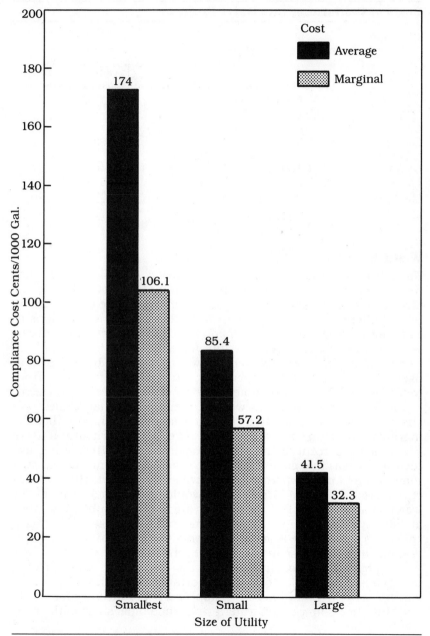

FIGURE 5–2

Treatment Costs for Meeting Safe Drinking Water Act.

Source: Stevie and Clark (1978), tables 3, 4, and 6, p. 14.

TABLE 5–5

Costs of California State Water Project

Facility	Total cost of construction (millions)	Marginal yield (mil AF)	Cumulative yield (mil AF)	Average capital cost/AF of yield ($)	Marginal capital cost/AF of yield ($)
Oroville	429	2.1	2.1	10	10
Peripheral Canal	540	0.5	2.6	23	78
Glenn	1,160	1.0	3.6	40	84
Colusa	910	0.5	4.1	52	143
Los Vaqueros	540	0.2	4.2	59	245

Source: Phelps, Moore, and Graubard (1978), table A.3, p. 65.

Water Reuse

Water users should pay only for what they consume, not for what they divert. Some customers do not consumptively use all the water diverted for their use, because a portion of the diverted water can be reused afterwards. A power plant may divert millions of gallons of water for cooling, but almost all flows back into the stream and can be reused for irrigation or by a municipality. In the lower Colorado River region, about 50 percent of the water "diverted" by agricultural users flows back into the river. By contrast, any return flow from water diverted for drinking water requires expensive waste treatment.

Accounting for reuse in water pricing means that farmers are charged less than residential or industrial users. Suppose that the marginal diversion cost were $75 per acre-foot. If agricultural users consume 50 percent of the water they divert, then their water use involves a marginal cost of $37.50 per acre-foot. If municipal customers consume 100 percent of the water they divert, their use incurs marginal costs of $75. Farmers would pay only half as much for water as households. But the farmers are not being subsidized, they are simply paying the true costs of the water they use.[14] Chapter 6 considers some of the legal impediments to integrating fully considerations of water reuse into a user-fee schedule.

Implementing possibilities of water reuse into water pricing must consider other factors, the importance of which varies among localities. Return flows need not appear instantaneously for reuse, and this affects how much water prices should fall short of the marginal cost of diversion.[15] The uncertainty of estimating return flows, however, does not limit their applicability. An uncertain estimate of a 30 percent return rate can be more accurate than implicitly assuming a zero rate, as would be done if return flows were neglected entirely.

PRICING SURFACE DELIVERIES

Efficient pricing of surface deliveries includes not only the full costs associated with delivering water, but also any costs associated with treating water after use. This section describes how these goals are achieved in the face of differences among users in how their use affects water quality, financial deficits resulting from scale economies, and the presumed inability of agriculture to pay the full marginal costs of water.

Pricing Restoration and Maintenance of Water Quality

Municipalities must meet wastewater standards that limit the bacterial content of both reclaimed water consumed by residential users and wastewater discharged. User fees should include the marginal cost of water treatment in the delivery charge. This may raise the price of water to residential and industrial customers relative to the price paid by agricultural users.

The "treatment surcharge" in user fees should reflect the actual wastes discharged by water users. If poultry processors discharge twice as much waste per cubic foot of water as fruit canners, they should pay twice the treatment surcharge. If fees are structured in this manner, industry will invest in new equipment or will modify their waste discharges to avoid paying discharge fees (Eldridge, 1972). The reduction in the volume of waste produced and the installation of private treatment facilities mean that the capacity of public waste-treatment facilities will not have to be as large.

Not all waste-treatment problems originate from water use. For example, improper storage of industrial chemicals can increase significantly the level of contaminants in a city's water supply. Levying fees on the private production of waste imperiling water supplies diminishes the discharge of wastes and, therefore, reduces the necessary investment in public treatment facilities. It also provides an additional source of revenue for backing debt.

Pricing Surface Deliveries Under Economies of Scale

Efficient pricing under conditions of economies of scale generates losses for the utility. Failure to use marginal-cost pricing has been

105

justified traditionally by the need to avoid operating deficits (Kahn, 1971). Only 2.2 percent of municipal water utilities employ uniform pricing, whereas 55.6 percent employ a minimum monthly charge and a declining block rate—the water price declines with the volume of use—and 25.6 percent impose a minimum charge and a uniform water price (*see* table 5-6).

Declining block rates subsidize large commercial and industrial users at the expense of small residental users, because the larger customers pay less than the marginal costs of service while smaller customers pay more than marginal costs (DeHaven, 1963). These fee schedules provide the wrong signals for water allocation. Charging residential users more than their marginal costs artificially limits water use in the residential sector. Charging commercial and industrial users less than their marginal cost leads to overuse of water in that sector. On balance, total water demand increases, because residential users are less responsive to water price than commercial and industrial users.

How can a utility cover deficits without cross-subsidization? The answer is a two-part tariff. The "first part" is a fee for being a customer of the system. The "second part" is a water price reflecting the marginal cost of service. To promote economic efficiency, the fee cannot be more than the amount by which the value of the water purchased exceeds payments made under the second part of the tar-

TABLE 5—6

Relative Frequency of Water Rate Schedules in United States

Schedule	Frequency (%)
Uniform rate	2.2
Fixed charge and	
Uniform rate	6.7
Decreasing block	4.4
Increasing block	3.3
Seasonal	1.1
Minimum charge and	
Uniform rate	25.6
Decreasing block	55.6
Increasing block	1.1

Source: Lippiatt and Weber (1982), table 1, p. 279.

TABLE 5-7

Structure of Monthly Water Charges in City of Dallas, Texas

Meter size (inches)	Customer charge ($)	
	Water	Sewer
⅝	1.10	2.15
¾	1.20	2.15
1	1.50	2.15
1½	2.00	2.15
2	2.55	2.15
3	17.65	2.15
4	26.01	2.15
6	51.35	2.15
8	95.68	2.15
10	149.58	2.15

Usage charge Residential	Rate ($) per 1,000 gal. of water delivered	
	Water	Sewer
<20,000 gal./month	0.61	0.38
>20,000 gal./month		
Winter	0.61	none
Summer	0.79	none

Source: Rice and Shaw (1978), table 00, p. 000.

iff, or the user will opt out of the system. Losing the business of these users reduces the utility's financial capacity, because it turns away users who could increase the net benefits of the water supply system.

A simple rule of thumb to avoid this problem employs different fees for different categories of users—defined according to their range of consumption. For example, the first part of the tariff may be a monthly charge of $1 for water use below 2,000 gallons, $2 for water use between 2,000 and 4,000 gallons, and so on. The tariff must be related to a *range* of consumption levels, not actual consumption, otherwise the tariff will simply be a price added to the second part of the tariff.

The city of Dallas imposes such a system (*see* table 5-7). Customers pay a monthly marginal charge for water use (shown in the lower part of the table) and a fixed charge that varies with the size of the meter installed—meter size is a proxy for the range of consumption. This type of pricing structure is equitable, because smaller residential users do not pay disproportionately more than larger commercial and industrial users. It also means that all users contribute to cover possible financial deficits resulting from efficient pricing of water.

Can Agriculture Pay User Fees?

Many observers question the economic viability of levying user fees on agriculture. Suppose a fee system that took account of reuse possibilities and differences in treatment costs charges agricultural users 50 percent less than municipal and industrial users. These prices still may exceed agriculture's apparent ability to pay because the necessary water expenditures would exceed the per-acre cash flow earned from farming.

There are two reasons why it may be hasty to conclude that agriculture would not survive under user-fee financing of water investment. First, estimates of how higher water prices increase the per-acre water expenditures by farmers generally neglect water conservation. For example, if the elasticity of demand for water per irrigated acre is only −1, then water expenditures per acre are unaffected by increases in the water price. The water purchased per acre declines by the same percentage that the water price increases. Second, the current cash flow earned by agriculture legitimately nets out mortgage payments from the revenues earned from sales. However, higher water prices reduce agricultural land values and thereby reduce the land costs incurred in farming. To be sure, individuals owning agricultural land will suffer capital losses from the reduction in their land values, but whether farming remains the highest-valued land use is a separate issue.

The relations among farming productivity, land values, and water prices also imply that local tax financing of water investment is not a viable alternative to user-fee financing for distressed economic areas. Suppose that the underlying economics of farming are so poor that farmers abandon agriculture if a new water project were financed by user fees. The local irrigation district's tax base would be equally weak, because the fundamental economic problem is low farming productivity. Lowering water prices increases taxation relative to the weak economic base, because the required tax revenues exceed the increased land values from lower water prices by the amount of the economic inefficiency created by water subsidies (see Smith, 1983).

So the crucial policy issue for user-fee financing is whether the decline in land values from increasing water prices should be imposed on farmers as a by-product of low-cost financing of water investment. If not, some form of grant program is required that will increase the overall financing costs of water investment (*see* chapter 7) or little-used efficient financing mechanisms based upon the conjunctive use of surface water and groundwater must be implemented.

GROUNDWATER EXTRACTION TAXES AND CONJUNCTIVE USE

Groundwater extraction—pumping water from underground reservoirs—is an important source of water for western states but traditionally has remained outside the control of water authorities. Formal water organizations rely on groundwater for only 1.9 percent of their total water supply (*see* table 2-4). Yet for many states, such as California, groundwater sources can account for 50 percent of a state's entire water supply (Phelps, Graubard, and Moore, 1978). In many areas, water is being withdrawn at rates far in excess of the rates at which aquifers (or underground reservoirs) are naturally replenished, leading to shortages and land subsidence.

Excessive pumping of groundwater can be curbed by allowing water authorities to tax extractions. This section examines the issues that must be addressed to set an efficient tax rate and argues that the tax revenues should be dedicated to finance the development of surface water.

Few water authorities have been created for groundwater management because the aquifer (or underground reservoir) provides a natural means of water distribution (Brown and McGuire, 1967). No diversion or delivery systems need be constructed. Each water user can simply install a pump and capture his or her own water supply.

Within the past few decades, declining water tables (the depth to which water users must pump for water) and higher energy costs have combined to increase significantly the cost of pumping groundwater. The resulting economic hardship has renewed interest in economically efficient groundwater management (*see* State of California's Governor's Commission to Review Water Rights, 1978).

The Economic Case For Pump Taxes

Excessive depletion of groundwater supplies can be attributed, in part, to the nature of pumping costs—the faster the pumping rate and the deeper the water table, the higher the costs per gallon.[16] The depth of the water table, in turn, depends on the natural rate of recharge, the return flow of used water, and the *total* amount extracted by all water users. Therefore, a water user's marginal cost depends on personal decisions—how much to pump—and the decisions of others pumping from the same aquifer.

People tend to deplete an aquifer at a faster rate than is economically efficient, because each pumper considers only how his or her costs are increased by the pumping and ignores how this action raises the costs of others.[17] Taxing groundwater extractions can limit this problem.[18] The tax increases each user's costs by an amount that could be set equal to the costs that a user's pumping imposes on others. The tax should, therefore, reflect three factors: 1) the effect of water depth on pumping costs of all water users; 2) the effect of net extractions from the aquifer on water depth; and 3) the effect of water use on net extractions.

Including the effect of water use on net extractions from the aquifer is analogous to allowing for return flows in the pricing of surface water. If 70 percent of user A's pumping percolates (returns) to the aquifer, then A's use of an acre-foot of water represents a net withdrawal of only three-tenths of an acre-foot of water from the aquifer. If only 30 percent of user B's water use percolates to the aquifer, then B's use of an acre-foot of water represents a net withdrawal of seven-tenths of an acre-foot of water. The pump tax should be 57 percent lower for user A than B, because their pumping activities have different effects on the depth of the water table.[19] If the tax is calibrated this way, an individual's decision would weigh the value of the water against the social costs of water extraction. The tax causes all users to pump less.

How should a water authority use the revenues generated by extraction taxes? Two considerations present a strong case for using the revenues to *subsidize* the delivery of surface water. First, surface water used on the aquifer's overlying lands percolates underground and raises the water table so that groundwater extractors enjoy lower pumping costs. Managing this interrelation between surface water and groundwater supply is termed *conjunctive use* (Maknoon and Burgess, 1978). Because surface water users do not consider how their consumption affects others' pumping costs, their consumption should be subsidized to encourage the most efficient use of ground- and surface-water together.[20]

The second justification for subsidizing surface water is the likely local opposition to groundwater taxation. If the water authority were to use the tax proceeds for purposes that did not directly benefit water users (for example, transferring the revenues to the general fund of a local or state government), then water users as a whole would lose from the pump tax. Tax revenues exceed the pumping costs saved by raising the water table (*see* Wetzel, 1978, pp. 25-29). Water users would be better off with the overdraft problem than they would be with groundwater taxation. Using the tax proceeds to subsidize surface deliveries allows water users to benefit from the economic efficiencies created by the pump tax.[21] The gains from lower surface water prices alone would make pumpers benefit from the tax scheme (Wetzel, 1978, p. 28). The recharge from surface water percolating into the aquifer is an additional bonus.

As with return flows among surface users, how much surface water should be subsidized to accommodate replenishment of aquifers depends on how quickly surface water becomes available as additional groundwater. The effects depend on the specifics of each situation, but slow percolation need not diminish the case for subsidization of surface deliveries.

To many in the West, conjunctive use is not a new idea. The *physical* relation between surface water and groundwater supplies is well understood. Conjunctive use as a resource-management device is neither new or unused. However, the *fiscal* relationship between controlling the overdraft problem with pump taxes and financing surface water development is less widely practiced. Properly implemented, conjunctive use becomes an additional fiscal tool for financing water investment.

Experience with Pump Taxes

As the overdraft problem intensified, some local and state governments implemented pump taxes. The experiences of the Orange County Water District in California (OCWD) and the state of Arizona illustrate how the basic principles of groundwater taxation work in practice.

Groundwater problems have plagued Orange County since the 1930s (Lipson, 1978). Urbanization and intensive cultivation increased groundwater pumping, creating overdraft and water-quality problems. Replenishment was originally believed to be the solution. OCWD initially used property taxation to finance the purchase of surface water to replenish underground aquifers. Over time, OCWD evolved toward the taxation and pricing schemes discussed above. In 1952, the district introduced a pump tax on groundwater extractions to pay for the surface water needed to replenish its declining water table. By 1977, the average pump tax was $25 per acre-foot pumped, although irrigators paid only $11 per acre-foot. The revenues from this tax—almost $5.5 million in 1978—have allowed the county to reduce property taxes. By the early 1970s the district was levying property taxes at only 35 percent of its authorized levels (Lipson, 1978, table 9, p. 68). The groundwater overdraft has disappeared, and the county (now the richest in California) is able to realize its growth potential despite its naturally arid environment.

The state of Arizona is a more recent convert to pump taxes. A growing overdraft problem and concerns about the future of its agriculture led to the passage of the 1980 Groundwater Act. The state levies a $2-per-acre-foot tax on groundwater extraction. Management plans indicate how much water—from each source—each acre of farmland may use. The state levies a withdrawal fee (per acre/foot) on extractions of groundwater that consists of three parts: 1) a fee—not less than 50 cents nor more than one dollar—to finance the administration of the Act; 2) a charge not to exceed two dollars for importation of water for artifical recharge of aquifers; and 3) a fee not to exceed two dollars nor levied before the year 2006 for the purchase and permanent retirement of irrigated land from agriculture if 500,000 acres of farmland are not retired voluntarily by 2020.

The Orange County and Arizona examples illustrate that pump taxation is indeed feasible. The OCWD tax has been in place long enough to indicate that taxing groundwater can both cope with the overdraft problem and raise revenues. Coordinating tax collections with the purchase or subsidization of surface deliveries can be managed effectively. The Arizona program is too new to draw conclusions from it.[22] However, the relatively low tax rate (in comparison to OCWD) and the failure to use revenues for conjunctive use may limit the benefits gained from the program. A policy of fiscal conjunctive use is worth considering, especially in light of the major investments required to complete the Central Arizona Project.

USER-FEE FINANCING OF MULTIPLE-BENEFIT PROJECTS

Skeptics question whether user fees can be applied to multiple-purpose projects. How can a fee structure be designed to raise revenues for dam safety or flood control? What price should be charged for hydroelectric power that is generated at little additional cost to a large-scale project? General tax revenues are usually used to finance dam safety and flood control because of the perceived difficulty of assigning a user fee. Yet pricing schedules can be designed and should be the preferred revenue source for securing low-cost financing. Pricing of hydroelectric power should reflect the costs of alternative sources of electricity supply.

Dam Safety

An efficient user-fee system would charge water users for maintaining dam safety, because protecting surrounding residents from damages is the responsibility of the water system. Returning to the example of Arid County, the costs of protecting residents below a newly constructed ACMWD dam should be paid by water users as one of the costs incurred in supplying water. The full cost of the project includes the explicit cost of labor, materials, right-of-way, and water rights, plus the cost of safeguarding nearby residents.

Past federal policy has obscured the connection between water development and safety, because federal monies financed the portion of project costs associated with dam safety. Contracts between water users and the federal government expressly absolved water users of any financial responsibility for maintaining safe dams.

User fees can pay for dam-safety costs in both new and existing water projects. Since federal policy is changing, states can no longer rely on the federal government to pay the costs of dam safety. As contracts are renewed or as new contracts are written, user-fee schedules can be established. The U.S. Army Corps of Engineers' recent review of dam safety indicates that many existing projects should undertake investments to improve dam safety, and user fees would be an effective way of financing them.

Flood Control

The benefits of flood control are related to the value of the protected property, not to the quantity of water consumed. Therefore, that part of a water project's cost attributed to flood control could be paid by a surcharge on the taxes for properties threatened with the flood and not through water charges—provided that a water project did not create the flood-control problem. If the project created the flood problem, then the costs of protection should be allocated to water users for the same reasons that water users should pay for dam safety.

Some may view the use of property taxes as a user fee to pay for flood control as farfetched. Can property owners select their levels of flood control? If they cannot, how can property taxes influence decisions about the degree of flood control? The answers depend, critically, on whether the beneficiaries reside in a single jurisdiction.

Flood-control programs protecting only local residents are usually financed through the creation of a special flood-control district where projects are voter approved in special elections. If payment for flood-control projects is divorced from benefits, then voters would approve even very expensive projects as long as the project were to provide some minor flood-protection benefits to a majority of voters, or reject projects whose benefits—while exceeding costs—are enjoyed by a minority of voters. Making those who benefit pay gives voters an incentive to weigh their benefits from flood control versus their apportioned share of project costs. Using *ad valorem* property tax financing ensures that a resident's balance of costs and benefits is roughly proportional to those of the project.[23]

The actual experience of flood-control districts illustrates the relevance of this point. Often, districts subdivide themselves into "improvement districts" to levy separate property taxes on different residential and industrial areas because not all of their projects benefit all areas. If the districts were not subdivided, voters would reject worthy flood-control projects. The Maricopa County Flood Control District in Arizona recently proposed a project that would protect only a portion of its district from floods. Voters defeated the project because the entire district was required to pay for it.

Intergovernmental cooperation is required for efficient financing of flood-control projects to protect residents of many jurisdictions. For example, the Pick-Sloan Project in North Dakota provides flood-control benefits to residents throughout the Mississippi Delta. If only North Dakota residents paid for the flood control, this would be cross-subsidization that would reduce the collateral behind project financing, similar in concept to the reduced collateral suffered by engaging in cross-subsidization of the delivery of surface water. The institutional form of the required cooperation can be varied—from intergovernmental grants (or payment for services rendered) to establishing a flood-control agency the jurisdiction of which extends beyond common political boundaries.

Hydroelectric Power

Federal policy also has obscured the economic issues surrounding the pricing of hydroelectric power generated by water projects. In past U.S. Bureau of Reclamation and Army Corps of Engineer projects, the federal government followed a "cheap power" pricing policy by purposefully using below-market interest rates in calculating the necessary revenues to be raised from users. Power-preference clauses in federal contracts allocated available power to favored users. Does it make economic sense for local public entities, operating in the post-federal-financing era, to adopt the same policy?

Charging the interstate power price instead of a cheaper rate for power of comparable quality and priority raises additional revenues to finance water development. This policy makes economic sense, because power produced by the project would substitute for more costly power sources. Total electricity demand would not increase

114

unless the availability of additional hydroelectric power reduced interstate market power prices. If cheap power pricing were adopted, then those enjoying preferences under the chosen power preference policy would expand their use of electricity to applications where the value of electricity was less than the interstate market price.

As with subsidizing water, subsidizing power intensifies the pressure for additional investments in hydroelectric generation. Financial collateral of water projects would decline, because cheap power pricing sacrifices revenues and increases the scale of necessary investment in hydroelectric power.

USER FEE FINANCING AND FUTURE PROJECT EXPANSION

Two pricing issues arise from it being cheaper to build a larger project today in anticipation of higher future demands for water. How should water be priced during the early years of operation when the system has excess capacity? Should existing residents be charged a water price lower than the price charged to newcomers, because the newcomers are the source of additional demand on the system? These questions can be answered by returning to the earlier hypothetical example.

Suppose Arid County were considering construction of a 5-million-acre-foot diversion project. Current growth plans indicate that water demand today is only 50 percent of what it will be in 25 years. So building the project today means that excess capacity will persist for at least a decade after the project's completion. Many would argue that water should be priced below its long-run marginal cost until water demand reaches its long-run potential (*see* Phelps, Graubard, and Moore, 1978).

Efficient water pricing need not dictate this "short-term" cheap water policy. ACMWD has the alternative of delaying its project and thereby incurring its construction costs at a later date. Delaying project construction saves financing costs because borrowing $10 million five years from now involves a smaller obligation, in present-value terms, than borrowing $10 million today.[24] ACMWD can use its financial capacity for other purposes—retiring its outstanding debt or investing its "extra financial capital" at current market interest rates. So building today to meet existing demands sacrifices the returns that could be earned by short-term investing.

The full analysis of whether to delay construction must include other considerations. Are construction costs expected to increase at a faster rate than the return that could be earned from short-term

115

investing? If so, then building today would be cost-effective, but the cost of supplying water demands at their embryonic stage of growth include the forgone investment opportunity.

Following this prescription for efficient water pricing reduces the financing requirements of the water project. If the cheap water policy were adopted, ACMWD would have to obtain even more short-term financing to cover the larger temporary "deficits" that must be incurred while awaiting Arid County's achievement of its full growth potential. Also, user fees generate a positive cash flow on the delivery of water to early users that would provide an additional financial cushion for ACMWD. Those funds would increase the district's bond quality and reduce its borrowing costs.

Efficient user fees require utilities to adopt connection fees that cover the costs of extending distribution systems and connecting new homes and businesses. It is these new demands for water service that create the costs, and unless faced with those costs, new residents will demand extension of service into territories with values less than the costs of service. If ACMWD chooses instead to "spread the costs" among all users, it threatens its financial collateral by undertaking investments with negative net benefits. The district would face the intense political debates that commonly surround cross-subsidization. (An example of the problem can be found in chapter 7's discussion of the political opposition to the Peripheral Canal in California.)

Efficient user-fee schedules, however, do not distinguish between original and new customers when setting prices for the development of additional supply sources. For example, ACMWD may extend its supply by building an additional 1-million-acre-foot diversion project. Both old and new customers contribute to the demand for that additional water and both have the ability to cut back their demands. Giving a price break to "original residents" reduces the financial capacity of the district, because the water supply will not be allocated to its highest-valued use. Residents receiving the price break will use water in lower-valued uses than residents paying higher prices.

CONCLUSIONS

User-fee financing promotes the design of economically efficient water investment without significant sacrifice of other policy objectives. Revenue bond financing is not inferior to general obligation bond financing. Nor does tax financing of water investment promote common equity goals. User-fee schedules can become complex as they reflect treatment costs, water reuse opportunities, and scale economies. Their potential for effective financing of water investment has not been exploited fully.

In agriculture, the *fiscal conjunctive use* of dedicated groundwater tax revenues for financing surface water development has yet to be adopted widely. In municipal settings, effluent charges have not been levied on discharges of industrial wastes into the water supply. Adopting both instruments can reduce borrowing costs and represent unexplored revenue sources for backing debt.

TEXT NOTES

1. Reconsider the source of revenues for the Metropolitian Water District in Southern California (table 4-3 in chapter 4): 52 percent of revenues come from user fees and 35 percent from property taxes.

2. The reader is referred to tables 3-20 and 3-21 in chapter 3 for representative evidence.

3. Due to capital market imperfections, it can be difficult for revenue bonds to generate the same number of bids as general obligation bonds. How state policies can overcome this problem is discussed in chapter 6. If this imperfection is removed, then financing water by revenue bonding can become cheaper than general obligation debt.

4. Standard & Poors rated San Diego water bonds as AA in January 1983 (S&P *Bond Guide*, 1983), so this water system is well regarded by the bond market.

5. This is the policy studied by Neuner, Popp, and Sebold, who only studied the initial effects in table 5-4. The results reported in the table differ from those in the reference because of different treatment of the gains and losses for accounts the authors were unable to match to utility files with property tax assessments. The authors specified the unmatched accounts as a separate user category. The analysis here excludes them on the theory that they represent an unknown combination of residential, industrial, commercial, and agricultural users.

   The computations on how lower water prices increase water use are based on the following assumptions about demand elasticities: residential (-0.5), and commercial, industrial, and agricultural (-1.0). So, a water subsidy that reduces prices by 25.8 percent is assumed to increase residential water use by 12.8 percent and water use by the other categories, by 25.8 percent.

6. The water authority must ration water if it choose not to expand system capacity. Rationing policies require even more complicated analysis than that for the subsidy policy. Generally, the costs of rationing destroy most of the initial gains reported in table 5-3 (Barzel, 1974). So the text considers the best case for using water subsidies for equity.

7. No individual water user has an incentive to limit water use to avoid these system losses, for the consumer would sacrifice gains from expanding personal water use, which would have only a negligible effect on the property tax rate.

117

8. The 91 cents property tax liability is inferred by comparing the initial net benefit for the residential sector as a percentage of its water bill (2.35 percent) to the 25.8 percent reduction in water bills from the water price break. The 95 percent loss from the residential sector's financing of economic inefficiency is computed by noting that total net gains (0.13 percent) are about 5 percent of the initial gain from the subsidy policy (2.35 percent).

9. The studies on the elasticity of water demand indicate that residential elasticities are about –0.5, whereas commercial, industrial, and agricultural elasticities easily exceed –1.0.

10. The reader is reminded that the data refer to 1971. Among the 22 residential areas, Rancho Bernado had the highest median family income ($17,473) and the downtown area of San Diego the lowest ($5,583) (Neuner, Popp, and Sebold, 1977, table 2, p. 43). The data in figure 5-1 are fitted values from regression analysis of the per-parcel net gain (measured in dollars per year) from the subsidy policy. The estimated equation is:
Net effect per parcel $=$ 14.78 (4.27) – 0.001 (–3.73) median income –0.324 (–2.50) percent aged. R^2 = 0.493. Standard deviation: dependent variable $=$ 5.49; residual $=$ 4.11.

11. The number of meters exceeds the number of accounts because many users—especially commercial and industrial—have more than one meter. So the estimates in the text understate the average loss suffered by commercial and industrial users.

12. The most obvious agricultural loser is the dry-farmer, who gains nothing from water subsidization but receives a property tax bill from the water utility. The local financing of water subsidization is important. If an outside source—state or federal government—financed the water subsidy, then all users still benefit from the reduction of their water bills but suffer smaller local tax burdens.

13. Scale economies are said to exist when the average cost of an activity declines with increases in its scale of use.

14. This aspect of marginal costs is commonly absent from discussion of efficient water pricing. Hanke (1978) outlines a method for integrating engineering with economic considerations in the planning process of municipal water pricing. His guidelines for pricing ignore the reuse element, and does not provide a user with a "credit" against his marginal cost of diversion. Following Hanke's procedure would mean overcharging agricultural users relative to the water price justified on grounds of economic efficiency.

15. The precise effect depends on whether the marginal cost of diversion in the future grows at a faster or slower rate than the nominal interest rate. Assume that it takes 10 years before return flows can supply another water user, that the marginal cost of diverted water grows at 15 percent per year, and that the nominal interest rate is 10 percent. Then agricultural use, by only consuming 50 percent of its diverted water, will reduce required diversions in 10 years, and its marginal costs would be $303 ($75 cost growing at 15 percent for 10 years). Saving $303 in 10 years is equivalent to saving $117 today at a 10 percent interest rate. So the "credit" given for a return flow rate of 50 percent would be $58.49 instead of the $37.50 given in the text's example. If the marginal cost of diversion grows at a smaller rate than the nominal rate of interest, then the subsidy would be below the $37.50 figure.

16. Brown and McGuire (1967) conducted an empirical analysis of actual pumping

costs in Kern County, California. They found that variation over time in the rate of pumping and the depth of the water table explains variation in actual costs incurred.

17. The excessive pumping by uncoordinated water users, sometimes called the *over-draft* problem, is well discussed in the literature (*see* Brown and McGuire, 1967; Brown and Deacon, 1972; Maddock and Haines, 1975; and Wetzel, 1978).

18. The many issues in calibrating the pump tax for solving the overdraft problem are outlined in Maddock and Haines (1975) and Wetzel (1978).

19. Suppose that an acre-foot withdrawal from the aquifer increases pumping costs by $25. Then user A pumping an acre/foot of water represents 0.3 of an acre-foot withdrawal and should be levied a tax of $7.50 ($25 multiplied by 0.3). User B, who pumps an acre-foot of water, represents 0.7 of an acre-foot withdrawal from the aquifer and should be levied a tax of $17.50 ($25 multiplied by 0.7). So, user A's tax is 57 percent lower than user B's tax.

20. Consider the situation of user A in the preceding footnote. His use of groundwater returns 70 percent to the aquifer: so the optimal pump tax equals $7.50. Assume that 70 percent of A's use of surface water also percolates to the aquifer; then his use of an acre-foot of surface water returns 0.7 of an acre-foot to the aquifer, which has a value of $17.50 (0.7 multiplied by the $25 value of reducing withdrawals from the aquifer). That $17.50 represents an economic credit for A's use of surface water. The optimal subsidy paid for surface water use is 2.33 times the optimal pump tax. The optimal subsidy of surface water and taxation of groundwater need not yield a balanced budget for the water authority.

Any resulting deficits, for example, could be financed by using multiple-part pricing schedules discussed in conjunction with pricing surface deliveries when there are economies of scale. Even if the authority uses a smaller subsidy (a level financed by the proceeds of the pump tax), this use of funds would still improve efficiency in the allocation of water (*see* note 21).

21. Wetzel (1978, p. 28) shows that subsidizing surface water improves the efficient allocation of water resources beyond that obtained by using the proceeds of the pump tax in nonwater uses. This situation occurs even if the subsidy paid to surface deliveries is the one that could be afforded by the collections from the pump tax.

22. This judgment must be viewed as preliminary, for the evidence is yet to be collected on the Arizona experience. It is important to note, however, that Arizona is even more arid than Orange County and has a lower water table. These factors would lead one to expect a *higher* tax in Arizona than in OCWD.

Political factors are undoubtedly important in limiting (the new) tax on groundwater. Perhaps the opposition is partly related to the use of the revenues (land retirement instead of financing surface supplies for conjunctive use). As mentioned in the text, water users are likely to suffer economic losses from efficient groundwater taxation unless the proceeds of the tax are used to subsidize surface deliveries.

23. The resident's share of project costs is the fraction his or her property's assessed valuation is of the district's total assessed valuation. The resident's benefits from flood control, in turn, are reflected in the increased value of his or her property. Some may believe that higher property values capture only how flood control protects property and neglect how it protects people. This belief is inaccurate because the safety of people residing in an area also affects property values. Urban residents should recall how their property values declined as crime in-

truded into their neighborhood, even though the physical attributes of their property remained the same.

24. If the municipality can earn 10 percent per annum on a five-year investment, then only $6.2 million must be set aside today in anticipation of having $10.0 million available for paying construction costs in five years (*see* further text discussion for some of the complications created by anticipated inflation in construction costs).

CHAPTER 6

FISCAL AND LEGAL CONSTRAINTS ON BUILDING AND MARKETING COLLATERAL

WATER PROJECTS MUST BE FINANCED within fiscal and legal constraints. Many state and local governments have constitutional and statutory restrictions on the amount and nature of public debt and on their tax and expenditure policies. States' water laws establish the rules under which water can be captured and transferred among users. State security and banking regulations dictate who may underwrite bond issues, who can purchase bonds, and how municipalities may choose their underwriters. This chapter examines how these policies affect financing costs.

The first section argues that financing of water investment is not compromised seriously by constitutional and statutory restrictions on debt, spending, and tax policies. Debt limitations influence the distribution of fiscal responsibility between state and local governments, without limiting the overall ability to raise revenues. The second section identifies how water law affects a jurisdiction's capacity to finance water investment. Disputes over water rights may increase financing costs by increasing uncertainty. The financial collateral of water investment can be improved by explicitly defining water rights in terms of consumptive use rather than diversion. Allowing individual users to transfer water among themselves increases the financial collateral backing water investment and reduces financing costs.

The third section examines how state regulation of securities, banking, and underwriting affects financing costs. Allowing commercial banks to underwrite revenue bonds stimulates competition and lowers financing costs. Reforming state trust regulation to allow trust investments in lower-grade municipal bonds reduces financing costs for smaller, riskier projects without jeopardizing the goals of trust regulation. Changing state regulation of how municipalities award their underwriting contracts from the net-interest-cost method[1] to the true-interest-cost method[2] reduces interest costs paid by municipalities.

FISCAL LIMITATIONS AND THE FINANCE OF WATER PROJECTS

In the past decade, statutory and constitutional restrictions on state and local governments have proliferated. Some fear that these restrictions have inhibited the financing of worthwhile public investment and jeopardize western water investment (*see* Congressional Budget Office, 1983). However, the municipal bond market has been more sanguine about these limitations than government policymakers because the limitations have protected future financial claims of current investors against dilution by additional future borrowing by state and local governments (Lamb and Rappaport, 1981, p. 21 and pp. 103-104). These limitations have affected, however, the distribution of fiscal responsibility between state and local governments. This section reviews evidence on how much statutory and constitutional restrictions affect revenue raising, debt outstanding, and revenue transfers of state and local governments, and the effect of California's Proposition 13 on municipal bond yields.

Restrictions on Local Governments

Western states limit local government tax and expenditure powers more than states do nationwide (*see* table 6-1): Forty-one percent of western states limit the overall local property tax rate; 71 percent place specific restrictions on the property tax rate; four—Arizona, California, New Mexico, and Oregon—limit how fast local governments can raise assessed valuations; three—Arizona, California, and Kansas—limit general expenditures by local governments; and three—Nebraska, Nevada, and Washington—limit general revenues raised by local governments.

Local governments in states with limitations on either overall property tax rates, and/or property tax levies, and/or assessment increases raised less revenue than local governments that did not face such limits:[3] An overall property tax limitation reduced local revenue collections by 15.1 percent; limiting property tax levies reduced local collections by 11.8 percent; limiting increases in assessed valuation reduced local collections by 14.2 percent; and limitations on the specific property tax rate, or general limits on total revenues or expenditures, had no effects on local government collections.

Local governments in 11 western states collected less revenue as a result of property tax limitations (table 6-2).[4,5] They raised 24.37 percent less revenue than local governments in states without property tax limitations. In all 17 western states, tax limitations reduced

TABLE 6—1

State-Imposed Restrictions on Local Fiscal Policies

State	Overall property tax rate	Specific property tax rate	Property tax levy limit	General revenue limit	General expense limit	Limit on assessment increases
Arizona	*		*		*	*
California	*				*	*
Colorado		*	*			
Idaho	*	*	*			
Kansas		*	*		*	
Montana		*				
Nebraska		*		*		
Nevada	*			*		
New Mexico	*	*	*			*
North Dakota			*			
Oklahoma	*	*				
Oregon			*			*
South Dakota		*				
Texas		*				
Utah		*				
Washington	*	*	*	*		
Wyoming		*				
Fraction of western states with restrictions	0.41	0.71	0.47	0.18	0.18	0.24
Fraction of all states with restriction	0.28	0.58	0.38	0.10	0.12	0.12

Source: Advisory Commission On Intergovernmental Relations, *Significant Features of Fiscal Federalism, 1980–1981*, table 20, p. 30.

local collections by an average of 15.12 percent, compared to the national average of 10.40 percent.[6]

Property tax limitations shift the responsibility for raising revenues from local to state governments. Western state governments collected 15.64 percent more revenue when local governments were subjected to revenue restrictions, and transferred 23.34 percent more revenues to local governments.

TABLE 6–2
Effect of Significant Local Fiscal Restrictions*

State	Local collections (%)	State collections (%)	State transfers (%)
Arizona	−41.1	42.1	63.1
California	−29.3	27.1	34.4
Colorado	−11.8	15.0	28.7
Idaho	−26.9	27.5	38.5
Kansas	−11.8	15.0	28.7
Montana	0.0	0.0	0.0
Nebraska	0.0	0.0	0.0
Nevada	−15.1	12.4	9.8
New Mexico	−41.1	42.1	63.1
North Dakota	−11.8	15.0	28.7
Oklahoma	−15.1	12.5	9.8
Oregon	−26.0	29.7	53.3
South Dakota	0.0	0.0	0.0
Texas	0.0	0.0	0.0
Utah	0.0	0.0	0.0
Washington	−26.8	27.5	38.5
Wyoming	0.0	0.0	0.0
West average	−15.12	15.64	23.34
U.S. average	−10.40	10.95	16.60

*Significant restrictions are limits on overall property tax rates, property tax levies, and on assessment increases (columns one, three, and six of table 6-1).

Since tax limitations exempt principal and interest payments for general obligation debt, they do not jeopardize debt financing of water investment (Advisory Commission on Intergovernmental Finance, *State Reports*). However, the trend toward increased intergovernmental revenue transfers in response to these limitations may make local general obligation bonds less attractive because the interest and principal payments would depend increasingly on a riskier tax base dependent on intergovernmental grants (*see* chapters 3 and 7).

Revenue bonds—debt backed by user fees—avoid any increased financing costs from property tax limitations because these limitations do not affect the power of the municipality to levy user fees. As limitations proliferate, the economic advantages of user fees intensify, because fees conserve general-obligation-bonding capacity for other public investments not as easily financed by user fees.

State restrictions on local governments' debt issuance generally apply to the referendum requirements necessary for debt authorization (see table 6-3). Western states require majority approval of a debt issue, with the exception of Idaho, North Dakota, Oklahoma, and Washington. Although winning voter approval is important for issuing new debt, local governmental debt is no lower in states with more stringent plurality requirements than in comparable states requiring simply majority approval.[7]

Fiscal restrictions on local governments do reduce their total outstanding debt: limiting increases in assessed valuation reduces outstanding debt by 31.8 percent; limitations on overall property tax rates and specific limitations on tax rate reduce local debt by minor amounts.[8] This implied reduction in the capacity to finance debt only would apply to general obligation and not to revenue bonding.

TABLE 6–3

Referendum Requirements for Issuing Local General Obligation Debt

State	Approval margin
Arizona	Majority
California	Majority
Colorado	Majority
Idaho	2/3
Kansas	Majority
Montana	Majority[a]
Nebraska	Majority
Nevada	Majority
New Mexico	Majority
North Dakota	2/3
Oklahoma	3/5
Oregon	Majority
South Dakota	Majority
Texas	Majority
Utah	Majority
Washington	3/5[b]
Wyoming	Majority

Source: Vaughan (1983), table 16, p. 86.

[a] Issue fails if turnout is less than 40 percent.
[b] No referendum required if within limit.

125

TABLE 6—4

Limits on State Government Fiscal and Debt Policies

STATE	Constitutional restrictions on tax/spending	Statutory restrictions on tax/spending	General obligation debt prohibited
Arizona	*		*
California	*		
Colorado		*	*
Idaho		*	
Kansas			
Montana			
Nebraska		*	*
Nevada			
New Mexico			
North Dakota			
Oklahoma			
Oregon			
South Dakota			*
Texas	*		
Utah		*	
Washington		*	
Wyoming		*	
Fraction of western states with restriction	0.18	0.29	0.29
Fraction of all states with restriction	0.16	0.20	0.16

Source: Advisory Commission On Intergovernmental Relations, *Significant Features of Fiscal Federalism, 1980–1981*, table 20, p. 30, and *Census of Governments.*

Restrictions on State Governments

State governments also operate under limitations on their tax, spending, and debt policies (*see* table 6-4). Three western states—Arizona, California, and Texas—place constitutional restrictions on tax and spending policies. Five states—Colorado, Idaho, Nebraska, Washington, and Wyoming—have statutory restrictions. Five—Arizona, Colorado, Nebraska, South Dakota, and Wyoming—are constitutionally prohibited from issuing general obligation debt. As with local limitations, western state governments are more likely to operate under restrictions than state governments nationwide.

Limitations on state governments are less effective than those on local goverments.[9] Neither constitutional nor statutory restrictions on state tax or expenditure policy reduces state revenue collections. Constitutional restrictions reduce state revenue transfers to local governments by 34.7 percent.

States with *constitutional restrictions* have 41.8 percent less debt outstanding than states without any restrictions on tax and expenditure policies. States with *statutory restrictions* have 41.8 percent more debt outstanding than states with no restrictions and 83.6 percent more debt outstanding than states with constitutional restrictions.

Constitutional prohibitions on state issuance of general obligation debt affect the composition, but not the total amount, of debt outstanding.[10] States operating under constitutional prohibition have 60 percent less debt outstanding than states that can issue general obligation debt. Local governments in states with prohibitions against state general obligation debt issued 22.4 percent more debt than local governments in states without this constitutional restriction. Total state and local government debt outstanding is unaffected by this restriction.[11]

As with fiscal constraints on local governments, fiscal constraints on state governments need not affect the financing of western water investments. Tax and spending limitations reduce state governmental transfers to local governments, but these transfers are not necessary for building collateral for water projects. Prohibitions against state general obligation bonds simply substitute local for state debt financing. Placing financial responsibility where the project's benefits and costs are experienced leads to better project selection and management. As with local fiscal constraints, none of the state fiscal constraints affects revenue bond financing.

The Effect of Proposition 13 on the Yields of California Municipal Bonds

Before its passage in 1978, Proposition 13 was viewed as the death knell for local governmental debt financing in California. It was feared that a shift from general obligation to revenue bonding would drive up borrowing costs (*see* Quint, 1980). These fears proved unfounded.

The borrowing costs of water utilities did not increase as a result of Proposition 13. Interest costs on new water utility bonds and the yield differential between water utility general obligation and

127

revenue bonds were unchanged by the passage of Proposition 13 (*see* Benson, 1980).[12]

Yields on traditional general obligation and revenue bonds were unaffected because the raising of revenues for debt service was explicitly exempted from the tax limitation. However, the cost of some "innovative" forms of financing did increase: the yields on lease purchase bonds rose by 75 basis points; the yields on tax-anticipation bonds—where the municipality uses future increases in assessed valuation anticipated from public investment as financial backing for the loan—increased by 250 basis points. This was due to the fear that Proposition 13 would destroy the ability of local governments to increase assessed valuations as assumed when the debt was issued (Beebe, 1979).

The lesson from Proposition 13 is that fiscal limitations per se do not increase financing costs (Beebe, 1979; Forbes, Fischer, and Petersen, 1981). Special allowances for future debt service and capital outlays guarantee that fiscal constraints present no problem for debt management.

WATER LAW AND FINANCIAL CAPACITY

A secure and stable water supply is a prerequisite to low-cost financing (*see* Lamb and Rappaport, 1981; and Medanich, 1963). Water supplies that fall below their planned levels jeopardize the jurisdiction's ability to service debt because conveyance facilities cannot deliver enough water to generate the required revenue. Clear and secure water rights help ensure a stable water supply and also help water authorities adapt to changes in future conditions in water demand.

This section discusses three current issues of water law that can influence financing costs: uncertainty of future water rights; definition of water rights according to consumptive use instead of diversion; and voluntary water transfers. These issues have been controversial for many years and promise to remain unsettled for some time.

Uncertainty of Future Water Rights

Many water projects are long-term investments with useful lives of 40 years or more. If the security of future water rights is in jeopardy, conveyance facilities may not be able to meet their financial obligations. Water law provides a framework for assuring supply, but controversies surrounding the law render it, at best, an imperfect mechanism.

Consider the plight of the Imperial Valley Irrigation District. Built on 1930's reclamation projects, agricultural crops in the Imperial Valley became among the most productive in California. Because of the success of the industry and its presumed long-term stability, the district had received an excellent credit rating.[13] In recent years the district has been threatened by potential legal problems.[14] It faced reductions in its water rights to the Colorado River and, until recently resolved, its exemption from the old 160-acre limitation on farms serviced by federal reclamation projects was jeopardized. These actions raised questions about the future economic viability of agriculture in the Imperial Valley and the district's financial capacity. Today, partly reflecting these legal uncertainties, the Imperial district has a BBB credit rating that has increased its costs of debt financing.[15]

The Imperial district's experience is only one example of how legal uncertainty affects financing costs. Litigation over Native American water rights poses similar problems. More than 50 court cases are pending concerning quantification of tribal claims from a 1908 U.S. Supreme Court case giving Native American water users precedence over most others. Tribal claims are estimated to account for 900,000 of the 8.5 million acre-feet (or 10.5 percent) of beneficial consumptive use allocated to the Lower Basin of the Colorado River.[16] These unsettled claims cloud western water investment and, as Governor Babbitt of Arizona argues, represent a significant item on the western water agenda that must be resolved to expedite investment.[17]

In the interim, financing costs for water investment will be higher, reflecting the greater financial risk bondholders must bear from the uncertainty over the final disposition of these cases.[18] Aside from expediting settlement, policymakers have two choices: delay investment until the uncertainty is resolved, or keep project development on schedule and absorb the higher financing costs.

Definition and Transferability of Water Rights

Two other dimensions of water rights influence the financial capacity of water investment: transferability of rights and protections of third-party interests. Both factors protect repayment revenues against adverse future events. Defining water rights in terms of consumptive use, instead of diversion, can enhance the contribution of water law to building financial collateral for water investment.

Improving the transferability of water rights should facilitate a more economically efficient allocation of water (Hirschleifer, Milliman, and DeHaven, 1962; and Phelps, Graubard, and Moore, 1978).

129

Transfers of rights occur when the value of water to the prospective seller is less than the value of water to the prospective buyer. Reallocating water from lower- to higher-valued uses increases the overall net benefits of the water project.

The gains from reallocating water to higher-valued uses are substantial. Allowing water transfers among the users of the California State Water Project, for example, could increase the efficiency of water allocation by at least $60 million annually, or $850 million over the life of the project (Phelps, Graubard, and Moore, 1978). Water transfers would increase financial capacity by 50 percent of the original $1.7 billion in bonds issued to finance project construction.

Flexibility to transfer water helps mitigate the financial risk from uncertainty. At time of construction, demands for water are calculated on projections of future income and population growth. Even the best models cannot be totally accurate. In 20 years the municipality might find itself with either greater or lesser demand than anticipated. Water transfers allow the system to balance itself by empowering those jurisdictions with less demand than anticipated to sell water to those jurisdictions with more demand.

Water transfers also improve financial collateral by reducing the scale of water projects. By more efficiently allocating water among users, water transfers allow a smaller-scale project to satisfy the water demands of prospective users (DeHaven, 1963, p. 543).

A concern about water transfers is that the trade between two water users may neglect the alteration of return flow patterns. The transfer can change the point of diversion or type of water use for a third party that relies on the return flow. In *Denver v. Fulton*, for example, the court held that the city of Denver (in this case a third-party user of return flows) was using water reasonably and was thereby protected under state water law (Trelease, 1974, p. 231). This ruling provides strong legal support for protecting return flows as part of an overall water-use and development strategy.

Permitting voluntary transfers, while protecting third-party interests, lessens the financial risk of water investment. For example, a municipal water utility could be asssured that the water rights supplying its conveyance facilities would not be diminished because a city upstream decided to resell a portion of its water supply to a new energy development that did not provide any return flows. Avoiding such future risks enhances the utility's financial capacity by limiting the prospect that future events—such as the above water sale—would reduce the utility's ability to service its own debt.

Water law does not consistently protect return flows in a way that promotes economic efficiency (Meyer and Posner, 1971). If the return flow from one water user is the source of water supply for another, water law generally places responsibility on the first user to maintain current water use if altering that use would jeopardize the water supply of another individual.

This approach does not provide a clear mechanism for balancing the gains from better resource allocation against the gains from protecting third-party interests (Posner and Meyer, 1971; and Gisser and Johnson, 1981). Policies that inhibit water transfers sacrifice potential gains from more efficient water allocation that exceeds the value of water used by protected third parties.

Defining water rights in terms of consumptive use rather than diversion alleviates this problem of restriction (Gisser and Johnson, 1981). Suppose a small municipality diverts 1,000 gallons per day from a river, 50 percent of which returns and becomes a 500-gallon water supply for an agricultural district. The municipality wishes to transfer 200 gallons a day to a new energy development with no return flow. If the transfer occurred, the agricultural district downstream would suffer a loss of 100 gallons a day (200 gallons used by the city returns 100 gallons, while 200 gallons used by the energy development returns nothing). In this case, no portion of the municipality's diverted 1,000 gallons per day could be resold without jeopardizing the rights of downstream users.

Suppose, instead, that the municipality's rights were defined in terms of consumptive use. The municipality would "own" rights to consumptive use of 500 gallons per day. Now the water transaction involves the municipality transferring 100 gallons of consumptive use to the energy development—in place of the original 200 gallons of diversion, which represented a sacrifice of 100 gallons of consumptive use.

To protect the agricultural district's water rights, the municipality must reduce its water diversion by 100 gallons per day. The 100 gallons not diverted after the water transfer protects the agricultural district's 500-gallon daily water supply. The district would receive 400 gallons from return flows from the 800 gallons the municipality still diverts for satisfying its remaining rights to a consumptive use of 400 gallons per day. The district receives its remaining 100 gallons from the municipality's smaller diversions from the stream.

For the energy-development project, water transfers become more expensive. Defining water rights according to consumptive use requires the company to purchase 200 gallons of consumptive use (or 400 gallons of diverted water) from the municipality for it to acquire 200 gallons of water for its own consumptive use. But this higher cost means that water *will be transferred* from municipal use to energy development *only if its value in energy development exceeds the value of sacrificed water uses* in the municipality *and*

131

the cost of protecting the agricultural district's water rights.[19] Voluntary water transfers under this system give due consideration to third-party interests.

Implementing this approach entails measurement problems. Current technology allows, at best, "educated guesses" at the true structure of return flows operating in an area's hydrology. However, ignoring the distinction between consumptive use and diversion effectively estimates return flows to be zero. The key policy question is whether the errors from assigning zero are greater or less than the errors encountered by relying on imprecise estimates—which always have the option of being zero.

Most western states administer water rights de facto on the basis of consumptive use (*see* Gisser and Johnson, 1981, pp. 286-287 for a discussion of New Mexico). However, this policy is not defined in law and is therefore, lacking the superior certainty of statutory protection, subject to changes in the administrative process. Codifying water rights in law rather than to tradition assures the bond market that subsequent changes in administrative personnel would not change the legal basis of water rights. It also allows all owners of water rights to have a clearer idea of what they own. Owners would not have to wait for administrative rulings on their attempts to transfer water. This reform reduces the uncertainty of future water rights and improves the financial capacity of water investment.

Making explicit the primacy of consumptive use in water law also removes legal impediments to designing user fees to account for return flows. Under current law, a water authority can use, and therefore charge for, return flows only if they result from an inter-basin transfer or remain solely within the authority's jurisdiction. In contrast, return flows created by an intrabasin transfer remain outside of the control of the water authority and limit its ability to price water according to consumptive use rather than diversion. The "financial credits" from return flows cannot be collected.

REGULATION OF SECURITY MARKETS AND BANKING

Developing strong financial capacity for water investment is only half the challenge in the struggle to lower interest costs. The other half is marketing debt on the best possible terms for the borrower by finding the buyer with the greatest willingness to pay.

Vigorous competition among underwriters is the surest way for borrowers to obtain good services at the lowest price (Stigler, 1968, chapter 2). The general features of the underwriting market foster competition (*see* chapter 3). However, government policies limit the degree of competition and prevent borrowers from enjoying the lowest-cost financing possible. This section reviews three major areas—regulation of securities; regulation of banking; and selection methods of some municipalities for underwriters. The discussion shows where reforms are likely to reduce financing costs for state and local governments.

Regulation of Securities and Banking

Federal regulation has led, unfortunately, to higher financing costs for state and local governments. The Glass-Stegall Banking Reform Act of 1933 prohibits commercial banks from bidding for underwriting contracts on revenue bonds (Lamb and Rappaport, 1981, pp. 35-36). Commercial banks can purchase these bonds for their own accounts, but they cannot make a secondary market (Kessel, 1971).

For governments issuing revenue bonds, this restriction limits the number of potential underwriters. This restriction on competition has meant that the average revenue bond receives about one bid fewer than the average general obligation bond (*see* Kessel, 1971; Cagan, 1978). Reducing the number of bids implies greater underwriting costs and higher interest costs paid by states and municipalities (*see* chapter 3).

State policymakers can take some actions to mitigate the effects of federal regulation. First, the Bush Task Group recently studied whether to relax these restrictions on commercial banks. They concluded that further deregulation at this time should be delayed because of the many other changes occurring in financial markets. This study is in the wake of the Hunt Commission (1973) and the Fine Commission (1979-81), which also agreed "in principle" to loosen restrictions on underwriting (Butcher, 1983). State and local governments could become important forces in the impending debate.

Federal administrative remedies also have been available in the past. During 1968, Mr. Saxon, comptroller of the U.S. currency, declared some bond issues to be "general obligation" that would have been categorized previously as revenue bonds. These "Saxon bonds" received 50 percent more bids for their underwriting contracts (an average of 4.7 instead of 2.9) than when earlier issues were classified as revenue bonds, making the issues ineligible for bidding by commercial banks. Fifty percent of those Saxon bonds were won by underwriting syndicates led by commercial banks. Increasing the number of bidders from three to five reduces interest costs of municipalities by 20.5 basis points.[20] That is, a municipality would receive about $51.1 million in proceeds from issuing a 25-year, $50-million bond (or 2.2 percent more) if it kept its coupon payment schedule the same.[21]

Increasing competition also saves, in this scenario, 20.6 basis points on interest costs for states and municipalities which issue revenue bonds on a negotiated basis (Cagan, 1978, p. 45). The competitive pressures from auctioning off underwriting contracts would lower the fees demanded on negotiated bids.

Although these findings pertain to all state and municipal debt, the gains from entry by commercial banks may be even greater for water bonds. The effects of increased bidding on interest costs are greater for utility bonds than for other types of municipal debt (Benson, 1980). Also banks' traditional clientele find that the financial characteristics of water bonds meet their investment demands (Cagan, 1978, p. 44). Forbidding commercial banks from making a secondary market for municipal bonds precludes a low-cost method of marketing water bonds to potential buyers.

North Carolina's Local Government Commission illustrates the potential for lowering financing costs by stimulating competition for underwriting contracts. Among its duties, more fully described in chapter 7, the commission coordinates the arrival of North Carolina's municipal bonds to the marketplace. By aggressively advertising, the commission has increased the number of bids received and reduced interest costs by 35 to 100 basis points (Twentieth Century Fund 1974, p. 32). A 100-basis-point savings translates into a municipality receiving $55.3 million for a 25-year, $50-million bond offering, if the issuing government does not alter its coupon repayment schedule.[22]

State trust regulation also has impeded the functioning of the municipal bond market. The "legal lists" of bonds qualifying for inclusion in trust accounts discriminates in favor of higher-quality bonds (Twentieth Century Fund 1974, p. 68). The top-four categories of bond rating can be included on trust balance sheets at par value without any investigation on the part of regulators. Lower-quality bonds, if they can be included at all, must be investigated in depth by regulators (Twentieth Century Fund 1974, pp. 65-66). The different regulatory treatment severely increases the cost to banks of including lower-quality bonds in trust portfolios. As the former head of the Federal Deposit Insurance Corporation observed (Twentieth Century Fund 1974, p.66):

> Now BAA is the dividing line and that is where we increase our activity in looking at the credit itself. Those rated in the A's take less verification to qualify them for investment by the banks.

Protecting trust accounts against speculative risk can be achieved without barring lower-quality bonds. Changing regulatory rules from requiring investigation into each security in a portfolio to standards about the *entire* bond portfolio concentrates regulation on the key point of trust accounts—overall performance. A portfolio's performance is not simply the sum of its parts (Fama, 1976). By concentrating on the parts, regulatory standards completely neglect the advantages of risk diversification.

Placing standards on overall performance of bond portfolios relieves banks from potential investigation on each bond purchase. Commercial banks would decide how purchasing a low-quality bond would contribute to meeting regulatory goals of portfolio performance. Bankers would have to defend their overall performance to regulators, not the details behind their business decisions.[23]

Indirect evidence indicates how trust regulation may distort the relative demands for high- versus low-rated bonds (*see* figure 6-1). For general obligation bonds—where commercial banks are eligible to participate in underwriting and to create secondary markets—AAA , AA , and A-rated bonds receive, respectively, 4.9, 4.3, and 1.8 more bids on underwriting contracts than BAA-rated bonds. For revenue bonds—where commercial banks are restricted—AAA-, AA-, and A-rated bonds receive, respectively, only 1.9, 1.9, and 1.1 more bids on underwriting contracts than BAA-rated bonds. Higher-quality bonds can be marketed through a more competitive underwriting environment than can lower-quality bonds, and, therefore, enjoy lower underwriting costs. If these regulations were changed, all levels of bond quality could benefit from the advantages of expanded competition.

State Regulations on Municipalities' Awarding of Underwriting Contracts

Many municipalities must award their underwriting contracts to the bidder offering the lowest "net interest cost" (the undiscounted sum of interest payments over the bond's life less any premium paid or plus any discount received on bonds relative to their par value). This method of awarding contracts does not necessarily select the low-cost bidder (West, 1968).

The flaw in the net-interest-cost measure is that it neglects the time value of money. A dollar paid 10 years in the future is not the same economic liability as a dollar paid today—the reason that interest rates are positive. If the 10-year interest rate is 7 percent, then the municipality can invest 51 cents today and, by reinvesting the accumulated interest, have one dollar in 10 years to repay its debt. In

FIGURE 6—1

How Bond Ratings Affect Number of Underwriting Bids.

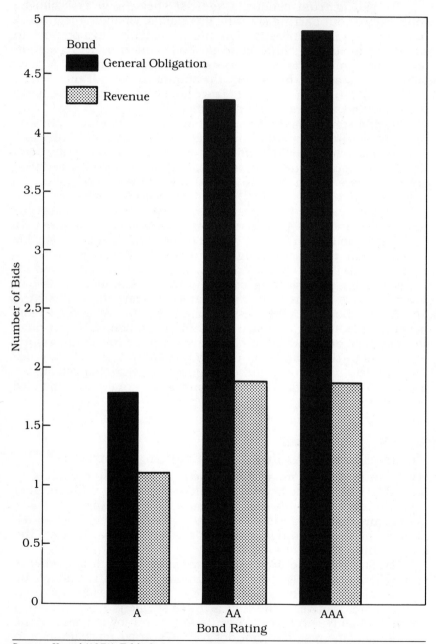

Source: Kessel (1971), Table 2.

the same manner, a dollar coupon repayment today is worth more to private investors than a dollar coupon repayment 10 years in the future.

When designing coupon repayment schedules, underwriters have an incentive to tilt interest payments toward earlier repayment. States and municipalities have attempted to limit this bias by restricting minimum price bids and the magnitude of coupon rates. Without restriction, competition forces underwriters to design coupon schedules that are clearly not in the borrowers' self-interest.[24]

For example, in 1972 the state of Minnesota sold $25 million of 20-year serial bonds without any restrictions on price bids or coupon repayments. Seven bids were received. The winning bid according to the net-interest-cost method had 50-percent coupon payments for the first four maturities and 0.1-percent coupon payments on the last seven maturities! The lowest true-interest-cost bid—taking into account the time value of money—ranked fourth even though it offered a 60-basis-point savings in financing costs (Hopewell and Kaufman, 1974).[25]

Placing coupon payments relatively early increases the municipality's revenue obligations before the project reaches its full revenue-raising potential.[26] The solution is to allow municipalities to award underwriting contracts on the basis of "true interest cost." This allows the time value of money to be included when computing which underwriter is offering the lowest-cost financing (Lamb and Rappaport, 1981, p. 25). This reform removes a statutory impediment to low-cost financing of water investment.

CONCLUSIONS

The institutions through which western water projects are financed have evolved to meet many different economic and social needs. They have not—and, for the most part, cannot—be redesigned solely with the purpose of reducing the financing costs of water projects. But some changes are possible without sacrificing other policy objectives. Policymakers can reform trust regulations, the method used by municipalities in selecting winning bids on underwriting contracts, and can define water rights according to consumptive use instead of diversion, without sacrificing the original purposes of these rules. Deregulating entry into underwriting collides with the goal of keeping commercial banks out of the business. Spending, tax, and debt limitations are not serious impediments on building and marketing water-investment collateral.

137

TEXT NOTES

1. The net-interest-cost method awards the underwriting contract on the basis of which vendor designs a repayment scheme with the smallest total interest cost over the life of the bond. This method neglects the time value of money—a dollar received 10 years from today is less valuable than a dollar received today. Competition among underwriters forces them to bid according to this rule, even though following the rule is not in the best interest of the borrower (see Kessel, 1971; and discussion below).

2. True interest cost awards the underwriting contract on the basis of which vendor designs a repayment schedule that minimizes the interest costs (taking into account the time value of money).

3. The discussion in the text relies on the findings from a regression study of the determinants of per-capita local and state governmental revenue collections and per-capita transfer of state revenues to local governments. The dependent variables are measured in natural logarithms. The estimated coefficients and t-statistics (reported in parentheses) are:

Explanatory Variable	Local Revenue Collections	State Revenue Collections	State Revenue Transfers
Population*	−0.03	−0.02	0.28
	(−1.00)	(−0.46)	(−3.85)
Income per capita*	1.26	1.09	0.39
	(5.09)	(4.02)	(0.97)
Revenue transfers			
From feds*	0.22	1.05	0.82
	(1.67)	(5.96)	(3.11)
From state*	0.30	——	——
	(4.18)	——	——
Western states	0.18	−0.09	0.24
	(2.63)	(−1.00)	(1.81)
Legal restrictions on local government			
Overall property rate	−0.15	0.12	0.10
	(−2.24)	(1.44)	(0.76)
Property tax levy	−0.12	0.15	0.29
	(−1.48)	(1.90)	(2.42)
Assessment increases	−0.14	0.15	0.25
	(−1.17)	(1.27)	(1.42)
Plurality required on general obligation debt	−0.20	——	——
	(−1.17)	——	——
Legal restrictions on state government			
Constitutional	——	0.04	−0.35
	(0.39)	(−2.34)	

Explanatory Variable	Local Revenue Collections	State Revenue Collections	State Revenue Transfers
Statutory	—— (–0.54)	–0.05 (–1.40)	–0.13
Constant	–7.43 (–3.66)	–9.16 (–3.81)	–0.51 (–1.40)
Summary statistics R^2	0.723	0.745	0.519
Standard deviation: Dependent variable	0.334	0.444	0.486
Residual	0.195	0.248	0.373

Explanatory variables with "*" indicate that they are measured in natural logarithms. All other variables are dummy variables equal to one if the stated condition prevailed, otherwise set equal to zero.

Adding variables measuring the presence of the other restrictions listed in table 6-1 (limitations on specific property tax rates, general revenues, and general expenditures) had small estimated effects—generally showing effects less than 2 percent on local collections—that were statistically insignificant—probabilities exceeded 70 percent that those estimated effects were consistent with the true effects being zero.

4. The entries in the table are estimated by adding together the effect of each state's restriction. For example, a state with both limits on the overall property tax rate and increases on assessed valuation has an estimated decline in local government of 29.3 percent (the 15.1 percent loss from the overall property tax rate limitation and the 14.2 percent loss from the limitation on increases in assessed valuation).

5. The other six states—Montana, Nebraska, South Dakota, Texas, Utah, and Wyoming—imposed restrictions that were estimated to have had no effect on local governmental revenue collections. If the reader prefers, he or she may place an * representing no significant restriction instead of the zeros for these states.

6. The greater likelihood of restrictions in the West means that local governments in western states exert even greater abnormal revenue collection efforts than indicated by the 9 percent in chapter 4. After controlling for the presence of tax limitations as well as population, income, and intergovernmental revenue transfers, western local governments collect 18 percent more than nonwestern states of comparable economic and legal environment. (See the statistical results reported in note 3).

7. The statement in the text and subsequent discussion of the determinants of local governmental debt are based on regression analysis of per capita local government debt (measured in natural logarithms). The estimated coefficients and t-statistics (reported in parentheses) are: population, 0.02 (0.23); income, 0.24 (0.51); West, 0.40 (2.91); federal transfer, 0.43 (1.65); state transfer, 0.48 (3.28); limit one, –0.05 (–0.37); limit two, –0.09 (–0.76); limit three, –0.32 (–1.65); limit four, 0.22 (1.41); Alaska, 1.30 (2.38); constant, –0.23 (–0.06). R^2 = 0.633. Standard deviation: dependent variable = 0.551, residual = .374.

The following variables are measured in terms of natural logarithms: population, income, federal and state revenue transfers to local governments. West, Alaska, and the following legal-restriction variables are measured as either one (indicating presence) or zero (indicating absence) of stated condition. Limit one = restriction on local overall property tax rate. Limit two = restriction on property tax levy. Limit three = restriction on increases in assessments. Limit four = prohibition against state issuance of general obligation debt.

Adding a variable showing the required plurality has an estimated coefficient that indicates that states with a three-fifths-required plurality for bond elections had 0.7 percent less debt per capita than states requiring only simple majority approval.

8. Local governments had 5.0 and 9.2 percent less debt outstanding, respectively, if they were subject to an overall limitation on property tax rates and limits on the property tax levy. (*See* statistical results reported in note 7).

9. All of the estimates discussed in the text refer to differences after controlling for state differences in intergovernmental revenue transfers, state population, per-capita income, western-versus-nonwestern states, and the presence of fiscal constraints on local governments. (*See* statistical results reported in note 3).

10. The text's discussion is based on the findings from a regression analysis of the determinants of per-capita state governmental debt (measured in natural logarithms). The estimated coefficients and t-statistics (reported in parentheses) are: population, -0.13 (-1.14); income, 2.06 (3.70); West, -0.47 (-2.71); federal money to state, 1.47 (3.66); federal money to local, 0.55 (1.71); state money to local, -0.39 (-2.04); limit one, -0.42 (2.03); limit two, 0.42 (2.29); limit three, -0.60 (-3.02); Alaska, -0.36 (-0.53); constant, -19.90 (-3.78). R^2 = 0.768. Standard deviation: dependent variable = 0.859, residual = 0.464.

Population, income, and intergovernmental revenue transfers are measured in natural logarithms. West, Alaska, and following limitation variables are measured as dummy variables (equal to one indicating presence of stated condition, and zero indicating its absence): limit one = constitutional limit on state government revenues; limit two = statutory limit on state government revenues; limit three = prohibition against state government issuance of general obligation debt.

11. As local governmental debt outstanding exceeds that of state governments, 60 percent less of the smaller state governmental debt approximately equals 22.4 percent more of the larger local governmental debt.

12. The estimated effects reported by Benson hold constant the bond's rating, maturity, number of bidders for the underwriting contract, and the general level of interest rates. He investigated but found no significant changes in pre- and post-Proposition 13 bond issues in these dimensions.

13. See any issue of Moody's *Government Manual* during the 1940s.

14. The purpose of the example is not to judge the legitimacy of Imperial Valley Irrigation District's claims in these disputes. The example simply shows how legal uncertainty becomes impounded into financing costs.

15. Standard & Poor's Corporation, *Bond Guide*, 1982, p. 168.

16. For an overview of the problem see *American Survey: Water In The West*, Economist, 14 May, 1983, pp. 41-49.

17. *See* Governor Bruce Babbitt, "The Future of The Colorado River." Address before the Colorado River Working Symposium 23 May, 1983, Santa Fe, New Mexico.

18. Analogous to the effects of California's Proposition 13, the consequences of legal uncertainty on financing costs may prove substantial. Recall that uncertainty about *future* assessment policies increases the yields on tax-allocation bonds. The effect of uncertain water rights is similar qualitatively. Water investment may become built upon water diversions the rights to which may be sacrificed in future litigation.

19. If the cost of protecting the agricultural district's water rights were less than the value of additional water to the energy company, then the company would purchase rights from the agricultural district as well. For example, it could purchase from the district the rights to the 100 gallons the municipality did not divert from the stream after its transaction with the energy company.

20. Cagan (1978) estimates that increases in the number of bids reduce net interest costs by 32 basis points divided by the original number of bids (so, the effect of increasing bids is smaller the greater the original number of bids). The 20.5-basis-point savings is estimated by computing the savings from increasing the average number of bids received from 2.89 to 4.74.

21. Table 3-19 in chapter 3 provides estimates of the economic value of basis points. The estimates in the text are computed by scaling up the $10.67 per $1,000 par value of bonds from saving 10 basis points on a 25-year bond when market interest rates is 8 percent.

22. Same computation procedure as described in note 21, except that the 100-basis-point savings was estimated by scaling up the estimated savings of 70 basis points.

23. Federal regulation of automobile emission standards is an excellent example of focusing on overall performance rather than how a business meets the standards. Each automaker must match a specified mileage goal for the entire fleet of automobiles sold. Regulation does not specify the required mileage of each model.

24. Two competitive reasons force underwriters to tilt the coupon schedule. First, if they did not, then any underwriter could offer the same net interest cost but shift forward in time the coupon repayments and make more money on the resale of the bonds. Second, as underwriters understand this, they will tilt coupon repayments and be willing to bid premiums over those underwriters who did not fall prey to the temptation. These tempted underwriters could offer the same undiscounted interest payments and bid a higher premium and thereby offer a lower net interest cost and be awarded the underwriting contract. As observed by Kessel (1971), underwriters who do not respond to the incentives prevailing under the net-interest-cost method would be committing "economic suicide."

25. Hopewell and Kaufman (1974) estimate that the selection of the wrong bids cost state and municipalities $20 million in higher interest payments on the $17 billion worth of bonds issued in 1972. The authors indicate this estimate may understate the gains from abandoning the net-interest-cost method for reasons related to the abnormal term structure of interest rates prevailing in 1972.

26. Hopewell and Kaufman (1974) neglect these added costs by assuming that states and municipalities can raise any additional money during the early years without suffering *any* allocative inefficiencies from inappropriate structuring of debt service relative to the ability to repay. Sacrificing the economic gains from prudent debt finance result in considerable economic cost to the borrower (see chapter 4).

CHAPTER 7

STATE AND LOCAL GOVERNMENTS' FISCAL RELATIONS

PARTNERSHIPS BETWEEN STATE AND LOCAL governments to finance water projects are unusual in the West. The most important exception is the California State Water Project. Although some states—such as Oklahoma, Texas, and Utah—aid poor communities in financing the matching portions of federal grants, localities generally finance their own projects through the municipal bond market or the U.S. Bureau of Reclamation. With reduced federal funding for water investment, more effective cooperation between state and local governments is required to finance water projects. There are five options to consider: 1) *technical assistance programs*—as in Texas, North Carolina, and Idaho—to improve the information provided to the municipal bond market by local governments; 2) *state assistance for local governments' purchase of bond insurance*, especially for small, high-risk communities; 3) *state-operated municipal bond banks*, through which state governments pool and resell small municipal issues; 4) *state grants*—either traditional grants-in-aid or an infrastructure bank through which federal and state funds are used to set up revolving low-interest loan funds; and 5) *state-constructed and operated water projects*.

The first two options reduce overall financing costs. Municipal bond banks, state infrastructure banks, and grants-in-aid programs shift financing costs to states from local governments and probably increase overall financing costs. State-owned and operated water projects can be an effective mechanism for financing water development. Policies and programs adopted by California, Idaho, Texas, Utah, and a number of eastern states illustrate the effects of these options.

TECHNICAL ASSISTANCE

The municipal bond market is quite different from other financial markets (*see* chapter 3). The number of bonds and the infrequency of transactions pose a gargantuan information problem for private investors. Although ratings help, investors may still question a municipality's future financial strength. Investors may wonder what is hidden behind poorly organized and nonaudited financial statements (Lamb and Rappaport, 1981).[1] The financial community seeks sound information on municipalities. Municipal bond statements carry poorer information than corporate bond statements (Zimmerman, 1977), and municipal bonds are riskier than equally rated corporate bonds (Fama, 1977). Therefore, municipal bonds pay greater yields than would be predicted by their tax-exempt status.[2]

Surveys of commercial banks and underwriters document the dissatisfaction with the quality of the information provided by municipal borrowers (Boyett and Giroux, 1978). Table 7-1 ranks, in order, the 21 most important factors for assessing the financial risk of municipal bonds. Only 2 of the top 10 appear regularly on financial statements. Information on overlapping debt is often omitted (*see also* Coopers and Lybrand, 1978). The low rank (19th) given to bond ratings illustrates how the investment community attempts to "pierce the veil" of bond ratings. Organizations interviewed for both studies stated that standardization of reporting practices and independent auditing could raise information standards for municipal issues to those of corporate bonds. This would lower financing costs.

The Municipal Advisory Council of Texas, for example, was formed in the 1950s by local bond dealers and banks to provide investors and rating agencies with better information about Texas municipalities. The organization provides standardized information and financial reports on hundreds of Texas municipalities. The council is credited with increasing the number of rated municipalities from 200 in 1955 to over 600 by the 1970s, with substantial savings in interest costs (Twentieth Century Fund, p. 135).

Experience in North Carolina illustrates how state governments also can improve the dissemination of information to the municipal bond market. The state established the Local Government Commission in 1931 in response to the default of several municipalities. The commission consists of the state treasurer, auditor, the secretary of state, the secretary of revenue, and five appointees. It offers staff assistance to municipalities in selecting rating agencies and issuing financial reports, conducts an *independent* audit of the information, and maintains and publishes data on the financial condition of local governments. The commission also assists localities by publishing and distributing their bond prospectuses. These activities have lowered the financing costs of local government in North Carolina (*see* chapter 6). This model is a concrete way of centralizing and disseminating information about municipal bonds.

Providing better information to investors is only one aspect of technical assistance. States can also assist localities in developing

144

TABLE 7–1

Important Information Demanded by the Bond Market

Rank	Item
1	. . . . Total debt outstanding
2	. . . . Debt/actual property value
3	. . . . Overlapping debt outstanding
4	. . . . Debt per capita
5	. . . . Tax collection history
6	. . . . Changes in financial position
7	. . . . Trends in population and resident income
8	. . . . Actual value of property in jurisdiction
9	. . . . Operating revenue
10	. . . . Assessed valuation
11	. . . . Tax rate limitations
12	. . . . Operating expenditures
13	. . . . Debt/assessed valuation
14	. . . . Accounting policies used
15	. . . . Principle taxpayers
16	. . . . Portion of tax rate applicable to debt
17	. . . . Tax rate history
18	. . . . Sinking funds applicable to debt
19	. . . . Bond rating
20	. . . . Current assets and liabilities
21	. . . . Fixed assets

Source: Boyett and Giroux (1978).

the collateral to support a bond issue. Many local governmental entities are small and have little experience in water finance. The state's technical assistance staff can supply information needed to design a water project, identify income flows, and design a financing package. North Carolina and New Jersey both assist localities extensively.

PRIVATE MARKET BOND INSURANCE

State governments also can inform local governments about cost-cutting innovations in the bond market. Private bond insurance appears to be a promising financing option for some municipalities and is growing in popularity. In 1982, 10 percent of total new municipal financing was insured through private bond insurance (Williams, 1982). Bond insurance has rapidly penetrated the market since its introduction following New York City's financial problems in 1974 (Geczi, 1976).

Private bond insurance protects investors' scheduled coupon and principal payments in the event of default. Currently, three organizations write bond insurance. MGIC Investment Corporation of Milwaukee, Wisconsin, has two subsidiaries offering services: American Municipal Bond Assurance Corporation (AMBAC), the leading private guarantor of mortgages for "higher quality" bonds, and MGIC Indemity Corporation, which guarantees the lower-rated bonds. The second insurer is the Municipal Bond Insurance Corporation (MBIA)—a joint venture of Aetna Casualty & Surety, Aetna Insurance (of Connecticut General), St. Paul Fire & Marine, and United States Fire. A new entrant is the Financial Guaranty Insurance Company (FGIC), backed by Merrill Lynch, Lehman Brothers, Kemper Group, General Electric Credit Corporation, and General Reinsurance Corporation.

Table 7-2 reports the type of issues eligible and the cost for various bond policies. All insure general obligation bonds. MBIA limits revenue bond eligibility to investments in municipal utilities. This does not preclude insuring western water projects. Once insurance is purchased, Standard & Poors automatically increases its rating to AAA. Moody's ignores bond insurance in its ratings because the service does not want to implicitly rate the insurance carrier.

Studies indicate that purchasing private bond insurance reduces the municipality's financing costs by as much as three times the premium payments (Carr, 1972; and The Twentieth Century Fund 1974, p. 137). There may be further savings because of the additional underwriting bids usually received by higher-quality bonds (Joehnk and Kidwell, 1978).[3] The benefits from private bond insurance can range from 40 to 95 basis points on financing costs at an expense of premium payments equivalent to 20 or 30 basis points (Roche, 1976). The "investment" in private bond insurance is particularly attractive for the smaller, lower-rated municipalities.

It is easy to determine whether private bond insurance is a profitable investment. A bond issuer can request that underwriters submit bids on an issue with and without bond insurance. If the rate differential exceeds the cost of the premiums, insurance is worthwhile. This procedure need not disrupt the traditional marketing process nor the issuer's relations with its bond counsel, financial advisors, and investment bankers (Joehnk and Kidwell, 1978).

State governments can help local governments by devising standard procedures for underwriters to participate in this new bidding process. State governments also can promote additional entry by other carriers into the bond insurance market. Expansion in the demand for insurance could exceed the ability of the existing insur-

TABLE 7–2

Selected Features of Private Municipal Bond Insurance

Program	Type of issue	Size of issue ($ million)	Quality	Cost
AMBAC	General obligation & revenue for existing facility	0.6 to 22.0 (total principal & interest)	S&P BBB or more	0.5 to 1.5% of original principal & interest
Indemnity corporation	General obligation & revenue	0.6 to 18.0 (total principal & interest)	any	0.5 to 3.5% of original principal
MBIA	General obligation & utility revenue	0.6 to 20.0 (principal)	S&P BBB or more	1 to 2% of principal only

Source: Joehnk and Kidwell (1978), exhibit 1, p. 31.

ance carriers to write policies without large increases in premium rates.[4]

MUNICIPAL BOND BANKS

In 1972, Maine formed its municipal bond bank to reduce financing costs by pooling the bonds issued by municipalities into one portfolio. It was believed that the portfolio of municipal bonds would enjoy greater marketability as a group than as separate issues because the pooling diversifies the financial risk borne by private investors. Table 7-3 reports the broad outlines of the five active municipal bond banks—in Alaska, New Hampshire, Maine, North Dakota, and Vermont. New York State also has a municipal bond bank program, but it has not been active due to lack of interest on the part of municipalities.[5]

A bond bank authority divides the sale proceeds from the bank's bonds and the interest rate obligations in proportion to the *face value* of each municipality's bonds. A municipality with bonds, the face value of which is $10 million of a $50-million bond bank issue, would receive 20 percent of the net proceeds from the sale and pay 20 percent of the interest payments. The proceeds available for distribution among the municipalities are the gross proceeds from the sale of the bond bank less the costs of administering and setting up of a reserve fund (generally equal to 15 percent of the maximum principal and interest payments due in any future year).

The share of municipal new issues channeled through bond banks varies from 17.5 percent in Alaska to 75.6 percent in New Hampshire (table 7-4). Outstanding debt of bond banks is small relative to the total debt outstanding of state governments (ranging from 5.1 percent of Alaska to 16.3 percent of New Hampshire state government's total long-term debt).

The backstop provided by state funds is a key feature of bond banks. By pledging—explicitly or implicitly—the taxing power of the state, bond banks transfer financing risk from local to state governments. This reduces financing costs of local governments. But it increases the financing costs of state governments, because they do

TABLE 7–3

Selected Features of Municipal Bond Banks

	Municipality				
Category	Vermont	New Hampshire	Maine	North Dakota	Alaska
Order of Backing	Reserve, state money, municipal money	Reserve, state money, municipal money	Reserve, supplement, state money	Special reserve, pledge of U.S. bonds held by bank	Reserve, state money, municipal money, tax
Bonds eligible	General opportunity	General opportunity, utility revenue, education revenue	General opportunity & revenue (property tax)	General opportunity	General opportunity, revenue, energy
Allocation of proceeds	Loans, reserve, operating account refund, notes of bank	Loans, reserve, operating account	Same as Vermont	Reserve, loans	Loans, reserve, refund, operating account
Size limit	$5 million minimum	$5 million minimum	None, usually $10 million	None	$150 million total bank

TABLE 7—4

New Issues and Debt ($ Millions) of Municipal Bond Banks

Issues by:	State				
	Alaska	Maine	New Hampshire	North Dakota	Vermont
Municipal bond bank					
1982 issues	48.5	26.8	28.3	None	9.6
Total debt	150.0	217.7	65.0	35.9	63.1
As of:	4/1/83	6/30/82	12/31/82	4/1/83	7/31/82
Municipalities 1982 issues					
(long term)	277.7	57.0	37.4	67.6	28.2
Total debt	2,825.0	611.1	444.1	605.6	180.3
As of:	12/31/82	6/30/82	12/31/82	4/1/83	7/31/82
State 1982 issues					
(long term)	934.0	187.3	173.3	0.8	69.3
Total debt	2,399.5	833.5	1,038.8	212.0	673.4

Source: Moody's Annual Reports of State Bond Banks.

not have unlimited financial capacity to assume the financial risks of local governmental investment.

Private investors apparently view bond banks as ultimately the responsibility of state governments, notwithstanding any language to the contrary in the enabling legislation. State funds are involved, either directly or indirectly, via an implicit form of state "equity participation" (Forbes, Fischer, and Peterson, 1981, p. 163). State legislators are authorized if not required to bail out a municipality that cannot meet its bond bank obligations. In 1972, municipalities in Vermont were experiencing finance problems that threatened their ability to meet their required debt-service payments to the Vermont Bond Bank. Both the state of Vermont and its bond bank suffered reduced ratings, partly due to the anticipation that the state would absorb the financial responsibility for its municipalities (Twentieth Century Fund 1974, p.136). Vermont's *statutory option* to bail out was viewed to be the same as a *political responsibility* to bail out.

Bond banks also redistribute financing costs among municipalities (*see* figure 7-1). Normally, bond banks receive a rating one

FIGURE 7–1

How Maine Bond Bank Affected Interest Costs of Cities.

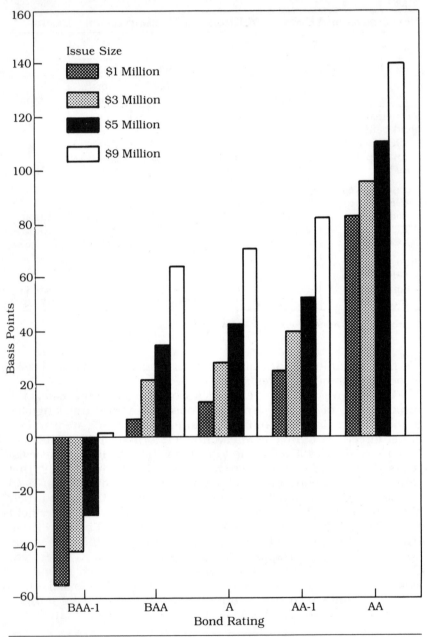

Source: Computed from Cole and Millar (1982), Exhibit 2, p. 74.

category below the state government's general obligation bonds (a practice consistent with the view that bond banks are ultimately the financial responsiblity of state government). All municipal bonds are treated the same, regardless of their individual financial strength. Lower-quality bonds enjoy lower financing costs and higher-quality bonds suffer higher financing costs because the bank "averages" high- with low-quality bonds. It is estimated that this commingling of municipal bonds raised the interest costs of AA-rated, larger issues by 140 basis points (almost 1.5 percentage points). A medium-sized, $5-million, A-rated bond suffers increased financing costs of 43 basis points. Only BAA-1-rated bonds enjoy reduced financing costs, ranging from savings of 56 basis points for a $1-million issue and disappearing for bond issues larger than $9 million.

This cross-subsidization occurs because bond banks are not a true means of risk diversification. Diversification occurs when a portfolio is constructed without the relative values of the constituent bonds being destroyed. Private investors can diversify risk by constructing their own *portfolio* of bonds. Normally, only a few securities—perhaps as few as 10 to 15—must be purchased to attain almost the full benefits of complete diversification (Fama, 1976).

Bond banks fail to diversify risk in an efficient manner because they require a municipality whose cost of capital is 10 percent to receive the same interest rate as another whose cost of capital is 12 percent. This "equal treatment of financial unequals" confuses cross-subsidization with the objective of risk diversification. By not allowing the market to separately price bonds with differing intrinsic values, bond banks are an economically higher-cost means of risk diversification.

This explains why bond banks do not reduce municipal borrowing costs (Kidwell and Rogowski, 1983). A study of borrowing costs for New England municipalities estimates that a municipality selling its bonds through underwriters selected by competitive bidding has slightly lower costs than one participating in a municipal bond bank (averaging the gains and losses in figure 7-1). Bond banks are only superior, on average, to municipalities selling their bonds on a negiotated basis to underwriters. There are more direct ways of introducing competition into underwriting than state governmental operation of a bond bank (*see* chapter 6).

The Mirror Bond Program in Idaho exploits real gains from coordinating local bond issues without engaging in the cross-subsidization found in bond banks. Small tax-exempt bond issues for irrigation projects are sold through standardized contracts placed privately with local lenders at very low cost. The Water Resource Board, which developed the contract, decides whether a project complies with the state's water plan, and when borrower and lender have agreed to financial terms, gets a bond attorney to state that the project qualifies as a tax-exempt issue. The loan agreement serves as the bond, thus avoiding printing and other issuing costs. The issuing costs under this program average about 1 percent of face value of the loan—much less than the 10 percent that many small bond issues cost.

GRANT PROGRAMS, REVOLVING FUNDS, AND INFRASTRUCTURE BANKS

State expenditures on local water investment are the most direct ways of substituting state for local governmental financial capacity. Although state transfers—in either direct grants or low-cost loans—benefit recipients, such transfers will increase, not reduce, the overall financing costs of water investment.

Intergovernmental Grants

State grants-in-aid programs *increase* total state and local governmental spending on water investment. By receiving a grant, local governments have more resources at their disposal and increase local governmental spending (Hyman, 1981). If the grant has a matching requirement, the locality covers a fraction of the costs of any project it builds and the grant covers the rest. Construction subsidies lead to overbuilding when incremental benefits are less than incremental costs to state and local governments. For localities, the more they spend the larger the transfer they receive from the state. This overinvestment in water projects reduces financial collateral behind project investment.

In practice, a dollar increase in federal transfers to local governments increases local spending by $3—the federal dollar stimulates local governments to raise an additional $2. A dollar increase in state transfers to local governments increases local spending by $1.44—the state dollar stimulates local governments to raise an additional 44 cents (*see* chapter 6). The difference between the effects of federal and state transfers is understandable. Federal transfers have larger matching requirements than state transfers. The latter are allocated through rigid formulae based on population (Advisory Commission on Intergovernmental Relations, 1982).

Grants-in-aid programs also increase perceived financial risk and thereby increase interest rates on water bonds (*see* chapter 3).

Intergovernmental grants transmit one government's financial problems to the other and introduce political considerations into future financing partly out of the control of local authorities. Intergovernmental grants must be justified as purposeful schemes to redistribute income among communities, not as low-cost financing mechanisms.

Revolving Funds and Infrastructure Banks

While still mostly proposals, state infrastructure banks are a new idea for allocating intergovernmental revenue transfers for public capital investment. They combine three functions: 1) a bond bank; 2) revolving loan funds for localities; and 3) technical assistance to localities for project design, financing, and debt marketing.

The first infrastructure bank emerged from New Jersey's Department of Environmental Protection, which faced requests for $2.4 billion to fund wastewater-treatment facilities and sewer-upgrading projects from 230 local communities. Federal grants from the Environmental Protection Agency would be, at most, $385 million between fiscal years 1982 and 1985. Instead of providing grants to a small fraction of the eligible communities (the state estimates between 11 and 13 projects could be funded), the bank would pool federal grants and state capital funds and provide loans on a revolving fund basis. The proposal was extended to fund other public investment in New Jersey after an analysis of projected capital investment showed that anticipated federal and state resources fell short of projected expenditures. State water supply investment, for example, was projected to be $1.3 billion while available funds were $350 million. The bank also would offer localities technical assistance in arranging leases and other service contracts with corporations.

Implementing the bank requires federal legislation to enable New Jersey to use federal funds in this new way. Three amendments are required of the Clean Water Act: 1) to permit states to use funds normally allocated under the act as grants in a revolving fund program; 2) to permit states to be the recipient of federal funds, rather than local communities as currently is the practice; and 3) to allow the federal government to provide a state's funding allocation in a lump-sum grant, rather than awards on a project-by-project basis.

The bank also requires extensive state-enabling legislation. A less ambitious proposal is being considered in Massachusetts, and many other states have established task forces and advisory groups to assess the feasibility of infrastructure banks. No other proposals have followed New Jersey's concept of intercepting existing federal grant programs and converting them into loans.

153

Utah recently funded a program similar to an infrastructure bank without relying on federal grants. The Water, Wastewater, and Drinking Water Bond and Loan Program Act authorized the state to issue $50 million of general obligation bonds. Twenty-million dollars will be administered by the Board of Water Resources, another $20 million by the Department of Health, and the remaining $10 million through the Utah Safe Drinking Water Committee. These administrative agencies will provide localities with funds for investments in the development of water projects and in meeting federal wastewater treatment and drinking-water-safety standards. Localities will enter into loan agreements with these agencies, which have discretion on the terms of the loan. Localities may back their loan with their general obligation or revenue-bonding power. Each year after issuance of the bonds, until all outstanding bonds are retired, there is levied a direct annual tax on all real and personal property within the state, sufficient to pay any applicable bond-redemption premiums and all interest and principal on the bonds as they become due. These proceeds, along with the payments from municipalities, are placed in a sinking fund to meet debt servicing of the state's general obligation bonds and provide funds for new loans.

The recently defeated water-development plan in Texas would have represented a greater commitment of state fiscal resources. The proposal would have established a special Water Project Assistance Fund to be administered by the Texas Water Development Board by using 50 percent of all undedicated state tax spending in each biennium. A loan assistance program would have used those funds to pay principal and interest obligations for local political subdivisions until the funded project entered its second year of operation. Then the local authority would repay the loan program with interest. The plan also would have had the state pledging $500 million of its general credit to guarantee the principal and interest payments of bonds issued by qualified local governments.

How well would infrastructure banks or revolving funds using dedicated general tax reveneus finance western water investment? As a bond bank, an infrastructure bank would redistribute financing costs among municipalities and between state and local governments. State governmental financial responsibility will be more transparent than in the case of bond banks. The state's contribution of up-front capital is an explicit financial responsibility in contrast to the implicit one in the state's role as a source of backing of bond banks. As a disburser of intergovernmental grants, any loan-repayment requirements provide municipalities with greater incentives to economize on project resources than grants-in-aid programs. Smaller-scale projects—better directed toward provision of public services—are more likely to be presented to the infrastructure bank than they are to an agency administering outright grants (Vaughan, 1983).

STATE WATER PROJECTS

In 1959 the California legislature passed the Water Resources Development Bond Act that authorized, subject to voter approval, construction of California's state water project. Voters approved, in 1961, plans to use California Water Resource Bonds—backed by signed contracts with prospective water users—to finance the construction of a conveyance system that now spans two-thirds of the state. By 1981, the system delivered 3.1 million acre-feet of water to 30 local water agencies—slightly less than 3 percent of the total amount of water conveyed by all California water organizations. The project has issued bonds with total face value of almost $2.5 billion. California's experience provides guidance for other states contemplating state-managed water projects as ways of financing future water investments.

In principle, project financing proceeds on a sound basis. The state uses *signed* contracts by water users as a planning tool for identifying likely sources of water demand. The repayment provisions in the contracts require water users to pay their proportionate share of project costs, including interest costs. The Water Development Bonds use these contracts as the first level of financial collateral—general taxes are used only if contractors fail to meet their obligations. The bond market views these contracts so favorably that financial assessments of the state of California subtract from the state's debt obligations the Water Resource Bonds backed by state water project contracts.

The project's pricing policy is controversial. The Department of Water Resources employs average historical cost instead of incremental replacement cost pricing (Phelps, Moore, and Graubard, 1978). This violates two of the pricing rules established in chapter 5. Given that the project's new development costs are much higher than its earlier ones (*see* table 5-6), project pricing policy makes water users serviced by new additions, as well as other users who receive no benefits, pay for new investment. Economically, this subsidizes new water development and reduces the overall financial collateral of the water system (Hirschleifer, Milliman, and DeHaven, 1963).

The political skirmishes resulting from this cross-subsidization are illustrated by the fate of Proposition 9 in the 1982 elections—the proposed financing for the Peripheral Canal. The voters rejected the proposition, 62 percent to 38 percent. Northern California voted 11 percent for and 89 percent against, while southern California voted 61 percent for and 39 percent against. To many, these patterns reflect longstanding competition between these regions. But the voting patterns really reflect the large degree of cross-subsidization implicit in project pricing policy. Water users of the Peripheral Canal would be charged less than $20 per acre-foot for water developed at an incremental cost of over $120 per acre-foot. Fresno and Merced counties, both heavily agricultural with strong philosophical ties to water development, but not significant beneficiaries, voted only 20.5 percent and 14.8 percent in favor of Proposition 9, respectively. Kern County, the destination of much of the proposed project water and also a stronghold of pro-development philosophy, voted 59.8 percent in favor of Proposition 9. Only three other counties—Los Angeles, Orange, and Riverside—voted more enthusiastically, their pluralities slightly exceeding 60 percent; their water districts would have been beneficiaries of the canal.

State governments that develop water projects to replace federal funding will find themselves at the nexus of debate about who should benefit and who should lose from cross-subsidization, unless they institute economically efficient user fees. The best prospect for wide support from localities are state-financed grants-in-aid programs, but these suffer from their own fiscal limitations.

CONCLUSIONS

State governments can aid local governments in water investment. The lowest-cost options—technical assistance on information and marketing—are the most effective ways of reducing total financing costs of water investment. State support to local governments for purchasing private bond insurance also would reduce financing costs. Bond banks are better at redistributing financing costs than at reducing them. If they impose explicit repayment responsibility on localities, infrastructure banks are more promising as a cheaper means of providing assistance than traditional grants-in-aid programs. Traditional grant programs for defraying local construction costs increase state financial responsibility and are the surest route to increased overall financing costs.

156

TEXT NOTES

1. If accurate information is not released, then market participants must estimate the missing information. Participants in financial markets are generally able to forecast correctly, which is the economic characteristic of an efficient market (Fama, 1976).

    Efficient financial markets, in the above sense of ability of participants to forecast accurately, does not imply that municipalities cannot gain from improving information. Better information will improve the match between financial characteristics of municipal bonds with the demands of private investors. The resulting improvement in the economic allocation of risk will be shared between lenders and borrowers, according to economic forces that need not detain us here.

    However, municipalities must live with the market's perceptions if they choose to withhold information. The release of even "bad" information can help the municipality because the information still places municipal problems in the proper perspective. Information withheld can create even greater problems, as the market wonders what "disasters" are being hidden. For example, the "voluntary disclosure" of grades under privacy programs in universities ultimately became a "mandatory" disclosure as competition among students for jobs and admission to graduate schools made interviewers assume the worst about the candidates withholding their records.

2. As discussed in chapter 3, if municipal and corporate bonds had the same financial risk, then municipal yields would roughly be 50 percent of corporate yields. At no time since World War II have municipal yields been this low. Also see the discussion in chapter 8.

3. A municipality improving its rating from BAA to AAA could reduce its underwriting spreads by 3 percentage points (Kessel, 1971). Improving its rating also would increase the number of bids it receives on its underwriting contract and could be another reason for lower underwriting spreads (Kessel, 1971).

4. The gains from private-market bond insurance need not diminish for municipalities as more high-risk debt issuers purchase insurance. The differential yields on bonds of different risk classes reflect both the inherent differences in risk of the bonds and the market's required risk premium. That premium depends upon the risk structure of the *entire* portfolio of stocks, bonds, and real assets in the economy and is not a factor operating in isolation from the municipal bond market. From this broader perspective, the increased relative supply of highly rated bonds has little, if any effect on the marketwide "price of risk."

5. Conversation with director of New York Municipal Bond Bank.

CHAPTER 8

TRANSFERRING FINANCING RESPONSIBILITY TO THE PRIVATE SECTOR

FINANCING AND MANAGING WATER PROJECTS need not be the responsibility of the public sector. There are many instances of privately owned and operated water-supply and water-treatment systems. Although considerable public attention has been focused on the tax benefits of private ownership, these gains are small and risky. The case for private ownership rests on potentially superior operating and financing efficiencies unrelated to manipulation of the federal tax code.

During the past decade, traditional boundaries between public and private ownership and management responsibilities have shifted. Private developers have built schools, water systems and roads, while some state and local governments have financed the development of private industrial facilities for the "public purpose" of creating jobs. State and local governments also have experimented with "contracting out" the management of health services, recreation facilities, transit, and other services that have been managed traditionally by the public sector. On the other hand, the public sector has established and managed development finance agencies that compete with private banks, and private industry is developing waste-management facilities.

This chapter establishes a framework for determining the potential gains from private ownership or management. These gains would result from a "fiscal dividend" when the proceeds from sale of assets exceed the value of keeping the enterprise under public ownership and management.

THE FINANCIAL ADVANTAGES OF PRIVATE OWNERSHIP

If a private company can enjoy financial benefits not available to a public entity, then it will be prepared to purchase the water utility from the public authority at a price that gives the seller a fiscal dividend. The bid received will exceed the financial value of keeping

159

the system under public ownership. There are two potential financial benefits from private ownership: first, the private owner may be able to take advantage of the preferential tax treatment of capital investments; second, the private corporation may be able to raise capital more cheaply than the public owner.

Tax Incentives for Private Ownership

The tax advantages of private ownership of a public facility have been subject to frequent changes in recent years as a result of congressional action and rulings by the Internal Revenue Service. As a result, tax benefits occurring under current law may differ substantially from benefits available in the near future. Prudent financial analysis considers both the level and riskiness of the tax incentives for private ownership.

In 1981, the National Economic Recovery Tax Act greatly liberalized the definition of a lease (Vaughan, 1983, chapter 5). Paper transactions allowed New York's Metropolitan Transit Authority to sell and lease back its buses from Metromedia Inc. Although this type of arrangement cannot be used for water facilities, certain types of leases—such as tax-exempt leveraged leases—can be used for water projects.

Such transactions benefit governments financially only if the proceeds of the sale exceed the future income that the government could have earned by running the enterprise itself. The analysis examines the circumstances in which tax considerations alone make public water systems more valuable to the private than to the public sector. The evaluation of the sale of tax benefits to the private sector assumes that the stream of future revenues, costs, and financial risk of the enterprise are unaffected by the transfer of ownership.

The U.S. tax system provides conflicting incentives to transfer public water systems to the private sector. Being exempt from income taxation, governmental entities keep any and all revenues that exceed their water system's operating and financing costs. Private firms, in contrast, pay taxes on any income they earn. Local governments benefit from selling their water systems to the private sector only if firms could reduce their total tax payments on income earned on other activities by purchasing a public water system. Otherwise, private firms would bid less than the value of keeping the enterprise under public ownership.

Three considerations determine how much a firm values the acquisition of a public water system for tax benefits. First, the firm pays federal and maybe state and local income taxes on the amount that the company's revenues from water sales exceed its operating costs. Second, the tax code allows the firm to deduct interest and depreciation expenses from its taxable income. Third, the firm earns an investment tax credit on its original purchase of the system and on any additional construction and rehabilitation. These provisions reduce the firm's tax obligations on the income earned from other activities.

The investment tax credit reduces the firm's tax payments by a percentage of original purchase price or on the costs of rehabilitation or additional construction. The applicable percentages vary with the nature of the investment in the following way: 3-year-class life equipment, 6 percent; 5 to 15-year-class life equipment, 10 percent; rehabilitation of structures 30 to 39 years old, 15 percent; rehabilitation of structures at least 40 years old, 20 percent; rehabilitation of certified historic structures, 25 percent; and investment in research and development in excess of the level of investment in 1980, 20 percent.

The Accelerated Cost Recovery System (ACRS) categorizes assets into the following four groups for defining how quickly firms can write off the purchase price of its assets: Transportation equipment and machinery previously depreciated over 4 years or fewer, 3 years; most other equipment, 5 years; investment by utilities, 10 years; and structures, 15 years. ACRS schedules can be applied only to the value of the asset net of the value of the investment tax credit.

Privatization generates tax savings for the firm only if the value of interest and depreciation deductions, added to the investment tax credit, exceed the income tax liabilities on revenues exceeding operating costs. Figures 8-1 and 8-2 illustrate how the ratio of the maximum theoretical bid by a private firm compares with the value to the government of keeping its water system under public ownership.[1] A bid ratio of 100 percent indicates that privatizing a water supply system offers no financial gains for the government. Only for ratios exceeding 100 percent will privatization produce a fiscal dividend for government.

The figures show how the potential fiscal dividend from selling tax benefits to the private sector are sensitive to the asset life for tax purposes (indicated by the differently shaded bars), the investment tax credit (ITC), the interest rate, and the corporate income tax rate. The base case assumes a 15 percent ITC, a 10 percent interest rate for debt financing, and a 50 percent combined federal and state corporate income tax rate.[2] The graphs report how the bid-value ratio varies with different write-off periods and departures from base case values for a specified feature of the tax code or interest rate. The middle collection of bars in each graph represents the base-case situation, to allow easier comparisons across the panels.

161

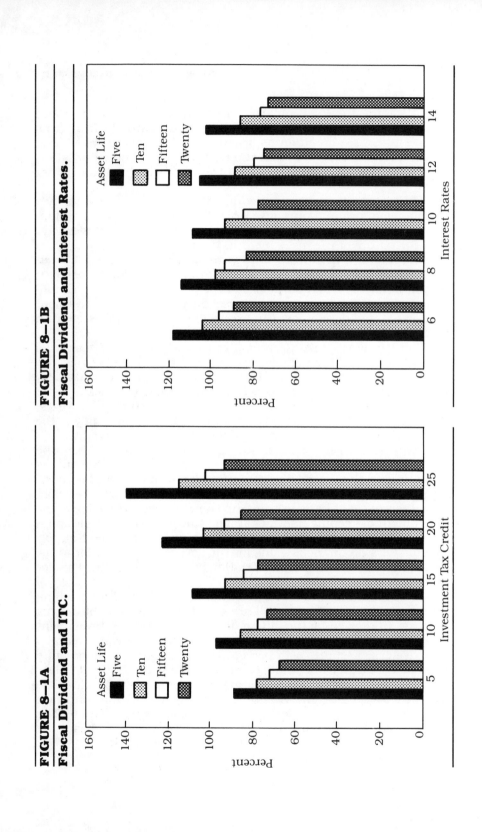

FIGURE 8–1A

Fiscal Dividend and ITC.

FIGURE 8–1B

Fiscal Dividend and Interest Rates.

FIGURE 8–2

Fiscal Dividend and Corporate Tax Rates.

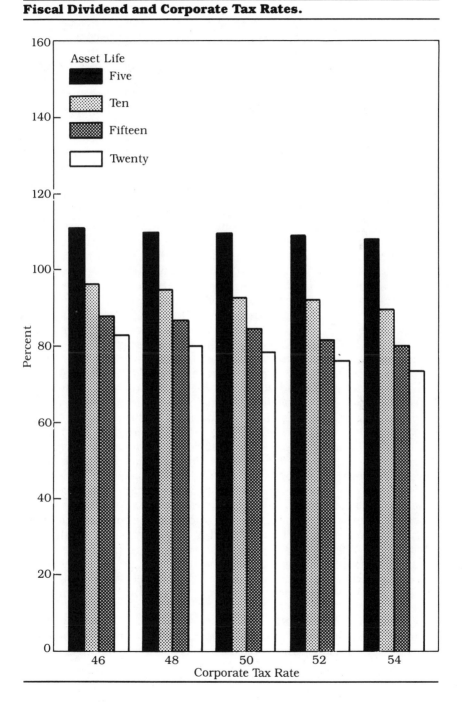

Privatization of a public-owned water system does not always create fiscal dividends for the government. In the base case, private bids would exceed (by 10 percent) the value to the government only if private firms could depreciate fully the purchase within 5 years. If the water system's assets are classified as utilities or structures, and depreciated over 10 years or 20 years, the greatest bids would equal 94 percent and 78 percent, respectively, of the value of keeping the water system under public ownership.

The fiscal dividend from selling the water system is greater for higher ITC rates (*see* the first panel in figure 8-1). ITC rates of 20 percent and 25 percent make profitable, respectively, the sale of assets that can be depreciated over 10 years and 15 years. However, these higher ITCs would be available only for rehabilitation of structures at least 40 years old under current tax law.

Even though state and local governments became interested in privatization as interest rates reached historical highs, the fiscal *dividend from privatization is greater* when *interest rates are low* (*see* the second panel in figure 8-1). Lower interest rates increase the value of accelerated depreciation, because the present value of the tax write-offs is increased. Selling public-owned assets that can be depreciated over 10 years creates a fiscal dividend for governments at 6 percent interest rates, but not if interest rates rise to 10 percent.

Finally, the fiscal dividend from privatization is slightly higher in jurisdictions levying no corporate income tax rates (*see* figure 8-2). Firms subject to a total corporate income tax rate of 46 percent—the federal rate and no state or local tax liability—would pay 6 percent more for public water systems than firms subject to a total corporate tax rate of 54 percent—federal and state income tax liability. *Lower corporate income tax rates increase the economic value of tax benefits,* because the value of the reduced tax payments on taxable income after deductions is greater than the value of the reduced tax payments saved by accelerated depreciation.[3]

Overall, the net tax benefits from transferring a public water system to private hands are slight—perhaps substantially less than 10 percent of the value of the system under public control. The most attractive projects are those involving substantial rehabilitation because the ITCs are highest. Private ownership of new facilities or machinery offers the lowest benefits, because the 10 percent ITC combined with the five-year write-off schedule would still yield a bid below the value of the investment under public ownership (*see* figure 8-1).

These modest potential gains—only captured by local government if the facilities are sold at competitive auction—may be more than offset by risks incurred through the common practice of indemnifying private investors against future adverse changes in the federal tax law. For example, suppose that a city sold its water system to private investors under conditions captured in the base-case assumptions. If all assets were eligible to be written off in 5 years, then the city could receive $88 million for a system worth $80 million under their control. A subsequent tax ruling that lengthens the write-off period to 10 years reduces the value of the sale to private investors by $4.8 million—or 60 percent of the municipality's gains from selling the tax benefits in the first place. A tax ruling that extends the write-off period to 15 years reduces the value of the system to private investors by $19.2 million! Indemnifying private investors, in this case, means that the municipality nets $68.8 million, after the adverse tax ruling, for the sale of a water system with an assumed value of $80 million under public ownership.

Tax gimmicks are not strong reasons for transferring ownership to the private sector. Corporate income tax obligations roughly offset the tax benefits from interest deductibility, accelerated depreciation, and ITCs.

Financial Incentives for Private Ownership

Private firms enjoy lower financing costs than public agencies. For comparably rated bonds, public borrowing costs averaged 20 percent more than after-tax private costs during 1978 to 1982.[4] The reasons why private firms have lower financing costs than public agencies are related to the rules of financial collateral discussed in earlier chapters.

First, private ownership erects greater collateral for debt financing than public ownership, because pricing and marginal costs of service are more closely related to each other under private ownership (De Alessi, 1975). The resulting smaller degree of cross-subsidization avoids economic inefficiencies that reduce financial collateral.

Second, the collateral behind private debt is more secure because revenues behind the repayment of principal and interest are less vulnerable to political manipulation, even if private firms are subject to state or local governmental regulation (Fama, 1977). Under private ownership, bondholder's financial interests are represented by the firm's financial interests in regulatory proceedings. Bondholders do not have this channel of influence under public ownership.

Finally, private firms provide the bond market with better information than public agencies. Shareholders monitor the operations of private firms more effectively than voters monitor public agencies (Zimmerman, 1977).

With lower financing costs, private firms would bid more for a municipal or rural water system than the government could earn from keeping it. For example, private firms enjoying 20-percent lower after-tax financing costs would bid 17.5 percent more for a public-owned water system.[5] A municipality would receive $94 million for selling a system with an $80 million value under public ownership.

OPERATING EFFICIENCIES OF PRIVATE OWNERSHIP

The strongest economic case for privatization rests on the superior ability of the private sector to deliver a lower-cost product than the public sector. There is a growing body of evidence suggesting that private ownership does lead to substantial cost savings. Bennett and Johnson (1980) summarize:

> Without exception, the empirical findings indicate that the same level of output could be produced at substantially lower costs if output were produced by the private rather than the public sector.

This section reviews the supporting evidence and shows that the likely magnitude of the savings in operating costs can exceed many times over the tax benefits.

Why would the private sector be a cheaper supplier of municipal services? The answer is not any presumed superiority of talent in private firms, nor any greater dedication on the part of private employees. Instead, private ownership means lower operating and construction costs, because *individuals in the private sector have greater incentives to be efficient* (Borcherding, 1982; De Alessi, 1974). Stockholders, both existing and potential, monitor the cost-performance of private firms to protect their financial interests (Manne, 1965; Easterbrook, 1981). A group of investors can acquire a controlling interest in a firm, reorganize personnel and operations as necessary, and enjoy the bulk of the financial rewards from improving the firm's efficiency by virtue of a large holding of stock.

A state's or locality's residents do not have comparable incentives to monitor the cost-performance of publicly owned enterprises (Zimmerman, 1977). Citizens cannot increase their ownership shares and harvest the financial rewards from improving the enterprise's cost-performance. Any cost-savings would be shared with fellow residents and customers, regardless of their individual contributions to the cost-reduction effort. Nobody monitors cost-performance of the public-owned firm, because residents await the effort by others (Olson, 1965).

This presumed superior efficiency of private ownership has been documented for the delivery of water. Public-owned municipal water systems incur 15 percent greater costs than privately owned, regulated water firms (Morgan, 1977). Crain and Zardkoohi (1978) concluded that publicly owned systems are 25 percent more expensive than privately owned municipal water systems.[6] Private firms also have been found to provide other municipal services at lower costs than public agencies.[7]

Because they can deliver water cheaper than a public agency, private firms would bid more for a municipal water system than the government could earn by keeping it under public ownership. Assuming that a private firm earns the same revenue stream as the municipality, the water system would have 30 percent greater value under private than it would under public ownership.[8] A municipality could sell its system worth $80 million for $104 million and earn a $24 million fiscal dividend.

IMPLEMENTATION PROBLEMS

Attempts to convert a publicly owned water system to private ownership and management will encounter many potential legal and political obstacles. But the process is possible. After all, private companies played a major role in the historical development of irrigation and in municipalities. The Congressional Budget Office found that 204 of the 756 systems in cities with populations greater than 50,000 were investor owned.

Agreements among state and local governments and private firms must comply with federal tax laws and regulations. This requirement may prove especially important for privatization efforts involving leasing and lease/saleback arrangements (Vaughan, 1983). Most important, the Internal Revenue Service will allow private firms to enjoy the tax benefits of leasing only if it can be established that the lessor would have a positive cash flow and profit independently of the tax benefits. Although tax considerations are not the driving financial factor for privatization, the loss of depreciation tax benefits, for example, would become a financial disadvantage that must be overcome by even greater savings in operating and financing efficiencies.[9]

Political impediments to privatization are only partly surmountable. Concerns that privatization "gives away" public assets can be partly assuaged by selling systems to the highest bidder in competitive auctions. Concerns that privatization "gives a monopoly" to the acquiring firms can be overcome in two ways. The bidding process can involve joint consideration of the amount of upfront money along with pricing schedules that would represent a long-term contract to supply water to the community. Alternatively, the municipality could continue to sell its system to the highest bidder, but under the condition that the firm would become regulated as a common carrier.

Most, if not all, private water systems currently operate under regulation, so this option does not involve breaking new regulatory ground. How regulation is structured will influence the efficiency of private companies. For example, rate-of-return regulation can increase costs above minimum economic levels (Averch and Johnson, 1961). However, studies showing that private ownership provides services at lower costs than public ownership invariably compare the operations of regulated private firms with those of public agencies.

Privatization conflicts with the interests of political supporters of water subsidization and public ownership. Not having the tax powers of governments nor the political incentives, private firms will not subsidize the provision of water to favored users. Public unions also oppose private ownership because private water companies rely on less labor-intensive technologies than do public agencies (Crain and Zardkoohi, 1978).

CONCLUSIONS

The analysis of the tax advantages assumes that the transfer of title from public to private ownership does not influence any other aspects of the water system—future streams of revenues, costs, or financial risk. The analysis concludes that privatization for tax reasons is more likely to provide a fiscal dividend for governments when the water project involves rehabilitation of aged systems, rather than construction of new structures. The net benefits tend to be lower when market interest rates are high, because the financial benefit from accelerated depreciation is lower. Municipalities expose themselves to considerable financial risk when they engage in the common practice of indemnifying private investors against future adverse changes in the federal tax code.

Most, if not all, financial advantages of private ownership result from the bond market's perception that private ownership involves less financial risk than public ownership. A private company may be able to raise capital 20 percent below the costs that a public entity would incur. These *real* efficiency gains are likely to be many times the level of the *paper* benefits that rest on the manipulation of the tax code.

The evidence on how turning over management responsibility to a private firm can reduce operating costs suggests that improvements in operating efficiency may reduce costs by at least 15 percent. This cost advantage could yield a fiscal dividend from privatization when the proceeds of sale exceed by 18 percent the value of keeping the water system under public ownership.

Awarding private ownership of water systems on the basis of competitive bidding is likely to yield the greatest revenues to municipalities. Local regulation can ensure that private firms do not exploit their potential monopoly position, provided that competing modes of water supply are not barred from serving the market. Despite local regulation, privatization will sacrifice political objectives promoted by cross-subsidizing water users allowed under public ownership— the same policies that reduce financial collateral (*see* chapters 4 and 5).

In summary, transferring financing and operating responsibility to the private sector may be a reasonable way of reducing the costs of meeting water demands. To do this successfully, state and local governments must insure that the proceeds from the transfer exceed the value of keeping the water system under public ownership. The case for privatization rests on fundamental economic grounds, not on exploiting tax gimmicks. Water systems can be more valuable in the hands of the private sector because of the resulting lower operating and financing costs. These factors may yield bids, from competitive auctions, that exceed by 30 percent the value of keeping the water system under public ownership. Regulating the price that private suppliers can charge may protect residents from monopoly pricing. The major political objection to privatization is that it will end the water subsidization policies that, in any event, have been found to diminish the financial collateral of public investment (*see* Chapters 4-7). If policymakers wish to promote economically efficient financing for public investment, they should seriously consider private ownership and management.

TEXT NOTES

1. The analysis assumes that the government would sell the water system at a competitive auction and receive the maximum theoretical bid. The value of the water system under private ownership is computed at the present value of the after-tax

cash flows earned from the investment. None of these assumptions understates the government's gain from selling tax benefits to the private sector.

2. The analysis assumes that the after-tax cost of corporate borrowing equals the government's tax-exempt interest rate, and that the firm finances its purchase by issuing bonds rather than stock. The reasons for these assumptions are discussed below in note 4.

3. To many readers it may appear that higher corporate income tax rates must increase the gains from selling tax benefits to the private sector. But accelerated depreciation only partly offsets the tax liabilities on the net revenues earned by private investors. Without the investment tax credit, tax benefits would always be negative from privatization: the more so the greater the corporate income tax rate. So, the investment tax credit is what makes privatization a potentially viable financing option.

4. Municipal bond interest rates are lower than corporate bond rates because the interest payments on the former are exempt from federal, and sometimes state, income taxes. If tax treatment were the sole difference between comparably rated private and public bonds, then the ratio of municipal to corporate bond rates should equal one minus the corporate income tax rate (Miller, 1977). As shown by Trezcinka (1982), municipal rates are consistently higher because of the higher financial risk of public bonds.

    The data in table 3-7 illustrate the differences. From 1978 to 1982, the ratio of municipal to corporate yields averaged 66.7 percent and exceeded the 55 percent ratio that would be expected because of tax considerations. So the tax-free interest rate on municipal bonds exceeded the after-tax interest rate on corporate bonds by 20 percent.

    How after-corporate-tax returns on corporate bonds compare with tax-exempt municipal rates is the relevant comparison for assessing the potential gains from privatization. Although investors demand higher tax rates on corporate debt because yields are taxed as personal income, corporations may deduct those payments from their own tax liability.

    The discussion also abstracts from the financial consequences of a private firm's use of equity in addition to debt financing. How the firm's cost of capital compares with its cost of debt depends on its debt-equity ratio and whether the returns earned on the water business are related to overall returns earned from investing in a diversified stock portfolio (Brealey and Myers, 1981). The firm's cost of capital will equal the cost of bond financing if the cash flow earned from the local water system is unrelated to the overall condition of the stock market: an assumption used in the following analysis.

5. Because water systems wear out, a 20 percent lowering of the interest rate does not increase the value of the cash flow to the private sector by 20 percent.

6. A recent study by Feigenbaum and Teeples (1983) concludes that there are no cost differences between privately and publicly-owned water systems. Two considerations, however, question the relevance of this study.

    First, the study held constant in its comparisons any differences between private and public firms in the wages they pay labor, the prices they pay for water and capital equipment, and the cost of financial capital. That is, after controlling for differences in the factors stressed by the debate over the gains from privatization, the authors conclude that there are no cost differences between private and public ownership.

    Second, the authors *do not report* the estimated cost differences between private and public water systems; the reader must rely on the "statistical insignificance" of estimated cost differences. However, the authors' conclusion is driven by their arbitrarily chosen 5 percent significance criteria. The reported tests indicate that the estimated cost differences have only a 10 percent chance of being random, so the differences barely miss the criteria of significance chosen by the authors. The authors do not report whether these excessively controlled, estimated cost differences are a "statistically insignificant" 2 or 50 percent. The wisdom of privatization revolves around these neglected issues.

7. Borcherding (1982) provides an extensive survey of the literature showing the superior efficiency of private ownership, including a summary of the methodological problems that invalidate the few studies showing equal efficiency of the private and public sectors.

    For example, private firms can provide the same quality of fire-protection services at 50 percent of the cost of publicly provided fire services (Ahlbrandt, 1973, 1974). Private firms can collect garbage 20 percent to 40 percent cheaper than public refuse-collection agencies (Savas, 1977; Stevens, 1978).

8. The computation assumes the following conditions for the two key considerations influencing the gain from privatization: 1) Private firms experience 20 percent lower costs than public agencies—an estimate consistent with the studies cited in the text; and 2) public water agencies enjoy a 38.7 percent net takedown (net revenues divided by gross revenues), the financial median of municipal water enterprises in 1982 (*see* table 3-12).

9. Recall that the income tax liabilities are roughly offset by tax benefits associated with depreciation, deductibility of interest, and the investment tax credit. Removing any of these offsetting tax-benefit factors will make privatization disadvantageous on tax grounds.

CHAPTER 9

CONCLUSION:
THE ROLE OF STATE GOVERNMENT
IN PROMOTING LOW-COST
FINANCING STRATEGIES

THE WEST FACES SEVERE PROBLEMS in financing water invest-ment. At a time when concern about the availability and quality of water supplies is growing, state and local governments are facing cutbacks in federal funds, unprecedented interest rates on bond issues, strong public sentiment for fiscal restraint, and, in light of the default of the Washington Public Power Supply System, growing doubts about their capacity to oversee major construction projects.

The evidence reviewed in the preceding chapters suggests that concerns over the capacity of the tax-exempt market to accommo-date significant increases in debt finance are misplaced. Even the largest default in the history of the municipal bond market has failed to prevent significant growth in new issues nor raised interest rates paid in municipal debt. Rather than focusing on concerns about the marketplace, policymakers should concentrate on devel-oping effective state policies to finance public investment.

Even the most enlightened state financing policy will not elimi-nate the growing scarcity of western water nor alter the fact that state residents will shoulder a larger share of costs. However, states can take measures to cope with scarcity sensibly, to use available supplies more effectively, to minimize the cost of expanding sup-plies, and to reduce the probability of a costly crisis situation.

Efficient water financing strategies must be developed to attain four objectives:

- Employing debt financing in favor of pay-as-you-go to minimize the economic burden of financing water investment and to assure that future residents—who also benefit from the system—will bear a portion of its costs.
- Strengthening local economies and tax bases by imposing user-fees such as water prices, pump taxes, benefit assessments for flood control, and effluent fees rather than general tax levies.
- Removing statutory and regulatory impediments to enable private capital markets to finance water projects as efficiently as possible.

173

- Supplying local governments with technical assistance in project planning, budgeting, management, and financing to assist them in building and marketing financial collateral.

This chapter describes policies that can meet these objectives—summarizing the discussions in earlier chapters. The first section describes statutory and regulatory reform—initiatives that do not require financial commitment by state governments. The second section outlines types of technical assistance that states can provide to local governments to help them build and market collateral. The third section describes how states can provide fiscal assistance to local governments most effectively. Most of the policies discussed rely on voluntary participation by private institutions and local governments. They can be of particular benefit to those small communities that have been the focus of greatest concern by policymakers.

STATUTORY AND REGULATORY REFORM

Statutory and regulatory reform can help build collateral by establishing an efficient market for water. They can help the marketing of collateral by promoting competition among the financial institutions that shape the market for municipal debt.

An efficient market for water is important because it ensures that existing water supplies flow to their highest-valued uses and it provides project planners with an accurate measure of the value of developing additional water supplies. Reforms to promote a market for water include:

- Authorizing powers to impose benefit assessments for flood control, to levy pump taxes, and to charge effluent fees;
- Clarifying water rights and defining rights in terms of consumptive use rather diversion of water;
- Providing local governments with the powers to transfer the ownership and management responsibility of water utilities into private hands.

A competitive financial market ensures that financial services are available to borrowers at lowest possible cost and that debt instruments can be sold to a wide market of investors. Reforms to achieve these goals include:

- Guaranteeing that major trust portfolios are not precluded from purchasing relatively low-grade bonds, and
- Maintaining competition in the underwriting industry

These policies are described briefly, in the following subsections.

174

Authority to Levy Pump Taxes, Effluent Fees, and Benefit Assessments for Flood Control

Imposing pump taxes and effluent fees not only build collateral by providing additional revenue sources, they also provide incentives for more efficient allocation of water. The appropriate pump tax induces users to weigh their benefits against the social cost of water, thereby encouraging conservation, reducing demands for new capacity, and ameliorating the overdraft problem. By making users bear the costs of water degradation, appropriate effluent fees provide incentives to reduce discharges and improve water quality.

Ideally, these taxes and fees should be levied at the local level. This policy would allow the taxes and fees to be coordinated with pricing strategies for surface water supplies. Opposition to state levies may appear unless revenues are properly earmarked to localities.

The proper level of government responsibility for financing flood control depends on specific circumstances. If flood damage results from a specific project, then protection costs are properly levied on project users through water pricing. In contrast, if a project provides flood protection, then protection costs should be paid through tax assessments levied on protected properties. For projects where benefits are localized, flood control districts can be formed as special local districts. If project benefits extend past jurisdictional boundaries, then intergovernmental cooperation is required. Either a grant system must be negotiated among local governments, or a new agency must be created whose jurisdiction extends beyond common political boundaries.

Clarifying Water Rights

Defining water rights in terms of consumptive use rather than diversion is another reform that can reduce financing costs. This reform would reduce uncertainty about a jurisdiction's actual rights, which today can only be established by an attempted sale. Explicit definition of water rights is also a necessary precondition to developing a market that allocates water to its highest-valued use. Future water projects would be less risky, and therefore less costly to finance, if statutes and regulations were reformed to ease the transferability of water rights.

Authorizing Powers to Privatize

Vesting municipalities with the power to transfer ownership and management of water systems to private firms is another measure that can build financial collateral. The "fiscal dividend" from trans-

175

ferring ownership to the more efficient private sector can only be realized if legal mechanisms are established for transferring title and selecting which regulations, if any, to impose on private firms.

Trust Regulation

Changing the regulations governing trust investments can improve the marketing of collateral in water projects. Defining guidelines in terms of the riskiness of whole portfolios rather than individual bonds would expand the market for lower-quality, high-risk bonds without sacrificing the goals of trust regulation. This reform would reduce financing costs for the small, high-risk communities who receive the attention of policymakers.

Increasing Competition in the Underwriting Industry

The costs of financing water projects would be reduced by repealing laws barring commercial banks from underwriting most revenue bonds and by permitting municipalities to select underwriters by the true-interest-cost method.

TECHNICAL ASSISTANCE

The regulatory and statutory reforms outlined above will have little effect unless municipalities have the knowledge and technical expertise to take advantage of them. State governments can promote the adoption of effective water policies by providing technical assistance to local governments—especially to those that lack extensive planning capabilities. The different types of technical assistance programs that can assist local governments are listed in table 9-1.

To set efficient water prices and pump taxes requires extensive knowledge of the return flows generated by each category of water user, the rate at which water percolates into aquifers, and how various discharges affect water quality. Since many municipalities possess neither the resources nor the expertise required to gather this information, and since some duplication of effort may occur, the states' water engineers and staff may be better suited to provide much of this hydrologic information. This information could aid local authorities who are responsible for the design of water pricing, groundwater tax schedules, and benefit assessments for flood control.

Marketing bonds is another area in which the states can provide municipalities with useful technical assistance. Anything that reduces the perceived risk of a bond on the part of investors will reduce financing costs to municipalities. The state can instill investor confidence by providing centralized information, standardized

TABLE 9–1

Technical Assistance Programs to Local Governments

Type of Information	Purpose
Hydrology: Return flows, percolation, waste discharges	Aids the design of efficient water prices, pump taxes, and effluent fees
Finance options: Pricing policies, pump taxation, effluent fees, general tax revenues	Assists in implementation of options
Bond market: Improving and disseminating data on local finances and policies	Overcomes the communication problems localities have with the bond market
Designing contracts for selecting underwriters	Provides expertise for the infrequent borrower
Sample bond prospectus	Same as above
Bond insurance	Coordinates the expansion of a worthwhile investment for high-risk communities
Privatization: Standardized procedures for sale of assets	Insures that the benefits accrue to the public sector
Standardized procedures for regulating private water companies	Insures that communities are not victimized by monopoly pricing of water

contracts, auditing local finances, and cataloguing operating procedures. Experience in Idaho, North Carolina, and Texas suggest that the savings from this type of assistance can be significant—sufficient to generate voluntary participation by municipalities.

Localities contemplating the transfer of ownership and/or management of water facilities to the private sector face a number of complex issues. How does the agency transfer title to a private firm? Does it require voter approval? Which public entity will oversee the administration of the contract and any local regulation? How shall the proceeds of the sale be divided among residents? Answering these questions is necessary before privatization can develop, rehabilitate, or rebuild western water systems.

State governments may provide useful technical assistance to localities anticipating privatization. States can collect, analyze, and disseminate case studies describing specific instances of privatization that have been attempted. The state could also help design regulatory policies governing the pricing and protection of water quality.

FISCAL ASSISTANCE

State programs—such as bond banks, dedicated tax revenues, and infrastructure or revolving-fund banks—create various degrees of state fiscal involvement. These policies *redistribute* the economic burden of financing, but—with the exception of state funding for the purchase of bond insurance by high-risk communities—they will increase, rather than reduce, overall financing costs.

Bond banks redistribute financing costs from high-risk, small-debt issuers to low-risk, large ones. Over the long-term, this pattern of cross-subsidization can continue only by mandating participation of all communities. Evidence suggests that bond banks raise borrowing costs for state governments because of the perceived contingent obligation to stand behind the debt issued by the bank. Nor will the cost of water finance necessarily be reduced by the use of dedicated tax revenues, such as mineral taxes. The risk associated with the dedicated tax may be far greater than that from project-related finance.

Because they entail the smallest sacrifice of financial collateral, infrastructure or revolving funds are the best way of disbursing state funds to support water investments. Moreover, the initial capitalization of the fund insulates it from political pressure, and making subsequent loans conditional on user-fee financing can reduce the chances of financing an inefficient project. Their major drawback, however, is that revolving-fund-financing approximates pay-as-you-go financing, because the original funds are raised from other tax bases unrelated to the ultimate benefits created by the project.

CONCLUSION

With the fragmentary evidence currently available, there is no assurance that the collection of policies recommended above will finance water projects at the lowest possible cost. Learning from experience is another crucial element of a water financing strategy. With planned investments in excess of $100 billion over the next 25 years, there will be ample opportunity to identify both effective and ineffective policies.

BIBLIOGRAPHY

Advisory Commission on Intergovernmental Relations. *Measuring the Fiscal Capacity and Effort of State and Local Governments.* Washington D.C.: U.S. Government Printing Office, 1971.

Ahlbrandt, Roger S. Jr. "Efficiency in the Provision of Fire Services." *Public Choice* Vol. 16 (Fall 1973): 1-15.

Allen, Eric. "Risk-Free Municipals: Underwriters Now Offer Insurance Against Default." *Barron's* (24 December 1973): 11-12.

American Water Works Association. *Managing Water Rates and Finances.* Denver, Colorado: American Water Works Association Management Handbook, 1980.

Anderson, Terry, editor. *Water Rights: Scarce Resource Allocation, Bureaucracy, and the Environment.* San Francisco: Pacific Institute for Public Policy Research, 1984.

Averch, Harvey and Leland Johnson. "Behavior of the Firm under Regulatory Constraint." *American Economic Review* Vol. 52, No. 5 (December 1962): 1052-1069.

Bain, J.S., R.E. Caves, and J.S. Margolis. *Northern California's Water Industry.* Baltimore: John Hopkins University Press, 1966.

Ball, Ray and Phillip Brown. "An Empirical Evaluation of Accounting Income Numbers." *Journal of Accounting Research* Vol. 6, No. 1 (Spring 1968): 159-178.

Barro, Robert. "Public Debt and Taxes." in Boskin (1979): 159-178.

Barzel, Yoram. "A Theory of Rationing by Waiting." *Journal of Law and Economics* Vol. XXVII, No. 1 (April 1974): 73-95.

Beebe, Jack. H. "The Effect of Proposition 13 on California Municipal Debt." *Federal Reserve Bank of San Francisco Economic Review* (Winter 1979): 25-38.

Bennett, J.T. and M.H. Johnson. "Tax Reduction without Sacrifice: Private Sector Production of Public Services." *Public Finance Quarterly* Vol. 8, No. 4 (October 1980): 363-396.

Benson, Earl D. and Robert J. Rogowski. "The Cyclical Behavior of Risk

Spreads on New Municipal Issues." *Journal of Money, Credit, and Banking* Vol. X, No. 3 (August 1978): 348-362.

Benson, Earl D. "Municipal Bond Interest Cost, Issue Purpose, and Proposition 13." *Governmental Finance* Vol. 9, No. 3 (September 1980): 15-19.

Borcherding, Thomas. "Toward A Positive Theory of Public Sector Supply Arrangements." in Prichard (1982): 100-183.

Boskin, Michael, editor. *Federal Tax Reforms: Myths and Realities.* San Francisco: Institute for Contemporary Studies, 1979.

Boyett, Arthur S. and Cary A. Giroux. "The Relevance of Municipal Financial Reporting to Municipal Security Prices." *Governmental Finance* Vol. 7, No. 2 (May 1978): 29-34.

Brazer, Harvey, D.B. Suits, and M.W. Converse. "Municipal Bond Yields: The Market's Reaction to the Michigan Financial Crisis." *National Tax Journal* Vol., 15, No. 1 (March 1962): 66-70.

Brealey, Richard and Stewart Myers. *Principles of Corporate Finance.* New York: McGraw Hill, 1981.

Brown, G. Jr. and R. Deacon. "Economic Optimization of a Single-Cell Aquifer." *Water Resources Research* Vol. 8, No. 3 (June 1972): 557-564.

Brown, G. Jr. and C. B. McGuire. "A Socially Optimal Pricing Policy for a Public Water Agency." *Water Resources Research* Vol. 3, No. 1 (First Quarter 1967): 33-43.

Brown, Gardner Jr. "An Optimal Program for Managing Common Property Resources with Congestion Externalities." *Journal of Political Economy* Vol. 82, No. 1(Jan./Feb 1974): 163-174.

Business Week. "A Fiasco that May Rock Municipal Bonds." *Business Week* (7 February 1983): 94-95.

Butcher, Willard C. "Market Forces Can't be Dammed Up." *The New York Times* Sunday, July 10, 1983: Section III, 2.

Cagan, Phillip. "The Interest Savings to States and Municipalities from Bank Eligibility to Underwriting All Non-Industrial Municipal Bonds." *Governmental Finance* Vol. 7, No. 2 (May 1978): 40-48.

Carleton, Willard T. and Eugene M. Lerner. "Statistical Credit Scoring of Municipal Bonds." *Journal of Money, Credit, and Banking* Vol. 1, No. 4 (November 1969): 750-764.

Carlson Richard G. "WPPSS' Forgotten Issue: Can the Customer's Pay." *The Bond Buyer* (30 September 1983): 18-19.

Carr, Frank. "Municipal Bond Insurance." Municipal Finance Officers Association Chicago: Municipal Finance Officiers Association Special Bulletin: March, 1972.

Clark, Robert M., Richard G. Stevie, and Gregory P. Trygg. "An Analysis of

Municipal Water Supply Costs." *Journal of American Water Works Association* Vol. 70, No. 10 (October 1978): 543-547.

Cohen, Kalman J. and Frederich S. Hammer. "Optimal Coupon Structures for Municipal Bonds." *Management Science* Vol. 12, No. 1 (September 1975): 68-82.

Congressional Budget Office. *Tax-Exempt Bonds for Single-Family Housing.* Washington D.C.: Government Printing Office, Committee Printing Office, Print 96-2, 1979.

Congressional Budget Office. *Efficient Investments in Water Resources: Issues and Options.* Washington D.C.: U.S. Government Printing Office, August 1983.

Conley, B.C. "Price Elasticity of Demand for Water in Southern California." *Annals of Regional Science* Vol. 1, No.1 (December 1967): 180-89.

Cook, Timothy and Patric Hendershott. "The Impact of Taxes, Risk, and Relative Security Supplies on Interest Rate Differentials." *Journal of Finance* Vol. 33, No. 4 (September 1978): 1173-1200.

Coopers and Lybrand. *Financial Disclosure Practices of the American Cities: A Public Report.* New York: Coopers and Lybrand and University of Michigan, 1976.

Council of Economic Advisors. *Economic Report of The President.* Washington D.C.: U.S. Government Printing Office, February, 1983.

Crain, W. Mark and Asghar Zardkoohi. "A Test of the Property-Rights Theory of the Firm: Water Utilities in the United States." *Journal of Law and Economics* Vol. 21, No. 2 (October 1978): 395-408.

De Alessi, Louis. "An Economic Analysis of Government Ownership and Regulation: Theory and the Evidence from the Electric Power Industry." *Public Choice* Vol. 19 (Fall 1974): 1-42.

De Alessi, Louis. "Some Effects of Ownership on the Wholesale Prices of Electric Power." *Economic Inquiry* Vol. 13, No. 4 (December 1975): 526-538.

DeHaven, J.C. "Water Supply, Economics, Technology, and Policy." *Journal of American Water Works Association* Vol. 55, No. 5 (May 1963): 539-547.

DeRooy, J. "Price Responsiveness of the Industrial Demand for Water." *Water Resources Research Bulletin* Vol. 10, No. 3 (June 1974): 403-406.

Demsetz, Harold. "Cost of Contracting." *Quarterly Journal of Economics* Vol. 82, No. 1 (February 1968): 33-53.

Easterbrook, Frank and Daniel Fischel. "The Proper Role of A Target's Management in Responding to A Tender Offer." *Harvard Law Review* Vol. 94, No. 6 (April 1981): 1161-1204.

Economist. "American Survey: Water in the West." *Economist* (14 May 1983): 41-49.

Elloit, R. D. and J.A. Seagraves. *The Effects of Sewer Surcharges on the Level of Industrial Water and Use of Water by Industry.* Raleigh, N.C.: Water Resources Research Institute 1972.

Ethridge, D.E. *An Economic Study of the Effect of Municipal Sewer Surcharges and Industrial Water.* Raleigh, N.C.: Water Resources Research Institute, November, 1970.

Etter, Wayne. "Municipal Credit Quality and the Property Tax." *Governmental Finance* Vol. 1, No. 2 (May 1972): 20-21.

Fama, Eugene F. *Foundations of Finance.* New York: Basic Books, 1976.

Fama, Eugene F. "A Pricing Model for the Municipal Bond Market." Chicago: unpublished manuscript, Graduate School of Business, University of Chicago. March 1977.

Feigenbaum, Susan and Ronald Teeples. "Public vs. Private Water Delivery: A Hedonic Cost Approach." *Review of Economics and Statistics* Vol. LXV, No. 4 (November 1983): 672-678.

Fischer, P.J. "Note, Advance Refunding, and Municipal Bond Market Efficiency." *Journal of Economics and Behavior* Vol. 35, No. 1 (September 1983): 11-20.

Fischer, Phillip, Ronald Forbes, and John E. Peterson. "Risk and Return in the Choice of Revenue Bond Financing." *Governmental Finance* Vol. 9, No. 3 (September 1980): 9-13.

Flack, J.E. *Water Rights Transfers: An Engineering Approach.* Palo Alto, California: Stanford University, 1965.

Foran, Robert and Ronald W. Forbes. "Some New Approaches to Financing Water Systems." *The Bond Buyer* (13 June 1983): 1.

Forbes, Ronald J. and John E. Peterson. *Costs of Credit Erosion in The Municipal Bond Market.* Chicago: Municipal Finance Officiers Assocation, 1975.

Forbes, Ronald, Phillip Fischer, and John Peterson. "Recent Trends in Municipal Revenue Bond Financing." *Kaufman* (1981): 149-186.

Fourt, L. "Forecasting the Urban Residential Demand for Water." Chicago: unpublished manuscript, Department of Economics, University of Chicago, February 1958.

Gallagher, D.R. and R.W. Robinson. "Influence of Metering, Pricing Policies and Incentives on Water Use." Canberra, Austrailia: Australian Government Publishing Service, Technical paper No. 19. 1977.

Gardner, B.P. and S.H. Schick. "Factors Affecting Consumption of Urban Household Water in Northern Utah." *Agricultural Experiment Station Bulletin* Logan, Utah: No. 499. November, 1964.

Geczi, Michael. "Bond Insurance and Fund Sales Jump Due to Fears Tied to N.Y. City Crises." *Wall Street Journal* (12 January 1976): 15.

Gies, Thomas G. "Problems With the Credit and Bond Rating Systems." *Governmental Finance* Vol. 1, No. 3 (August 1972): 14-16.

Gisser, Micha and Ronald N. Johnson. "The Definition of A Surface Water Right and Transferability." *Journal of Law and Economics* Vol. XXIV, No. 2 (October 1981): 273-288.

Gottlieb, M. "Urban Domestic Demand for Water: A Kansas Case Study." *Land Economics* Vol. 39, No. 2 (May 1963): 204-210.

Graeser, Henry J. "Financing System Changes." *Journal of American Waterworks Association* Vol. 70, No. 9 (September 1978): 492-495.

Grima, A.P. "Residential Water Demand: Alternative Choices for Management." Toronto, Canada: unpublished paper. University of Toronto, Department of Geography. 1972.

Gysi, Marshall. "The Effect of Price on Long Run Water Supply Benefits and Costs." *Water Resources Bulletin* Vol. 7, No. 3 (June 1971): 521-528.

Hanke, Steven H. "Demand for Water Under Dynamic Conditions." *Water Resources Research Bulletin* Vol. 6, No. 5 (October 1970):1253-1261.

Hanke, Steven H. "A Method for Integrating Engineering and Economic Planning." *Journal of American Water Works Association* Vol. 70, No. 8 (August 1978): 487-491.

Hastie, Larry K. "Determinants of Municipal Bond Yields." *Journal of Financial and Quantitative Analysis* Vol. 7 No. 3 (June 1972): 1729-1748.

Haywood, Robert W. Jr. "The Place of Multi-Purpose Reservoirs in Water Supply." *Journal of American Water Works Association* Vol. 55, No. 3 (March 1963): 263-266.

Hedges, Trimble R. *Water Supplies and Cost in Relation To Farm Resource Use: Decisions and Profits on Sacramento Valley Farms.* Berkeley, California: Giannini Foundation, March 1974.

Heins, A. James. "The Interest Rate Differential Between Revenue Bonds and General Obligation Bonds: A Regression Model." *National Tax Journal* Vol. 15, No. 4 (December 1962): 399-405.

Hempel, George. "An Evaluation of Municipal Bankruptcy Laws and Proceedings." *Journal of Finance* Vol. 25, No. 5 (December 1972): 1012-1039.

Hendershott, Patric H. and David S. Kidwell. "The Impact of Relative Security Supplies: A Test with Data from A Regional Tax-Exempt Bond Market." *Journal of Money, Credit, and Banking* Vol. X, No. 3 (August 1978): 337-347.

Herrington, P.R. "Regional Cross-Section Analysis of Public Water Supply

183

Consumption in England and Wales." Leicester, England: University of Leicester, Department of Economics. August 1972.

Hirschleifer, Jack, James DeHaven, and Jerome Milliman. *Water Supply: Economics, Technology, and Public Policy.* Chicago: University of Chicago Press, 1960.

Hoffland, D.L. "The New York City Effect on the Municipal Bond Market." *Financial Analysts Journal* Vol. 33, No. 2 (March/April 1977): 36-39.

Homer, Sidney and Martin Leibowitz. *Inside The Yield Book: New Tools for Bond Market Strategy.* Englewood-Cliffs: Prenctice-Hall, 1972.

Hopewell, Michael H. and George C. Kaufmann. "Costs to Municipalities of Selling Bonds by NIC." *National Tax Journal* Vol. XXVII, No. 4 (December 1974): 531-541.

Howe, C.W. and F.P. Linaweaver Jr. "The Impact of Price on Residential Water Demand and Its Relation to System Design and Price Structure." *Water Resources* Research Vol. 3, No. 1 (January 1967): 13-32.

Hutchins, Wells. *Mutual Irrigation Companies in California and Utah.* Washington D.C.: U.S. Farm Credit Administration, Cooperative Division, October, 1936.

Hyman, David N. *Public Finance: A Contemporary Application of Theory to Policy.* Chicago: Dryden Press, 1982.

Jantscher, Gerald. *The Effect of Changes in Credit Ratings on Municipal Borrowing Costs.* Washington D.C.: Brookings Institution, 1970.

Joehnk, Michael D. and David S. Kidwell. "Determining the Advantages and Disadvantages of Private Municipal Bond Guarantees." *Governmental Finance* Vol. 7, No. 1 (February 1978): 30-36.

Joenhk, Michael D. and David Minzi. "Guaranteed Municipal Bonds—Their Performance and Evaluation." *Review of Business and Economics Research* Vol. XII, No. 1 (Fall 1976): 1-18.

Johnson, J. Chester. "Current Financial Condition and Capital Financing Options for State and Local Governments." *Governmental Finance* Vol. 11, No. 3 (September 1982): 52-55.

Kahn, Alfred. *Economics of Regulation: Principles and Institutions.* New York: John Wiley & Sons, 1970.

Kane, Edward J. "Tax Exemption, Economic Efficiency, and Relative Interest Rates." *Kaufman* (1981): 1-12.

Kaufman, George, editor. *Efficiency in The Municipal Bond Market: The Use of Tax-Exempt Financing for "Private" Purposes.* Greenwich, Connecticut: JAI Press, 1981.

Kessel, Reuben A. "A Study of the Effects of Competition in the Tax-Exempt Bond Market." *Journal of Political Economy* Vol. 79, No. 4 (August 1971): 706-738.

Kidwell, David S. and Timothy W. Koch. "The Behavior of the Interest Rate Differential Between Tax-Exempt Revenue and General Obligation Bonds: A Test of Risk Preferences and Market Segmentation." *Journal of Finance* Vol. 37, No. 1 (March 1982): 73-86.

Kidwell, David and Robert J. Rogowski. "Bond Banks: A State Assistance Program That Helps Reduce New Issue Borrowing Costs." *Public Administration Review* Vol. 43, No. 2 (March/April 1983): 108-112.

Kidwell, David and Charles A. Trezcinka. "Municipal Bond Pricing and the New York City Crisis." *Journal of Finance* Vol. 37, No. 5 (December 1982): 1239-1246.

Kidwell, David S. "The Ex-Ante Cost of Call Provisions on State and Local Government Bonds." *Journal of Economics and Business* Vol. 30, No. 1 (Fall 1977): 73-78.

Kieschnick, Michael. *Taxes and Growth.* Washington D.C.: Council of State Planning Agencies, 1981.

Kormendi, Roger and Thomas Nagle. "The Interest Rate and Tax Revenue Effects of Mortgage Revenue Bonds." *Kaufman* (1981): 117-148.

Lamb, Robert and Stephen Rappaport. *Municipal Bonds: The Comprehensive Review of Tax-Exempt Securities and Public Finance.* New York: McGraw Hill, 1980.

Larkin, D.G. "The Economics of Water Conservation." *Journal of American Water Works Association* Vol. 70, No. 9 (September 1978): 470-482.

Leshy, John. "Irrigation Districts in a Changing West: An Overview." *Arizona State Law Journal* No. 2 (1982): 345-376.

Lippiatt, Barbara C. and Stephen F. Weber. "Water Rates and Residential Water Conservation." *Journal of American Water Works Association* Vol. 74, No. 6 (June 1982): 278-281.

Lipson, Albert J. "Efficient Water Use in California: The Evolution of Groundwater Management in Souther California." Santa Monica: RAND Corporation, R-2387/2-CSA/RF, November, 1978.

Maddock, T. III and Y.Y. Haimes. "A Tax System for Groundwater Management." *Water Resources Journal* Vol. 2, No. 1 (February 1975): 7-14.

Maknoon, Reza and Stephen J. Burges. "Conjunctive Use of Ground and Surface Water." *Journal of American Water Works Association* Vol. 70, No. 8 (August 1978): 419-424.

Mann, Patrick C. and Donald L. Schlenger. "Marginal Cost and Seasonal Pricing of Water Service." *Journal of American Water Works Association* Vol. 74, No. 1 (January 1982): 6-11.

Manne, Henry G. "Mergers and the Market for Corporate Control." *Journal of Political Economy* Vol. 73, No. 2 (April 1965): 110-120.

Marshall, W. N. "Funding Improvements with Debt Capital and Revenues."

185

Journal of American Water Works Association Vol. 74, No. 9 (September 1982): 456-459.

Maxwell, James and J. Richard Aronson. *Financing State and Local Governments.* Washington D.C.: The Brookings Institution, third edition, 1977.

Mead, Elwood. *Irrigation Institutions.* New York: Macmillan Co., 1907.

Medanich, Frank J. "Low Cost, Long-Term Financing." *Journal of American Water Works Association* Vol. 55, No. 4 (April 1963): 418-422.

Metcalf, L. "Effect of Water Rates and Growth in Population Upon Per Capita Consumption." *Journal of American Water Works Association* Vol. 15 , No. 1 (January 1926): 1-21.

Meyers, Charles J. and Richard A. Posner. *Market Transfers of Water Rights: Toward An Improved Market in Water Resources.* Washington D.C.: National Water Commission, Legal Study No. 4, NTIS No. NWG-L-71-009: July, 1971.

Miller, Merton. "Debt and Taxes." *Journal of Finance* Vol. XXXII, No. 2 (May 1978): 261-275.

Moody's Investor Services, Inc. *Pitfalls in Issuing Municipal Bonds.* New York: Moody's Investor Services, 1977.

Morgan, W. D. "Residential Water Demand: The Case from Micro Data." *Water Resource Research Bulletin* Vol. 9, No. 4 (August 1973): 1065-1067.

Morgan, W.D. "Investor Owned vs. Publically Owned Water Agencies: An Evaluation of the Property Rights Theory of the Firm." *Water Resources Bulletin* Vol. 13, No. 4 (August 1977): 775-781.

Musgrave, Richard and Peggy Musgrave. *Public Finance in Theory and Practice.* New York: McGraw Hill, 1980

Neary, Robert E. "North Carolina Local Government Commission Cuts Municipalities' Borrowing Costs." *The Daily Bond Buyer* (August 30, 1972): 32.

Neuner, Edward, Dean Popp, and Fred Sebold. "User Charges vs. Taxation as a Means of Funding a Water Supply System." *Journal of American Water Works Association* Vol. 69, No. 1 (January 1977): 39-45.

Oates, Wallace. *Fiscal Federalism.* New York: Harcourt Brace Jovanovich, 1972.

Okun, Arthur. *The Trade-Off Between Efficiency and Equity.* Washington D.C.: Brookings Institution, 1975.

Olson, Mancur. *The Logic of Collective Action.* Cambridge: Harvard University Press, 1965.

Pagano, Michael and Richard J. Moore. "Emerging Issues in Financing

Basic Infra-Structure." Washington D.C.: U.S. Department of Commerce, September, 1981.

Pascal, Anthony. *Fiscal Containment of Local and State Government.* Santa Monica: RAND Corporation, September 1979.

Pechman, Joseph A. *Federal Tax Policy.* Washington D.C.: Brookings Institution, third edition, 1977.

Peterson, George. *Tax-Exempt Financing of Housing Investment.* Washington D.C.: The Urban Institute, 1979.

Phelps, Charles E., Nancy Moore, and Morlie Graubard. *Efficient Water Use in California: Water Rights, Water Districts, and Water Transfers.* Santa Monica: RAND Corporation, R-2386-CSA/RF, November 1978.

Prichard, R., editor. *Public Enterprise in Canada.* Toronto: Butterworth, 1982.

Public Securities Association. *Fundamentals of Municipal Bonds.* New York: Public Securities Association, 1981.

Quint, Michael. "Tax-Exempt, Cost Crunch, Steer Banks to Revs." *American Banker* (February 27, 1980): 1.

Rees, T.A. "Industrial Demand for Water: A Study of South East England." London, England: London School of Economics, Research Monograph No. 3, 1969.

Renshaw, Edward F. "The Demand for Municipal Water." Chicago: unpublished manuscript, University of Chicago, Department of Economics, June 1958.

Renshaw, Edward F. "Conserving Water Through Pricing." *Journal of American Water Works Association* Vol. 74, No. 1 (January 1982): 2-5.

Rice, I. M. and L.G. Shaw. "Water Conservation—A Practical Approach." *Journal of American Water Works Association* Vol. 70, No. 9 (September 1978): 480-482.

Ridge, R. "The Impact of Public Water Pricing Policy on Industrial Demand and Reuse." General Electric Technical Information Series, 1972.

Roche, Peter. "Use of Municipal Bond Insurance Gains Among Localities Seeking to Sell Debt." *Wall Street Journal* (January 13, 1976): 15.

Rubenfeld, Daniel. "Credit Ratings and the Market for General Obligation Municipal Bonds." *National Tax Journal* Vol. XXVI, No. 1 (March 1973): 17-27.

Sang, Wong H. "The Financial Impact of Water Rate Changes." *Journal of American Water Works* Association Vol. 74, No. 9 (September 1982): 466-469.

Savas, Emmanuel, editor. *The Organization and Efficiency of Solid Waste Collection.* Lexington, Mass.: Lexington Books, 1977.

Schelhorse, Larry D. *The Market Structure of the Southern California Water Industry.* La Jolla, California: Copley International Corporation, June 1974.

Seidel, H.F. and E.F. Bauman. "A Statistical Analysis of Water Works Data for 1955." *Journal of American Water Works Association* Vol. 49, No. 12 (December 1957): 1531-1566.

Sharpe, William E. "Why Consider Water Conservation?" *Journal of American Water Works Association* Vol. 70, No. 9 (September 1978): 475-479.

Smith, Rodney T. *Housing Assistance and Welfare Reform.* Santa Monica: RAND Corporation, December 1978.

Smith, Rodney T. "The Economic Determinants and Consequences of Private and Public Ownership of Irrigation Facilities." in Anderson (1984): 167-217.

Smith, Wade. "A Case for the Present Rating System." *Governmental Finance* Vol. 1, No. 3 (August 1972): 5-9.

Sorenson, Eric. "Bond Ratings Versus Market Risk Premiums." *Journal of Portfolio Management* Vol. 6, No. 3 (Spring 1980): 64-69.

Starr, Frank C. and Ronald W. Forbes. "The Role of Investment Banking Firms in Managing Water Project Financing." *Journal of American Water Works Association* Vol. 74, No. 9 (September 1982): 451-455.

State of California. *Governor's Commission to Review Water Right Law.* Sacramento, California: Governor's Office, December 1978.

Stevens, Barbara J. "Scale, Market Structure, and The Cost of Refuse Collection." *Review of Economics and Statistics* Vol. LX, No. 3 (August 1978): 438-448.

Stevie, Richard G. and Robert M. Clark. "Costs for Small Systems to Meet The National Interim Drinking Water Regulations." *Journal of American Water Works Association* Vol. 74, No. 1 (January 1982): 13-17.

Stigler, George. *The Organization of Industry.* Homewood, Illinois: Richard D. Irwin, 1968.

Stone, Brian G. "Suppressing Water Use by Physical Means." *Journal of American Water Works Association* Vol. 70, No. 9 (September 1978): 483-486.

Swenson, Phillip R. "The Cyclical Behavior of the Net Interest Cost Differentials Between General Obligation and Revenue Bonds." *National Tax Journal* Vol. 27, No. 1 (March 1974): 23-40.

Tiebout, Charles. "A Pure Theory of Local Expenditures." *Journal of Political Economy* Vol. 64, No. 5 (October 1956): 416-424.

Trelease, Frank. *Water Law: Resource Use and Environmental Protection.* St. Paul, Minnesota: West Publishing Co., second edition, 1974.

Trezcinka, Charles A. "The Pricing of Tax-Exempt Bonds and the Miller Hypothesis." *Journal of Finance* Vol. 37, No. 4 (September 1982): 907-923.

Turnovsky, Steven J. "The Demand for Water: Some Empirical Evidence on Consumer's Response to a Commodity Uncertain in Supply." *Water Resources Research Bulletin* Vol. 5, No. 2 (April 1969): 350-361.

Twentieth Century Fund Task Force on Municipal Bond Credit Ratings. *The Rating Game.* New York: Twentieth Century Fund, 1974.

U.S. Department of Commerce. *A Study of Public Works Investment in the United States.* Washington D.C.: Government Printing Office, 1980.

U.S. Department of Commerce, Bureau of Census. *Governmental Finances.* Washington D.C.: Government Printing Office, 1982.

U.S. Department of Commerce. *U.S. Statistical Abstract, 1982-1983.* Washington D.C.: Government Printing Office, 1983.

U.S. Department of Justice. *Merger Guidelines.* Washington D.C.: U.S. Department of Justice, 1982.

Van Horne, James C. *Financial Market Rates and Flows.* Englewood-Cliffs: Prentice-Hall, 1978.

Vaughan, Roger J. *State Taxation and Economic Development.* Washington D.C.: Council of State Planning Agencies, 1979.

Vaughan, Roger J. *Rebuilding America: Financing Public Works in the 1980s.* Washington D.C.: Council of State Planning Agencies, Volume 2, 1983.

Ware, J. E. and R. M. North. "Price and Consumption of Water for Residential Use in Georgia." Atlanta, Georgia: Bureau of Business and Economic Research, School of Business Administration, Georgia State College, October 1967.

West, Richard R. "The Net Interest Cost Method of Issuing Tax-Exempt Bonds: Is It Rational?" *Public Finance* Vol. XXIII, No. 3 (Fall 1968): 346-354.

Western States Water Council. *State/Local Financing and Western Water Resource Development.* Western States Water Council, November 1981.

Wetzel, Bruce. "Efficient Water Use in California: Economic Modelling of Groundwater Development with Applications to Groundwater Management." Santa Monica: RAND Corporation, R-2388-CSA/RF, November, 1978.

White, Wilson Jr. *White's Tax-Exempt Bond Market Ratings.* New York: International Data Corporation, annual.

Williams, Paul C. "Creative Financing Techniques for Water Utilities." *Journal of American Water Works Association* Vol. 74, No. 9 (September 1982): 443-449.

189

Wong, S. T. and J. R. Sheaffer. "Multivariate Statistical Analysis of Water Supplies." American Society of Civil Engineers Water Resource Engineering Conference, May, 1963.

Wong, S.T. "A Model of Municipal Water Demand: A Case Study of Northeastern Illinois." *Land Economics* Vol. 48, No. 1 (February 1972): 34-44.

Yawitz, Jess B. "Risk Premia on Municipal Bonds." *Journal of Financial and Quantitative Analysis* Vol. 13, No. 3 (September 1978): 475-485.

Young, Edwin C. "The Economics of Municipal Waterwater Reuse." *Journal of American Water Works Association* Vol. 74, No. 7 (July 1982): 358-361.

Young, R. A. "Price Elasticity of Demand for Water: A Case Study of Tucson." *Water Resources Research Bulletin* Vol, 9, No. 4 (August 1973): 1068-1072.

Zimmerman, Jerry. "The Municipal Accounting Maze: An Analysis of Political Incentives." *Journal of Accounting Research* Vol. 15 (Supplement): 107-144.

Index

Accelerated Cost Recovery System (ACRS), 161–65

Agriculture; amount and growth of, by irrigation status, *14*; and conjunctive use, 108–09; effects of water subsidies on, 98–99; and protection of water rights, 131–32; and users fees, 108–09

Alternative revenue bases. *See* Revenue bases, alternative

American Municipal Bond Assurance Corporation (AMBAC), 146

Appropriative doctrine, compared to riparian, 12

Arbitrage, 45

Arizona, 1, 2, 11, 111–12, 129; amount and growth of irrigated agricultural acreage in, *14*; annual precipitation in, *13*; effects of local fiscal restrictions in, *124*; investment in irrigation facilities in, *26*; irrigation organizations in, *15*; limits on fiscal and debt policies in, *126*; nature and growth of debt in, *29*; outstanding debt in, *28*; referendum requirements for issuing general obligation debt in, *125*; restrictions on local fiscal policies by, *123*; share of conveyed water by irrigation organizations in, *20*; share of irrigated acreage by method of irrigation in, *22*; share of irrigated acreage by organizations in, *19*; share of municipal utilities' long-term debt in general obligation in, *77*; sources and distribution of revenue in, *73, 74*; sources of water supply for irrigation organizations in, *16*; total debt and share owed to USBR, *27*; water use and revenues collected in, *21*

Army Corps of Engineers (U.S.), 113, 114

Babbitt, Bruce, 129

Basic points, 59–62; economic value of saving, *59*

Bond banks; and risk diversification, 151

Bond insurance, 145–47; introduction of, 145; selected features of, *147*

Bond market; and privatization, 165

Bond rating; and changing issuer's financial status, 54–55; and debt analysis, 51–54; and debt assessment, 51–54; methodologies, 51; and number of underwriting bids, *136*; and relationship to yield, 61; and size of issue, by percent, *50*

Borrowing costs; and default of WPPSS, 63; and lessons from general market trends, 59–61; how determined, 59–62; how Maine bond bank affected, of municipalities, *150*

Bureau of Indian Affairs, 16

Bush Task Group, 133

California, 2, 11, 91, 96, 102, 109,

icies in, *126*; nature and growth of debt in, *29*; outstanding debt in, *28*; referendum requirements for issuing general obligation debt in, *125*; restrictions on local fiscal policies by, *123*; share of conveyed water by irrigation organizations in, *20*; share of irrigated acreage by method of irrigation in, *22*; share of irrigated acreage by organizations in, *19*; share of municipal utilities' long-term debt in general obligation in, *77*; sources and distribution of revenue in, *73, 74*; sources of water supply in, *16*; total debt and share owed to USBR, *27*; water use and revenues collected in, *21*

Moody's Investors Service, Inc., 50, 51, 146

Municipal Advisory Council of Texas, 144

Municipal bonds, 33–63, 147–52; actual and predicted yields, *41*; call provisions and yield, 62; coupon repayment schedules for, 137; effect of Proposition 13 on yields of, 127–28; effect on, by default of WPPSS, 63; factors for assessing financial risk, *145*; and infrastructure banks, 153–55; and intergovernmental grants, 152–53; issue size and yield of, 62; level of interest rates for, 38–42; private insurance for, 145–47; new issues of, *44*; number of bidders and relationship to yield of, 61–62; rating of, 49–55; recent trends in, 34–38; and revolving funds, 153–55; and technical assistance for local by state governments, 143–45; types of, 35; uses of, 35–38; yield differentials between different risk classes of, 45–48; yield differential on, compared with corporate bonds, 42–45; yield differential on individual issues of, 61–62; yields on,

according to market conditions, *40*; yields on new issues of, *61*; *see also* General obligation bonds; Municipal debt; Revenue bonds

Municipal bond banks; effect of on interest costs to municipalities (Maine), *150*; debt of, *149*; new issues of, *149*; and perceived responsibility of state governments by investors in, 149–51; reasons for, 147–52; selected features of, *148*

Municipal Bond Insurance Corporation (MBIA), 146

Municipal debt; incurred by governmental entities, *38*; interest rates on, 38–49; long-term borrowing for, by purpose, *39*; magnitude of, 34–35; new issues of, *37*; ownership of, 34–35; reasons incurred, 37–38; recent trends in, 34–38; types of, 35–37; *see also* Municipal bonds

Municipal enterprises, financial medians of, *54*

National Economic Recovery Tax Act (1981), 160

Nebraska; amount and growth of irrigated agricultural acreage in, *14*; annual precipitation in, *13*; effects of local fiscal restrictions in, *124*; investment in irrigation facilities in, *26*; irrigation organizations in, *15*; limits on fiscal and debt policies in, *126*; nature and growth of debt in, *29*; outstanding debt in, *28*; referendum requirements for issuing general obligation debt in, *125*; restrictions on local fiscal policies by, *123*; share of conveyed water by irrigation organizations in, *20*; share of irrigated acreage by method of irrigation in, *22*; share of irrigated acreage by organizations in, *19*; share of municipal utilities' long-term debt in general obligation in, *77*; sources